LOWER YOUR TAXES—

BIG TIME!

LOWER YOUR TAXES—

BIG TIME!

Wealth-Building, Tax Reduction Secrets from an IRS Insider

2007-2008 Edition

Sandy Botkin, CPA, J.D.

McGraw-Hill

New York Chicago San Francisco Lisbon London
Madrid Mexico City Milan New Delhi San Juan
Seoul Singapore Sydney Toronto

ISBN-13: 978-0-07-147868-7
ISBN-10:   0-07-147868-X

Editorial, design, and production services provided by CWL Publishing Enterprises, Madison, Wisconsin, www.cwlpub.com.

This publication is designed to provide accurate and authoritative information in regard to the subject matter covered. It is sold with the understanding that neither the author nor the publisher is engaged in rendering legal, accounting, or other professional service. If legal advice or other expert assistance is required, the services of a competent professional person should be sought.

From a Declaration of Principles jointly
adopted by a Committee of the American Bar
Association and a Committee of Publishers

McGraw-Hill books are available at special quantity discounts to use as premiums and sales promotions, or for use in corporate training programs. For more information, please write to the Director of Special Sales, McGraw-Hill, Two Penn Plaza, New York, NY 10121. Or contact your local bookstore.

Contents

How would you like to completely deduct the equivalent of your kids' college education, room and board at college, and their weddings? You can, with income shifting. This chapter also deals with a great tax planning technique called the gift-sale technique and the "Botkin Trust," which allows a double deduction for equipment—and has been approved in numerous Supreme Court cases. I love this chapter!

Learn the five methods of IRS-bulletproofing your automobile deductions. This is a must if you use your car for business.

This chapter explains how to convert your home into a tax-deductible money machine, using little-known audit-proofing strategies. One of my students told me that this chapter reduced her taxable income by $100,000.

What do you do when you get a letter from the IRS "inviting you in for a chat"? This chapter covers what your chances are of being audited, your audit rights, how to reduce your chances of being audited, what to do if you don't have the money to pay the IRS, and much more. This is a great chapter and you should read it carefully.

This chapter illustrates the practical steps necessary to withstand any "hobby attack" by the IRS. I have been so successful with clients who have used this information that many accountants have asked me for copies of this book because of this chapter alone. If you are running a business out of your home, this chapter could save you a bundle and prevent lots of IRS problems.

Chapter 14. Fringe Benefits You Will Love, Part 2   212

This chapter continues the discussion of tax-free fringe benefits from Chapter 13, with parking, transit passes, vanpools, cafeteria plans, qualified profit-sharing plans, SEPs, SIMPLE IRAs, and more.

Part 4. Miscellaneous Tax Strategies   233

Chapter 15. The Four Most Overlooked Real Estate Tax Deductions in America   235

Here are the big four: 1) the large deduction for mortgage points, 2) the new universal exclusion that will allow you to avoid up to $500,000 of gain on your properties every two years, 3) choosing to make "repairs" vs. "improvements" on your property, and 4) one of the biggest tax deduction mistakes in divorce situations. In fact, do not get divorced without reading this chapter!

Chapter 16. Making Colleges Less Expensive With Tax Planning   249

This chapter highlights qualified tuition plans for your kids future education,which will enable you to pay for college with tax free savings. This chapter also explains the benefits of both the Lifetime Learning Credit and the Hope Tax Credit, both of which result in a dollar-for-dollar reduction in your taxes. The chapter also covers the rules of deducting student loan interest, and shows how to deduct up to $4,000 of college expenses each year.

Chapter 17. The Top 10 Tax Questions   261

This is one chapter you don't want to miss.

Introduction

Rich or Poor—Your Choice

When a person with money meets a person with experience, the person with experience will get some money and the person with money will get some experience.

—Harvey MacKay,
How to Swim with Sharks Without Being Eaten Alive

This is not a financial planning book or a book about money. However, it will probably put more money in your pocket *each year* than any other book you've read. This is also not a book about investing or wealth building. However, the information contained here could probably create more wealthy people than any wealth-building book. Finally, this is also not a book that will show you how to do your own taxes. In fact, there are no tax forms in this book. However, it will probably reduce your taxes more than any idea that an accountant has given you and more than any idea that you may have read about in any other book.

Lower Your Taxes—Big Time! is a practical book on tax strategies and IRS audit-proofing techniques. You will not only learn to significantly reduce your taxes with proven strategies developed over many years; you will, at the same time, lower your chances of being audited and make your tax return "IRS-bulletproof." This sounds contradictory, but I promise you that these statements are true.

Read the quote at the beginning of this chapter again. I intend to give you the experience you need so you can become both "a person with money" and "a person with experience." There are costly ways to gain experience, as anyone who has been thoroughly audited will tell you, and not-so-costly ways. This book is the not-so-costly way for you.

The idea for this book began to develop when I was a trainer of IRS attorneys. While working at the IRS, I realized that many people were overpaying their taxes due to a lack of knowledge or lack of information. In fact, the turning point of my life occurred as a result of reviewing a friend's tax return. My friend knew that I was an attorney for the IRS and asked me to review his tax return for omitted deductions. Although his return had been prepared by a major accounting firm, I recommended that he file an amended return and get back over $16,000! As a result of this refund, my friend and his wife had their first vacation outside the U.S.

This experience led me to start my own company, Tax Reduction Institute of Germantown, Maryland (TRI Seminars, Inc), which teaches people how to significantly and legally reduce their taxes and, at the same time, IRS-bulletproof their records.

The Problem

I have seen time and again many people spending hours fighting over a $200 overcharge by their credit card company, yet spend little or no time learning how to reduce their tax bite by thousands of dollars, which would be very easy to do. I often have 100 people in a seminar where I can guarantee tax savings of at least several thousand dollars a year, but some motivational speakers can have thousands in a financial seminar with few or no guarantees. I used to wonder why most people don't understand the importance of tax strategies. As a result of many interviews, studies, and phone conversations, I came to realize that there were several myths that were impoverishing a great majority of people in this country.

Myth 1: I didn't make a lot of money this year so I don't need to know about tax planning! This is absolutely false. If you are a consultant or have a small or home-based business, you have access to the last great tax shelter left in this country. (If you don't have a home-based business, read Chapter 1, where I'll convince you why you should start one!) If your deductions in your business exceed your income, you can use that business loss against any form of income that you or your spouse have, such as rents, dividends, pensions, or even wages.[1]

Example: John and Mary earned $40,000 in salary but had a side home-based business that generated a loss of $15,000. They may use this loss to offset their salary in computing their taxable income. Thus, they only pay tax on $25,000 of income.

If your business losses exceed your whole year's income, don't fret. The government actually allows you to carry back all business losses for two years. (In 2002 you get an extended carryback of up to five years for your business losses.) You can also offset the last two years of federal taxes and, in most cases, state taxes that you paid in the last two years. Or you can carry over business losses 20 years and offset up to the next 20 years of earnings.[2]

Example: John has a net loss from his business of $10,000. If John had $40,000 of taxable income that he paid tax on two years ago, he can use this $10,000 loss and reduce his taxable income to $30,000. This is treated as if he had earned only $30,000 two years ago instead of the $40,000 that he earned and paid tax on. The result is that he will get a refund due to the carryback of the loss. In fact, even if he paid no taxes in prior years, he can carry over this loss and offset the next 20 years of earnings.

Isn't life grand! My point is, knowing about tax planning strategies is important regardless of your income level.

Myth 2: My home-based/small business has to have a profit at least three out of five consecutive years. Did you believe this myth too? Hundreds of people, including accountants, have said this to me. This is absolutely false. Congress simply wants you to run your business like a business and not like a hobby. If you do, you can have losses for many years.[3] This will be discussed in depth in Chapter 8.

Myth 3: My accountant takes care of my taxes. A similar myth is **"My spouse takes care of my taxes."** This is the biggest myth of all. These seven words impoverish more people than any other myth. It's like saying, "My doctor takes care of my body." Wouldn't it be great if we never had to exercise and could eat all the fattening foods and, once a year, our doctors would give us a "Roto-Rooter" job? The point is that the tax savings your accountant can find for you after December 31 are small compared with what you can save if you are pursuing your own tax strategies before December 31.

Myth 4: Tax knowledge won't save me that much money anyway. Did you know that taxes are the number-one expense in this country? If you add up your federal, state, and Social Security taxes, you may find that what you pay in taxes rivals or exceeds what you pay for food, lodging or mortgage payment, transportation, and clothing combined![4]

In a great book entitled *The Millionaire Next Door: The Surprising Secrets of America's Wealthy*[5], the authors analyzed the mindset of multi-millionaires in order to determine what makes them tick. They found a number of interesting correlations among millionaires. First, most millionaires are frugal and live beneath their means. Sam Walton, for example, drove a pickup truck. Second, most millionaires believe that if you want to get rich, you must get your taxes down to the legal minimum.

They know that we have two tax systems in the U.S. You may be thinking, "Right—one for the rich and one for the poor." No, that's not correct. There is one tax system for employees and for those who don't know the rules. This system is designed to take your wealth. The second tax system is for self-employed people who know the rules. This tax system is designed to create economic growth.

It has been estimated that small businesses generate the majority of job growth in the U.S. It isn't IBM or Microsoft, but small and home-based businesses. Thus, when lobbyists come to Congress to get some good tax laws passed for small businesses (and there are good tax laws), the small business lobbyists can sometimes get what they want. The reason is that Congress knows that small business is the economic engine behind our economy. In fact, states that have low taxes on business tend to be more economically successful because they attract business and jobs. The key is to take advantage of these good tax laws, which means that you have to know about them. The problem is, as a professor of mine many years ago said, "We don't know what we don't know." This is, unfortunately, especially true about tax knowledge.

The authors of *The Millionaire Next Door* concluded that most people who became millionaires didn't win a lottery, inherit a lot of money, or make a big stock market gain. They were, for the most part, average folks who saved a little bit each year, probably from the taxes saved with good planning, and invested the money in an average investment for 30 or more years.

At first, I didn't believe this. I ran the long-term growth numbers based on an average mutual fund. I picked the Vanguard Growth and Equity Fund and used the long-term growth rates that they actually experienced.[6] Based on a 30-year investment of $4,000 per year, the amount at retirement would have been $1,387,000. If you had invested $2,000 every six months into this fund for 40 years, it would have been worth a whopping $5,084,000! This means that everyone who learns the information in this book and invests the savings for retirement can become a millionaire. The rich know this analysis is true, and that is one big reason why they are rich and many people are not. Tax knowledge is lucrative.

What This Book Will Cover

We will be covering a wide area of tax knowledge.

Chapter 1. Why You Would Be Brain Dead Not to Start a Home-Based Business (if You Don't Already Have One) explains why everyone who is employed should have some kind of business, preferably a home-based business. If you don't have one, you are losing thousands each year.

Chapter 2. How to Deduct Your Fun deals with entertainment—how to deduct golf, sports tickets, movies, and plays and how to audit-proof all these deductions. You will also learn some IRS inside secrets related to Dutch treat meals and learn about the great $75 exception to keeping receipts as well as the home entertainment exception. You will love the information in this chapter, since you will be having twice as much fun by deducting your fun.

Chapter 3. How to Turn Your Vacation into a Tax-Deductible Write-Off deals with how to deduct your travel expenses and how to convert almost any vacation into a deductible business trip. This chapter will put thousands in your pocket.

Chapter 4. Income Shifting and Income Splitting: One of the Greatest Single Wealth-Building Secrets is for anyone who is married or who is single with children, whether young or adult, or people with friends. How would you like to completely deduct the equivalent of your kids' college education, room and board at college, and their weddings? You can, with income shifting. This chapter also deals with a great tax planning technique called the "gift-sale" technique. In fact, if everyone in the country knew about this one technique, it could reduce the IRS treasury legally by billions of dollars! No kidding. Finally, we will cover the "Botkin Trust," which allows a double deduction for equipment and has been approved in numerous Supreme Court cases. I love this chapter.

Chapter 5. How to Turn Your Car into a Tax-Deductible Goldmine is a must if you use your car for business or incur automobile expenses for the job. Automobiles are the area that the IRS audits most frequently because they are big-ticket items. You will learn how to make your car into a tax-deductible goldmine and learn the five methods of IRS-bullet proofing your automobile documentation.

Chapter 6. Home Office: The Misunderstood Key to Saving $15,000 Every Five Years explains how to convert your home into a tax-deductible money machine. It focuses heavily on little-known audit-proofing strategies required by the IRS and shows a great way to claim a home office year after year and pay very little tax on the sale of the home. One of my students told me that this chapter reduced her taxable income by $100,000. It is a very important chapter for anyone who works out of the house.

Chapter 7. Beating the Dreaded IRS Audit deals with a situation that worries far too many taxpayers. What do you do when you get a letter from the IRS "inviting you in for a chat"? This chapter will cover what your chances are of being audited, what your audit rights are, how to reduce your chances of being audited, what to do if you don't have the money to pay the IRS, and much more. This is a great chapter and should be read carefully.

Chapter 8. How to Shield Yourself from the IRS Weapon of Classifying a Business as a Hobby deals with an IRS tactic that has become a major issue nationwide. The IRS can eliminate virtually all business losses if you don't run your endeavor correctly. This chapter will illustrate all the practical steps necessary to withstand any "hobby attack" by the IRS. I have been so successful with clients who have used this information that many accountants have asked me for copies of this book primarily because of this chapter alone. If you are running a business out of your home or have a side business, this chapter could save you a bundle and prevent lots of IRS problems. It is well worth reading this chapter several times.

Chapter 9. Finding the Best Corporate Entity for Your Business will give you a great overview of the pros and cons of incorporating vs. being a sole proprietor or being a limited liability company. You will learn the inside secrets of what to look for in deciding whether incorporating is right for you.

Chapter 10. Forming a Nevada Corporation or a Limited-Liability Corporation in Nevada provides some little-known information. Many well-known, wealthy personalities (and many con artists) incorporate in Nevada. You will learn exactly why. This has been a well-kept secret until now!

Chapter 11. How to Eliminate up to 40 percent of Your Social Security and Medicare Tax with an S Corporation deals with one of the best-kept secrets among accountants and wealthy clients for years. Now you can learn exactly what the rich have known for years and learn a great way to substantially reduce those pesky, large Social Security and Medicare taxes.

Chapter 12. How to Get Assets and Money into a Corporation Tax-Free deals with avoiding some of the pitfalls of forming a corporation. It will also emphasize what should and, as important, what should not be transferred to a corporation. It covers a *very* widespread and crucial area that has killed many businesses: dealing with co-owners and partners. Finally, if you terminate your corporation at a loss, it explains a method that will give you an ordinary loss rather than a less-valuable capital loss.

Chapter 13. Fringe Benefits You Will Love, Part 1 deals with most of the wonderful, tax-free fringe benefits that you can have in almost any small business that are not covered in other chapters. I will discuss such perks as payment for parking, transportation, exercise equipment, employee achievement awards, and much more.

Chapter 14. Fringe Benefits You Will Love, Part 2 deals with some of the drawbacks to being a corporation such as personal service corporations, accumulated earnings taxes, and more. It's essential for every person who's thinking of incorporating to be aware of these hidden congressionally mandated tax traps.

Chapter 15. The Four Most Overlooked Real Estate Tax Deductions in America deals with four major real estate problems that affect almost every American at some point in their lives. It explains the large deduction for mortgage points, deals with the new universal exclusion that will allow you to avoid up to $500,000 of gain on your properties every two years, describes ways to dramatically increase your return on investments with the right choice of repairs and improvements, and finally reveals one of the biggest tax mistakes in divorce situations. In fact, do not get divorced without reading this chapter!

Chapter 16. Making College Less Expensive With Tax Planning addresses frequently asked questions concerning the deductibility of educational expenses and details great tax credits available for education. This chapter will also cover the prepaid tuition plans that will enable you to save money for your kids' education on a tax-free basis.

Chapter 17. The Top 10 Tax Questions addresses some of the most universal tax issues in America. I've also chosen some questions due to their inherent appeal. It will undoubtedly address some questions that you have asked yourself at some point or are currently wondering about. This is one chapter that you don't want to miss.

When I started writing this book, I had several goals in mind. First, I wanted to show readers, especially consultants, small business owners, and home-based business owners how to save thousands of dollars on their taxes. Second, I wanted to present the material in a simplified format without any of the "accountant jargon" or "gobbledygook." Finally, I wanted to emphasize the little-known, audit-proof documentation strategies needed to survive any IRS audit. As you will see, practicality is the theme of this book, which includes hundreds of practical tips and suggestions that will save you a bundle each year.

This book is a product of thousands of lectures I have delivered to over 100,000 students over the years. In these lectures I constantly ask my students to evaluate what was scary to them or what they didn't understand. Thus, *Lower Your Taxes—Big Time!* is the result of an evolutionary process of 16 years of work.

I have also provided all the IRS annotations, which are the legal footnotes for everything that will be discussed. Everything in this book will be supported with the appropriate documentation; thus, there will be nothing that will trigger any audit. If there were any "gray" areas, I omitted them from the discussion.

Finally, throughout the book, you will find icons that looks like this: These indicate a concept, strategy, or action you can take to lower your taxes—big time!

I hope that you get as much enjoyment from reading this book as I got in writing it.

Dedication and Acknowledgment

I would like to dedicate this work to my wife, Lori, and my children, Jeremy, Mathew, and Allison, for their endless patience, and to my many students who have helped craft this work with feedback and suggestions. I wish to thank Mary Glenn, my editor at McGraw-Hill, for her input and timely suggestions. Finally, I also want to dedicate this book to the U.S. Congress, which makes this work not only possible, but necessary.

Notes

1. Section 162 of the Internal Revenue Code (IRC) and Regulations.
2. Section 172 of the IRC.
3. Section 183 of the IRC and Regulations thereunder.
4. The Tax Foundation and *The Tax Adviser* (American Institute of Certified Public Accountants), May 2000.
5. *The Millionaire Next Door: The Surprising Secrets of America's Wealthy* by Thomas J. Stanley and William D. Danko (Longstreet Press, 1996).
6. From the Vanguard prospectus, the Growth and Equity Fund had a 10-year rate of return of 12.90 percent. I should note that I am not necessarily recommending Vanguard. There are many good funds, such as Fidelity, AIM, Janus, T. Rowe Price, and others.

Part 1

Wealth-Building Tax Secrets for Small and Home-Based Business Owners

1

Why You Would Be Brain Dead Not to Start a Home-Based Business (If You Don't Already Have One)

There are really two sets of tax laws in this country. One is for employees; it allows deductions for normal employee items, such as individual retirement accounts, 401(k)s (if you have one set up by your company), interest and property taxes on your home, and charity. Then there are the laws for small and home-based business people who conduct their business either full or part time. In addition to the tax deductions employees can get, small business people can deduct, with proper documentation, their house, their spouses (by hiring them), their business vacations, their cars, and food with colleagues. They can also set up a pension plan that makes any government plan seem paltry by comparison and deduct most of their "vacation" trips if they combine them with an appropriate amount of business. (See the discussion in Chapter 3.)

Chapter Overview
- You will *never* get rich until you learn to get your taxes down to the legal minimum.
- There are two tax systems in this country—one for salaried employees, one for small/home-based business owners.
- A home-based business will make you better off than a second income.
- Traditional job security has declined over the years and will continue to do so, making home businesses more attractive.
- You will probably save $2,000–10,000 per year by starting your own part-time business.

The example below shows how a woman named Lori, who earned a $15,000 salary, took home only $1,156 after she deducted all her work-related expenses. Yet she could have netted the entire $15,000 had she earned it in a home-based business. This is an increase of almost 13 times her take-home pay as an employee.

It illustrates why having more than one job in a family does not produce any major effect on most people's bank accounts because of the tax laws. This was well illustrated by Jane Bryant Quinn in a *Woman's Day* article on "How to Live on One Salary."[1]

Quinn assumed that the husband earned $40,000 per year, which is $3,400 per month and his wife (I'm calling her Lori) wasn't working. They had more month than money. (Sound familiar?) Lori subsequently got an administrative job for $15,000 per year. When Quinn examined the economics of getting this extra income for the family, the results were startling!

Lori had to pay federal and state taxes on her new income. Since they filed jointly, the family's combined income was what established their tax bracket. She paid $4,500 in new federal and state taxes, most of which were nondeductible.

Lori had Social Security withheld from her paycheck at the rate of 7.65 percent, which amounted to an additional nondeductible amount of $1,148 being extracted from her. She also has to commute to work 10 miles a day round trip, which is probably conservative for most people. This results in nondeductible commuting costs (in 1995) of $696.[2]

Lori also had child care expenses that give a partial tax credit. Quinn figured that the amount spent over and beyond the tax credit was $4,250 per year.

Lori also ate out each day with colleagues, spending an average of $5 per day for lunch, five days per week. This results in a nondeductible expense of $1,250 a year.[3] (I would love to know where she ate for only $5!)

Now that Lori has a job, she has to have better clothing and much more dry cleaning. Quinn assumed that Lori's increased expenses here were an extra $1,000 per year, nondeductible, of course.

Finally, with both spouses working, Lori wasn't in the mood to cook, somewhat akin to my own life. Thus, there were more convenience foods and more eating out. This resulted in increased food costs of a nondeductible $1,000 per year at the minimum.

Add it all up and Lori's take-home pay was a paltry $1,156 a year, for which she had to put up with the commute and the boss and the corporate hassles. (See the following summary of all these numbers, so you can do the math yourself.)

Gross Income *LESS:*	$15,000
State and Federal Taxes	−$4,500
Social Security Taxes	−$1,148
Car expenses (at 29 cpm—50 miles per week)	−$ 696
Child care (net of the credit)	−$4,250
Lunches at the job	−$1,250
Business clothing and dry cleaning	−$1,000
Higher food expenses (eating out, snack foods, etc.)	−$1,000
Net take-home pay:	$1,156

No wonder more and more people are starting up home-based and consulting businesses. In fact, according to author David D'Arcangelo, there are currently an estimated 37 million people working from their home, "representing a 20-fold increase over the last 10 years. What's more is that number is expected to grow by 15 percent annually and keep on growing!"[4] This has become and will continue to become one of the greatest mass movements in the U.S.

If Lori started a home-based business, she would not be spending dramatically more money then she is currently spending. She would eat out anyway, go on trips, and have the same car expenses for repairs, gas, and insurance as she did before. If she has a home-based and/or consulting business, however, many of her expenses become deductible. This concept is known as "redirecting expenses." With a home-based or consulting business, she can now deduct some of the expenses that she is incurring anyway.

More Reasons to Start a Home-Based Business

In recent years, the era of large corporate profits and economic growth came to an end. Moreover, many economists believe things won't be getting better any time soon.

Remember the American Dream? You worked hard for one employer, saved your money, and retired with dignity and security. Today, young and middle-aged alike are realizing that their dream of having a job with a company forever is an illusion. Just pick up any national paper and you will see companies downsizing, rightsizing, and capsizing. (Remember Enron and WorldCom.)

Finally, if this isn't bad enough, under recent tax laws, employees are shafted more than ever with limits and thresholds for their employee deductions and higher Social Security tax limits. This results in more couples working than ever before and, on many occasions, working at more than one job. It is now almost impossible to have only one job in the family and make ends meet!

Finally, with both spouses away from the home most of the day, we have more children fending for themselves until their parents get home and less discipline in the home. (I wonder if some of the shootings that occur in school today aren't caused, in part, because many parents aren't home to take care of their children and supervise them properly.)

The reasons so many people are going into a home-based business or becoming consultants rather than joining a traditional business are many. There is no commute (unless you have a really big home), no boss, little if any chance of lawsuits, much less overhead, and no employees or very few employees. It is for these reasons, according to *Entrepreneur Magazine*, that 95 percent of the home-based businesses succeed in their first year and achieve an average income of $50,250 per year, with many earning much more.

I should note that, in addition to all the benefits noted above, Congress will subsidize you while you're growing your small business. If your business produces a loss in the first year or so, you can use that loss against any other income that you have. It can be used against wages earned as an employee, dividends, pensions, or interest income, or against your spouse's earnings if you filed a joint return. If the tax loss exceeds all your and your spouse's income for the year, no problem. You can carry back the loss two years and get a refund from the IRS (and from some states) for up to the last two years of income taxes paid or you can carry over the loss 20 years. You read it right: you can offset up to 20 years of income!

Example: Mike earns $50,000 in a job with the government. If he starts a home-based business that generates a tax loss of $10,000, he pays tax on only $40,000.

In fact, if everyone in America who is employed full-time got a part-time business and used the strategies suggested in this book, each employee could easily reduce his or her taxes from $2,000 to $10,000 or more each year. If all the employees and small business people applied this information, the tax bite in the U.S. would be reduced by a whopping estimated $300 billion each year. (Of course, Congress would have to change the laws if this occurred.)

What Types of Businesses Should I Consider?

This is one of my most frequently asked questions. Actually, starting a business is not as hard as most people think. In most cases, there is little or no licensing required and you can operate it out of your home with few or no overhead costs. The key is deciding what type of business is right for you.

The best business for most people is the one that excites them and/or about which they have substantial knowledge. Consider the things that you are good at or really like to do. Consider your hobbies. I know one person who became an antique dealer because he and his wife loved collecting antiques. Perhaps you like writing and want to be a freelance writer or freelance editor. Tutoring and training such as giving SAT lessons or music lessons from the home are becoming fast-growing businesses.

Many people become distributors of products or services out of their home. If you are good with people, you should also consider one of the many good network marketing companies. Why? These companies have proven products and sales literature and you usually don't have to store or finance inventory or even ship it to customers. The company does all that for you. It will even give you an account of all your sales and of all your distributors' (downline) sales. There is no overhead, such as rent and employees, so there's no liability exposure, which can occur in traditional businesses. Moreover, just about every product that you can think of is currently being marketed using the network marketing approach.

In addition, most network marketing companies provide some form of residual income that provides a continual stream of income from your distributors from year to year and month to month. Finally, you get the same or even better tax benefits with network marketing than you would with any traditional business.

The only downside to network marketing is that some of these operations are shaky. If you go this route, you want to associate with a company that has been around a while and has a proven track record of success and proven marketing programs. Many of these companies have a very high failure rate within the first two years of operation. I would recommend that you consider only companies that have been around and continuously successful for at least two years. Check out the various distributors that you want to be associated with. You want successful people who will teach you and support you. Your best friend may or may not be the ideal person.

> **Strategy**
> Get LUCK—
> Labor Under
> Correct
> Knowledge.

Research has constantly shown that it is rarely the business that determines success or failure. It is usually the business owner. Why does one person succeed and another fail at the same business? Two words: *knowledge* and *action*. Some people want the benefits of having their own business, but they don't take action. The result is business failure. Then there are the people who are always working. They take action all day but still fail. The reason is that they are not taking the correct actions, the knowledgeable actions that will bring the desired results. Again, the result is business failure.

It's like drilling for oil. If you set up a drilling rig in your backyard, it's going to fail to produce oil unless your backyard is in Texas or Alaska. The same rig in a good oil field will produce a gusher because it was placed where oil was known to exist.

The point is that most people who start businesses or become consultants do so without all the necessary knowledge. Consequently, many people quit before they acquire through experience the knowledge that they need—and also without realizing that they are getting substantial tax breaks.

The choice between being rich and being poor, for you and for millions of others, is the opportunity that starting your own consulting or small business offers. If you have one going already, then you need to make sure that you're enjoying the many tax advantages your brilliance in so doing offers you.

Summary

- Job prospects are declining and will continue to do so.
- You will never get rich unless you get your tax affairs down to the legal minimum.
- There are two tax systems in this country: one is for employees and one is for small businesses, consultants, and home-based businesses.
- Everyone should have a home-based business immediately!

Notes

1. Jane Bryant Quinn, "How to Live on One Salary," Woman's Day, November 1, 1994.
2. In 1994, the IRS conservatively estimated that cars cost 29 cents per mile to own and operate. The allowed figure for 2007 is 48.5 cents per mile. This means that the automobile costs cited by Quinn are much lower than they would be today.
3. This assumes a two-week vacation.
4. David D'Arcangelo, Wealth Starts at Home (McGraw-Hill, 1997), p. 13.

2

How to Deduct Your Fun

Taxes are the price that we pay for civilization.

—**Oliver Wendell Holmes, Jr.**

I'm proud to be paying taxes in the United States. The only thing is, I could be just as proud for half the money.

—**Arthur Godfrey**

You are going to love this chapter. It deals with deducting your fun and audit-proofing your records for the Internal Revenue Service (IRS). It also will cover some exceptions that most people and even most accountants don't even know about. It will apply to you if you have a small business but also if your job requires you to entertain prospects or subordinates in order to obtain more business or to help motivate employees.

I should note that prior to 1987, you were allowed to deduct 100 percent of any entertainment cost for you or a

Chapter Overview
- Deduct your meals.
- Learn when you need a receipt and when the IRS doesn't require receipts.
- Deduct theater tickets, golf, plays, and other associated entertainment.
- Deduct season tickets.
- Know when a spouse's meals would be deductible.
- Understand the rules when you go "Dutch treat" with a prospect.
- Know how to audit-proof all entertainment for the IRS.
- Deduct home entertainment.
- Learn about a special exception for parties at home.
- Learn how to deduct large parties without ever discussing business.
- Provide lunches for employees.

prospect. However, as a result of some "tax simplification laws," your entertainment deductions normally are limited to 50 percent.[1] (In fact, whenever you hear that a member of Congress wants "tax simplification" or "tax reform," it doesn't mean what you think it means. It

Chapter Overview (Cont.)
• Deduct business club dues and dues to civic organizations.
• Find out about the "sales seminar at home" exception.

doesn't mean what you think it means. It normally means "stick it to the taxpayer.") There are some exceptions to this 50 percent rule, which will be outlined in this chapter. However, unless noted, the deductions in this chapter will be limited to 50 percent.

A question that comes up frequently in my seminars is, "When do I have to keep receipts?" The IRS has been very taxpayer-friendly lately with respect to receipts. No receipts are needed for entertainment expenses under $75 per expense.[2]

Example: John takes Mary out for a prearranged lunch and discusses business. John spends $25 on pretzels. (Hopefully, they're good pretzels!) John does not need a receipt because the cost of the entertainment is under $75.

Example: If John spent $85 for lunch, which includes drinks, he then would need a receipt.

Author's note: Although you technically don't need entertainment receipts for under $75, I would keep them anyway. IRS agents love seeing receipts, and it will avoid most problems. If you lose a receipt or forgot to get one, you can always use this IRS regulation in an audit.

Strategy 1
Discuss business when you eat.

There are several legal requirements for you to deduct your meals with prospects. First, tax law requires that a business meal be arranged for the purpose of conducting specific business. Your prospect must reasonably expect a business reason for the meal or entertainment.[3]

Example: Sam went to Greasy Lloyd's Restaurant for lunch and happened to discuss business with the waitress. This would not be a deductible business meal because Sam didn't have business intent to meet with the waitress, nor did she reasonably expect to discuss business with Sam as part of the lunch.

Example: Let's assume the same facts as above, but the waitress was Sam's neighbor and told Sam to stop by the restaurant where they could discuss Sam's services as a financial consultant. As part of the discussion, Sam also orders lunch while he is talking with her. This would be a deductible business meal because this was clearly a prearranged meeting with an actual business discussion.

A second requirement of the tax law is that you must discuss business before, during, or after a business meal to qualify for the business meal deduction.[4] This was put in because before the tax simplification law (1986 Tax Reform Act), you could have a quiet business meal and not say anything.

As long as your prospect was a legitimate prospect, this meal was deductible. The law was changed to require you to discuss some specific business. *The key is that you must have and document a clear and specific business discussion.*

The third requirement is that the meal must take place in surroundings conducive to a business discussion.[5] The IRS presumes that the active business discussion requirement is not met if the business meal occurs under circumstances where there is little or no possibility of engaging in business.[6] Eating dinner in a nightclub with a continuous floorshow is an example of a nonbusiness setting; the same would be true for a large cocktail party.[7] Food purchased at the theater would not be a business meal either.

The final requirement is that you must substantiate your meal or entertainment adequately even if a receipt is not required.[8] Here are the exact five questions that you will need to audit-proof your entertainment forever[9]:

- *Who was entertained* (business relationship)? The IRS wants you to identify the person or persons entertained, with names, occupations, official titles, and other corroborative information to establish the business relationship.
- *Where did the entertainment take place?* The nature and place of the entertainment (dinner at Greasy Lloyd's) must be described. When a charge slip or receipt is obtained, the nature and place usually are self-evident.
- *When did the entertainment take place?* The definition of time is usually the date when the entertainment takes place. When entries are made in a diary-type of document, the date on the diary page is adequate support for time.
- *Why did the entertainment take place* (business purpose)? Of the five elements, this is the most important. State the exact nature of the business discussion or activity. Be brief but specific—very specific. If you simply say "prospect" or "goodwill," this will not be enough.[10] You must be more specific. For example, it would be good enough if you said, "Tried to get a listing or referral," "Talked about using my services," "Talked about disability insurance needs or financial needs," or "Talked about opportunity or health care needs."
- How much *did the entertainment cost?* The cost of the entertainment must be recorded someplace. As I noted earlier, when the cost is $75 or more, you must retain documentary evidence, such as a receipt, voucher, or credit-card copy.

There is also one other requirement for all entertainment expenses that was not included in the preceding list. You must record the answers to these five IRS questions in a timely fashion, which means at or near the time of the expenditure[11] in some kind of notebook, diary, or tax organizer. You don't need to do this daily, but the closer in time you document your deductions, the better IRS agents will like it.[12]

Author's note: If you follow everything that I noted above, you will never have to worry about an IRS audit. You will have peace of mind in the face of any audit.

Author's tip: I have found that if people don't have something to trigger them to write down these things each day after each expense, they forget to do it, which results in no deduction. A tax diary or organizer is not only required by the IRS but also quite useful. Think of a tax diary as audit insurance or life insurance.

An interesting case happened when I was working at the IRS. There was a consultant who was being audited for his 1985 expenses in 1987. His accountant told him that he needed to keep some form of tax organizer. He thus converted his appointment book into a diary by backdating all his mileage and entertainment and travel questions using six pens of different colors. Some of the pages looked like they were dragged through the mud. Agatha Christie would have been proud! However, he made one mistake: He used a 1987 diary for his 1985 expenses!

Don't wait until you get audited. Get into the habit of filling out a tax organizer or daily diary, and you will save thousands—and you will have that peace of mind of never worrying about an IRS audit.

Generally, Congress and the IRS want you to discuss business in surroundings conducive to a business discussion. Thus, when you discuss business at a theater, on a golf course, and in a nightclub, this is not deemed conducive surroundings.[13]

The *Internal Revenue Code* allows you to deduct "associated entertainment."

Author's note: I never could understand why Congress wouldn't use wording that everyone understands, such as "fun" instead of "associated entertainment." No wonder few people know a lot about the tax strategies that are available to them.

The question that you may have is, "What exactly is 'associated entertainment'?" The answer is simple: Associated entertainment, also called *goodwill entertainment*, takes place in a nonbusiness setting.[14] No business discussion occurs during the entertainment. The key IRS requirement for you to deduct your fun is that the entertainment must either *precede* or *follow* a substantial and bona fide business discussion during the same day as the entertainment.[15]

Strategy 2
Deduct theater tickets, golf fees, movies, sports tickets, and other "associated entertainment" expenses. Putting it more plainly, this means deducting your fun!

Example: Lee has a business lunch with Karen and discusses business over lunch. If Lee suggests that they go play golf after the lunch, he may deduct 50 percent of all his golfing costs.

Author's tip: Remember, entertainment is 50 percent deductible unless there's a specific exception. When in doubt, you can deduct only 50 percent of the total expense. You would report the full amount of the entertainment to your accountant, alerting him or her that this is 100 percent of the entertainment. He or she will then deduct 50 percent on the tax return. If the entertainment deduction comprises one of the exceptions noted below, this would have to be separated from other, normal entertainment.

To audit-proof your associated entertainment, you must have a link between the business discussion and the entertainment showing that you discussed business either before or after the fun on the same day as the fun.[16] See the example in Figure 2-1 that came from the Tax Reduction Institute's tax organizer.

Note that the business discussion occurred in a proper business setting during dinner and was followed by entertainment *associated with* the dinner discussion. Some examples of associated entertainment that can be linked to business meals and other direct business discussions include entertainment in the following places:

- Nightclubs
- Golf courses
- Theaters
- Sports events

Season's tickets and box seats to theaters and sports events are treated according to the individual events.[17] Each event is treated separately.

Example: Jim holds season's tickets for a professional team. These tickets allow him to attend 10 games during the year. If he brings prospects to 8 of the games and talks business with them before or after the game, he treats 80 percent of the cost of these tickets as being business-related. He thus may deduct 50 percent of the 80 percent of the cost, for 40 percent. (Entertainment is 50 percent deductible unless I state that this is an exception.)

> **Strategy 3**
> Deduct season tickets by event.

The deduction is limited to the face value of the ticket plus any state and local taxes.[18] Thus, if you pay a scalper fee that is more than the face value, any deduction will be based on the face value of the ticket and not the scalper's price.

Author's note: It is amazing that someone in Congress actually thinks up this stuff!

ENTERTAINMENT						
ACTIVITY 1 Who?						
Where?						
Why?						
Breakfast		Home		Other		
Lunch		Golf/Etc.				
Dinner		Cocktails				
Total		Total		Total		

ACTIVITY 2 Who? **J & S Rock**						
Where? **Palm and Kennedy Center**						
Why? **Johnson referral at dinner followed by theatre**						
Breakfast		Home		Other		
Lunch		Golf/Etc.		Theatre	**120**	**00**
Dinner	**235 : 00**	Cocktails	**15 : 00**	Park, etc.	**11**	**00**
Total		Total		Total	**381**	**00**

ACTIVITY 3 Who?						
Where?						
Why?						
Breakfast		Home		Other		
Lunch		Golf/Etc.				
Dinner		Cocktails				
Total		Total		Total		

Figure 2-1. Documentation of a business meal followed by a theater performance. (Note how the theater is linked to the meal with the word *followed.*)

Charity Events

There is one interesting IRS twist to this: If you buy tickets for a charitable event, you are not limited to the face value of the ticket if the following three conditions apply[19]:

- The event is organized for the primary purpose of benefiting a tax-exempt charity.
- All the net proceeds of the event are contributed to the charity.
- The event uses volunteers for substantially all the work performed in carrying out the event.

Thus a charitable golfing event where all the net funds raised go to the Heart Fund or the United Way, for example, would be a qualifying event. (I should note that no matter how needy you may feel that you are, you, personally, are not a qualifying charity.)

One big question that most people have is whether they can deduct the cost of a meal alone with their spouse. The answer is very clear-cut: Absolutely not! The IRS has what is known as a "closely connected" spouse rule.

> **Strategy 4**
> Deduct for feeding and entertaining your spouse.

Author's note: At least the government acknowledges that your spouse is closely connected to you. This rule prevents you from deducting meals out alone with your spouse. Is there a way to deduct the cost of a spouse? The answer is yes! The closely connected spouse rule allows you to bring your spouse and deduct his or her costs whenever you are entertaining another couple.[20] In other words, if your business guest brings a spouse or a guest, you are entitled to bring yours.[21] In addition, if you are not married, you may bring your "significant friend" to help entertain the other couple. Naturally, you must be entertaining the business guest during the ordinary course of your business, and you must meet the business discussion and documentation requirements that I noted earlier in this chapter. I guess that if you are single but living with someone or dating someone, this would be classified as the "closely connected significant friend rule."

Author's elaboration: In case you are curious as to why this deduction for your spouse or significant friend is allowed when your guest has a companion, the rationale for this distinction is that your spouse or significant friend can keep the companion busy while you have a one-on-one conversation with your guest. The key is to note in your tax organizer or diary the name of the other couple and what you discussed. Moreover, this rule can be carried another step. If the other couple brings their children, you probably could bring your kids to keep the prospect's kids busy. This is probably one of the least understood areas for most people and even for accountants. In fact, when I have lectured to accountants and ask about this, very few have heard of this issue.

Strategy 5
Deduct for
Dutch-treat
meals.

The general rule is that if you pay for the meal for you and your guest(s), you can deduct 50 percent of the total cost of the meal. However, if you split the bill, you come under what is known as the *Dutch-treat rules*. A Dutch-treat meal is where you split the meal bill with someone or get two receipts. If you discussed business during the meal and you split the bill, you can deduct your share of the bill that exceeds what you normally would have spent at home or eating out when you don't discuss business. In other words, what you can deduct is the excess of what you normally spend for breakfast, lunch, or dinner when you don't have a business meal.[22] If, for example, you attend a Chamber of Commerce luncheon meeting and the lunch costs more than you would normally spend for lunch, you may claim the excess as a Dutch-treat business lunch.

Author's note: All this presumably would be subject to the 50 percent rule. You can deduct 50 percent of this excess amount over what you would have spent for the meal anyway.

Strategy 6
Document
your personal
meal costs to
support your
Dutch-treat
meals.

The key to this deduction is to document what you ordinarily would spend on breakfast, lunch, or dinner when you don't discuss business. Entries in your diary or tax organizer are strong evidence.[23] What I recommend is to keep a copy of your grocery receipts and note what you spend when you eat out alone or with your family for 30 consecutive days.

There are two methods of tracking the costs of your average personal meals:

Method 1: Write down the actual items consumed, and determine the cost of each item. For example, two eggs for breakfast, when a dozen eggs cost $2.40, would cost $.40. If you need to determine the actual costs only a few times during the year, it's easy to simply to write down the actual items consumed.

Strategy 7
Avoid the
Sutter Rule.

Method 2: I have found that a general rule that has been used in IRS audits is to make an allocation for meals from your grocery bills as follows: 50 percent for dinners, 30 percent for lunches, and 20 percent for breakfast. Sorry, nothing is allocated for snacks! If, for example, the grocery bill for a week amounts to $140, you can estimate the cost for breakfast, lunch, and dinner using the 50—30—20 rule. Thus approximately $70 would be for dinner. You would divide this over the seven days in a week, giving $10 per day. If there were two people in your household, the average cost per person for dinner would be $5. This would be your cost for the year for purposes of determining your Dutch-treat deductions and maximum disallowance. Thus any time you would split the dinner check with a prospect, the amount over $5 would be deductible multiplied by 50 percent. This may seem like a lot of work for a few dollars of deductions, but if you have a Dutch-treat dinner twice a week for 50 weeks, this could amount to thousands just for the dinners! You also would be allowed approximately 100 Dutch-treat lunches and 100 Dutch-treat breakfasts. In fact, you could figuratively eat away your taxes!

The IRS may at its whim invoke the *Sutter rule*. The Sutter rule allows the IRS to disallow a portion of your business meals when such meals absorb substantial amounts of your typical living expenses.[24]

Author's note: There was a case that a former IRS colleague had that involved a doctor who claimed $35,000 in meals in one year. This doctor was the biggest example of what we CPAs call the "P-I-G rule." His lawyer argued at a hearing that "he only eats for business reasons." Obviously, all his deductions were disallowed under the Sutter rule.

Exceptions to the 50 Percent Deduction Rule

There are a couple of exceptions to the 50 percent rule for deducting meals. In these exceptions, you can deduct 100 percent of the meal cost.

The IRS uses an objective test to determine whether an activity is of a type to constitute entertainment, which is 50 percent deductible, or more like business promotion, which is 100 percent deductible. Thus, attending a movie or theatrical performance normally would be considered entertainment. However, it would be 100 percent deductible and not deemed entertainment if done so by a professional theater critic or movie critic.[25] Similarly, a golf club sales rep or golfing consultant who plays golf and demonstrates his or her golf clubs, golfing equipment, or golf training should be able to deduct 100 percent of the greens fees, cost of golf balls, caddie expenses, etc.

> **Strategy 8**
> Some entertainment can be deemed business promotion.

Travel agents would be another example of people who would fall into this category on some expenses. If you were a travel agent and went to various cities to check out the hotels, restaurants, accommodations, and meeting facilities, you would be able to deduct all your expenses and not be subject to the 50 percent rule. Obviously, it would be important to document that you send clients to these places on vacations, document who you met with (such as the director of catering or the convention service),

> **Strategy 9**
> Use entertainment tickets as business gifts to avoid the $25 ceiling.

document that you had made some appointments in advance to meet with these people, etc.

Tax law limits your maximum deduction to $25 for business gifts to any one person during the year.[26] This limitation applies to gifts of tangible personal property and not money,[27] and even worse, a husband and wife are deemed to be one taxpayer for purposes of the $25 limit.[28]

Example: Alan, a consultant, gives a client a housewarming gift of flowers and a giant vase that cost him $300. He may deduct only $25 of the cost of this business gift. Ugh!

One interesting exception is that gifts made to a business where there is no single person designated to receive or benefit from the gift have no limit.[29]

Example: I do a lot of programs for Tony Robbins' Wealth Mastery seminars. Every year I send to the marketing department and the production department of Robbins Research a big basket of candy and fruit that cost several hundred dollars each. Since they are sent to each department without mentioning any names, the entire cost of the baskets would be deductible and not be subject to the $25 limitation.

If you give gifts of entertainment, you have several alternatives for treating the cost of the tickets. You have the choice of treating a gift of theater tickets either as an entertainment expense or as a business gift.[30] As an entertainment expense, you could deduct 50 percent of the cost of the ticket and avoid the $25 limit. As a business gift, you could deduct 100 percent of the gift up to the $25 limit.[31] Moreover, when giving tickets to an event, you need not be present,[32] as you would have to be if you gave away gift certificates to restaurants, which is discussed below. So how do you decide whether to treat gifts of tickets as entertainment or as business gifts?

The answer is very simple. If the face value of the ticket is less than $50, you should treat it as a business gift and deduct 100 percent of the cost up to $25. This would result in a greater deduction than if you classified this as a gift of entertainment, which allows only a 50 percent deduction. However, if the cost is $50 or greater, you would want to classify this as entertainment and deduct 50 percent of the ticket cost *without limit*.

As a result of the tax simplification law (remember that this term means you have been shafted by Congress), gifts of entertainment or meals are no longer allowed if you are not present.[33] You are entitled to a tax deduction for a business meal only if you are present during the meal.[34]

Without question, the most overlooked type of entertainment is home entertainment. This is just as deductible as having a business meal in a restaurant and in some cases even more deductible.

Your home is already deemed to be a setting conducive to a business discussion.[35] If you have a couple in your home for dinner, it's easy to have a one-on-one conversation. You do not need to spend more time trying to conduct business than you spend on entertaining your guests.[36] In fact, there's no time limit for the business discussion.

Strategy 10
Deduct your entertainment at home.

Example: Sam and Mary entertain Bob and Alice. Sam has a five-second discussion about getting referrals, and the party lasts four hours. Bob may deduct the cost of the party. There is no time limit to the business discussion.

Moreover, if you entertain at home and have only a few people for dinner, you probably won't spend more than $75 and thus won't need a receipt.

Author's tip: You have to discuss business to deduct any entertainment. Here's one suggestion that I give: Most people will start out the discussion with some variation of "How's business?" You should respond, "Business is unbelievable," because this response covers the state of your business either way! However, you need to add one other line, which is, "However, I never have enough business" or "I never have enough referrals" or "I never have enough clients." This is quick and to the point, and it suffices as an appropriate business discussion if it's clear that you're asking for business or referrals.

Hot Tip
Don't have all your home entertainment be $74.99!

Your home entertainment deductions are secure when you discuss specific business with guests.[37] You don't even need to discuss business with your spouse or closely connected significant friends to deduct them too.[38] Keep the guest list small (fewer than 12 people). Then you can talk to everyone with whom you need to discuss business. With small groups, you can easily discuss business with everyone there.

When you invite 12 people or more to your home, you will be hard pressed to prove to the IRS that you had specific business discussions with everyone in attendance. Therefore, you must establish some other type of commercial motivation. It's not that you can't talk business with everyone and document this fact in your diary. It's just that it would be difficult to do.

Strategy 11
Give small parties at home.

One approach to this problem is to display products on the wall. If you entertain a group for the purpose of showing a display of your business products or services, commercial motivation generally is deemed to be clearly established.[39] When you combine the display of products with an invitation that invites the guests for a specific business reason, you greatly improve your chances for deductibility.[40] It is also best that you have little social or personal relationship with the guests—the less social the better.[41]

Strategy 12
Deduct entertainment for large groups.

One note of caution in home entertainment: Never, never combine a personal event with a business entertainment event. A birthday party for your 10-year-old with business guests in attendance won't cut the mustard with the IRS.[42] The bottom line is that home entertainment, especially when large groups are involved, is deductible only when you can firmly establish a business motive.[43]

Example: Wanda (I've changed the person's name for privacy reasons), a real estate professional, invited 100 people over to her home for cocktails to celebrate being in real estate 20 years. This establishes a business agenda for the party. At the party, she has a buffet with pictures of properties above the food. She then has her husband take a picture of people looking at the displays while they're getting their food. This establishes a clear business setting and motive. Finally, when she goes shopping, she obtains two receipts from the grocery store: one for the party food and one for the general household. She staples them together and labels which is which. She clearly would be allowed to deduct the entire cost of the party (multiplied by the 50 percent limitation).

| **Strategy 13**
Give sales seminars and presentations in your home. | Normally, food and entertainment provided in your home as part of a business discussion are only 50 percent deductible, as with the general rule for entertainment deductions. However, food served at a seminar would be an exception to the rule—100 percent deductible.[44] In addition, there was a tax court decision[45] that noted that all food and beverages served to prospects are 100 percent deductible if provided at home during a sales presentation or sales seminar. |

Example: Juan holds sales presentations in his home for his network marketing business. If Juan provides food and drinks, he may deduct 100 percent of the cost of this entertainment.

Author's note: The key to this 100 percent deduction is documentation. Again, you have to show the who, where, when, why, and how much of the entertainment, as discussed earlier. You should note in your diary or tax organizer who attended (or have your guests sign a register), the date, what was discussed, what was served, and the cost of the food.

| **Strategy 14**
Give parties for employees. | The reasonable cost of providing social or recreational parties for employees, year-end holiday parties, or a summer outing that is primarily for employees and their families is 100 percent deductible.[46,47] You must, however, invite all employees. No discrimination is allowed.[48] Thus, if you have several workers and have a year-end celebration that they, their families, and you and your spouse attend, you may deduct the whole cost of the party. If it were just you and your spouse, it would not be deductible. The key is that the social outing be primarily for employees other than for the owners and their families. |

If you have any employees, you may provide lunches to your staff on a tax-free basis if you provide lunch for over half the employees and any one of the following conditions holds[49]:

> **Strategy 15**
> Provide lunches for employees.

1. There is a short lunch period[50] (generally no more than 45 minutes in length).
2. The employees are available for emergencies (such as ambulance services).[51,52]
3. There are insufficient eating facilities nearby.

Also, meals must be furnished on normal workdays.[53]

You deduct dues paid to business clubs when such payment is in the ordinary and necessary course of business.[54] The terms *ordinary* and *necessary* mean that the expenses are customary, usual or normal, and helpful or appropriate.[55] Dues to your local Chamber of Commerce almost always would be appropriate.[56] Dues paid to your professional societies, such as the Board of Realtors, Life Underwriters, enrolled agents societies, consultant societies, etc., are deductible.[57] Trade association dues also would be deductible if the association's purpose is the furthering of the business interests of its members.[58] Dues to community clubs organized to attract tourists and new members to your locality are deductible.[59] Dues to civic organizations such as the Rotary Club, Kiwanis, and Lions Club are deductible.[60]

> **Strategy 16**
> Deduct dues to business and civic organizations.

Country Club and Health Club Dues

As a result of tax simplification, Congress eliminated the deduction for country clubs and health clubs.[61] However, strange as it may seem, you can get a deduction for these kinds of clubs if the company reimburses the employees for the dues to the extent that they are used for business as a working-condition fringe benefit.[62]

Example: Cornell's consulting company provides Peter with a country club membership worth $20,000, which he does not record as compensation. If he substantiates that 60 percent of the time that he uses the club is for business, he may exclude 60 percent of the $20,000 cost of the club and be taxed on only $8,000. Cornell's company may deduct the entire cost of the membership. I should note that this would work for your employees regardless of what entity you conduct your business under and should work for you if you are incorporated.

Author's tip: The key here is documentation. You must show when you or your employee used the club and to what extent it was used to entertain prospects and discuss business. A tax diary or tax organizer is a necessity here. A little documentation goes a long way.

Author's tip: Regardless of the deductibility or nondeductibility of the club dues, any meal would be deductible (at 50 percent) if you discuss business during the meal. Again, the key is documentation and writing down the five elements of substantiation.

Summary

- **Strategy 1:** Discuss business when you eat—and document everything with the five elements of documentation—who, where, when, why, and how much.
- **Strategy 2:** Deduct theater tickets, golf fees, movies, sports tickets, and other "associated entertainment" expenses.
- **Strategy 3:** Deduct season's tickets by event.
- **Strategy 4:** Deduct feeding and entertaining your spouse.
- **Strategy 5:** Deduct for Dutch-treat meals.
- **Strategy 6:** Document your personal meal costs to support your Dutch-treat meals.
- **Strategy 7:** Avoid the Sutter rule.
- **Strategy 8:** Some entertainment can be deemed business promotion.
- **Strategy 9:** Use entertainment tickets as business gifts to avoid the $25 ceiling.
- **Strategy 10:** Deduct your entertainment at home.
- **Strategy 11:** Give small parties at home.
- **Strategy 12:** Deduct entertainment for large groups.
- **Strategy 13:** Give sales seminars and presentations in your home.
- **Strategy 14:** Give parties for employees.
- **Strategy 15:** Provide lunches for employees.
- **Strategy 16:** Deduct dues to business and civic organizations.

Notes

1. Internal Revenue Code (IRC hereafter) 274(n)(1).
2. Section 1.274-5(c) of the Income Tax Regulations (ITR hereunder); IR 95-56; notice 05-50, 1995-42 IRB.
3. Section 274 (a) of the IRC; 1.274-2(c)(4) of the ITR and J. Flaig v. Commissioner, 47 TCM 1161.
4. Section 274 (a) of the IRC.
5. Section 1.274-2(f)(2)(i)(a) of the ITR.
6. Section 1.274-2(c)(7) of the ITR.
7. Ibid.
8. Section 1.274-5T(c) of the ITR.
9. Ibid.
10. Section 1.274-2(d)(3) of the ITR; J. B. Walliser v. Commissioner, 72 TC 433 (1979); P.H. Leon v. Commissioner, 37 TCM 1514 (1978).

11. Section 1.274-5T(c)(1) and (2) of the ITR.
12. Section 1.274-5T(c)(2) of the ITR.
13. Section 1.274-2(c)(7) of the ITR.
14. Section 1.274-2(d)(1) of the ITR.
15. Section 1.274-2(d)(1)(ii) of the ITR.
16. Section 1.274-2(d)(3)(i) of the ITR.
17. Revenue Ruling 63-144, 1963-2 C.B. 129, Q&A 50.
18. Section 1.274(l)(1)(A) of the ITR and Section 274(n)(1) of the IRC.
19. Section 274(l)(1)(B) of the IRC.
20. Section 1.274-2(d)(4) of the ITR; Revenue Ruling 2000-45, IRB 2000-41; 46 RIA Weekly Alert, No. 39 (9/21/2000).
21. Ibid.
22. For example, Sutter v. Commissioner, 21 TC 170 (1953), acq. 1954-1 C.B. 6.
23. Section 1.274-5(c)(2) of the ITR.
24. Revenue Ruling 63-144, Q&A 31, 1963-2 C.B. 129; Sutter v. Commissioner, 21 TC 170 (1953), acq. 1954-1 C.B. 6.
25. Section 1.274-2(b) (i) and (ii) of the ITR.
26. Section 274(b)(1) of the IRC.
27. Section 274(j)(3)(A) of the IRC.
28. Section 274(b)(2)(B) of the IRC.
29. Section 1.274-3(e)(2) of the ITR.
30. Sections 1.274-2(b)(1)(i) and 1.274-2(b)(1)(iii) of the ITR.
31. Ibid.
32. Section 1.274-2(b)(1)(iii)(b) of the ITR.
33. Section 274(K)(2) of the IRC.
34. Section 274(K)(1)(B) of the IRC.
35. Section 1.274-2(e)(2) of the ITR.
36. Section 1.274-2(f)(2) of the ITR.
37. Section 1.274-2(d)(4); Revenue Ruling 63-144, cited above, Q&A 26-28.
38. Ibid.
39. Section 1.274-2(c)(4) of the ITR.
40. Ibid.
41. Steel v. Commissioner, 28 TCM 1301 (1969).
42. Sections 1.274-2(c)(4) and 1.274-2(c)(7)(ii) of the ITR.
43. Section 1.274-2(c)(4) of the ITR.
44. Sections 274(n)(2)(A) and 274(e)(8) of the IRC.
45. Robert Matlock v. Commissioner, TC Memo 1992-324.
46. H. Rept, 99-842, P. II-28, Section 274(e)(4) of the IRC and Section 1.274-2(f)(2)(v) of the ITR.
47. Ibid.
48. Ibid.
49. Section 119(b)(4) of the IRC and Section 1.119-1(a)(2) of the ITR.
50. Section 1.119-1(a)(2)(ii)(b).
51. Section 1.119-1(a)(2)(ii).
52. Ibid.
53. Section 1.119-1(a)(2)(i) of the ITR.
54. Section 274(a)(2)(C) of the IRC.
55. Section 162(a) of the IRC and regulations thereunder.
56. Section 274(a)(2)(C) of the IRC.
57. Section 1.274-2(e)(3)(ii) of the ITR.

58. Section 1.274-2(e)(3)(ii) and 1.274-2(f)(2)(i) of the ITR.
59. Roland J. Hymel, Jr., 86-1 U.S. TC Section 9419 (5th Cir. 1986).
60. Section 1.274-2(a)2)(iii)(b) of the ITR.
61. Section 1.274-2(a)(2)(iii)(a) of the ITR.
62. Section 1.132-5(s) of the ITR.

3

How to Turn Your Vacation into a Tax-Deductible Write-Off

The politicians' promises of yesterday are the taxes of today.

—Mackenzie King

Read my lips, no new taxes.

—George Bush

I have no intention of raising taxes.

—Bill Clinton

At my seminars people often ask whether they can deduct their meals while eating alone. The answer is yes, if you are on business travel, because that will allow a deduction for meals for each day that you are traveling on business. So, when are you traveling on business?

You are on business travel, according to the IRS, when you are traveling from home, overnight, or for a period of time sufficient to require sleep.[1] For example, assume that you live in Washington, DC, fly to New York City in the morning, and return that evening.

Chapter Overview

- Understand when you are on business travel.
- Understand the difference between business transportation and "on the road" expenses.
- Know how to deduct your spouse's or significant friend's expenses to any business convention and have the IRS bless those expenses.
- Know how you can maximize your business car usage with conventions travel, especially when you take family members with you on the trip.
- Understand the IRS dry cleaning rule.
- Learn how to avoid the congressional trap of taking courses on the wrong ships!
- Learn how to deduct the expenses for all weekends without doing any work on the weekends.

You would not be deemed on business travel since you were not away from home overnight on business. The IRS would classify this trip to New York as a non-travel trip. On this trip you would be allowed to deduct only your transportation costs of getting to the city.[2]

> **Chapter Overview (Cont.)**
> - Learn about four time-tested reasons to deduct most business trips anywhere in the world.
> - Learn how to audit-proof your travel expenses for the IRS.

Although the IRS doesn't specifically state that you must sleep overnight on your business trip, for all practical purposes, this is usually required. You may be able to get around this if you take a daily trip to a job location for several weeks that might be 170 miles away, for example.[3] In this situation, even if you didn't sleep overnight somewhere, the IRS may deem this to be business travel. However, to save yourself any uncertainty or challenge, you are better off sleeping somewhere overnight.

Author's elaboration: I call this the "strange bed" rule. I encourage people who want to establish "business travel" status to stay overnight in a strange bed, … conducting business. This can be a hotel, a friend's home, or a family member's home. The key is that you rarely stay there and that you are sleeping at your business location.

Notice, however, that it doesn't have to be in a hotel. If you choose to stay with friends or a relative, this would be "staying overnight," as long as you were on a business trip with a business motive. You should document in your tax organizer where you stayed and deduct any out-of-pocket expenses that you incurred.

I should note that there is no geographic limit to the business travel. For example, I gave a seminar in Gaithersburg, Maryland, that is about six minutes from my home. However, I stayed in the hotel the evening before the meeting to avoid potential car and traffic problems. I was considered to be on business travel.

I should note at this juncture that there is a lot of confusion between *transportation* expenses and *on-the-road* expenses. Many people and many accountants seem to combine this under one set of rules. However, they are treated differently; each category has its own separate rule base. It is possible to take a business trip where transportation expenses are not deductible but on-the-road expenses are deductible.

What are the differences? Transportation expenses are those costs that you incur in getting to and from your destination.[4] The actual cost of your airfare or car costs, if you drove to your destination, would come under this category. The on-the-road expenses include all costs necessary to sustain life while on your trip.[5] These expenses comprise lodging, meals, laundry, dry cleaning, and similar expenses.[6]

Author's tip: Not only are your dry cleaning and laundry expenses deductible while you are on business travel, but you can deduct the first laundry and dry cleaning expenses you incur when you get home, as long as your clothing was soiled on the business trip. You do not need to get your clothes dry-cleaned and laundered while away on the trip.[7]

The tax law rule is that, for every day you are on business travel, you may deduct 100 percent of your on-the-road expenses[8] but only 50 percent of your meal costs.[9] An example will illustrate this.

Example: Allison incurs the following on-the-road costs while on business travel:

$400 for hotels
$50 for dry cleaning
$20 in tips
$300 in food

She may deduct all of the hotels, dry cleaning, and tips but only $150 of the meal costs, which are limited to 50 percent.

You may *not*, however, deduct the cost of any entertainment where there was no business motive or prospecting.[10] Thus, if you were to go to a movie alone while on the business trip, the movie would not be deductible. (Darn!)

Moreover, the IRS has a convenient new ruling for travel-related receipts that I mentioned in a previous chapter. The IRS has stated[11] that you don't need receipts for travel if the expenditure is less than $75 per expense.

Example: Kim spends the following on her business trip:

$6.00 for drinks on the plane
$4.00 in skycap tips
$6.95 for breakfast
$12.00 for lunch
$50.00 for a fabulous dinner
$300.00 for airfare

She would only need to keep a receipt for the airfare, which is the only expense that was $75 or more. She would, however, need to have to document these expenses in some diary or tax organizer.

Strategies to Increase Travel Deductions and Add More Fun

Hire your spouse or significant friend. If you want to take trips with your spouse or significant other and deduct the travel expenses for both of you,

you must have a legitimate business reason for bringing along that person.[12] If he or she is in an entirely different business than you, taking your spouse to one of your business conventions would not result in tax deductions for your spouse. He or she would need to have a business reason for being on the trip, independent of being your spouse.

If you want to take your spouse or significant friend on a business trip or to a convention, you can do so if he or she is licensed in your business (such as real estate or securities or insurance) or—and you will like this— can make money for you at the convention! But what does "make money for you" at the convention or on the business trip mean?

Interestingly, Congress actually defined what this means. Starting in 1994:

- Your spouse or significant friend must be a bona fide employee of your business, and
- Your spouse or significant friend must be traveling for a bona fide business purpose, and
- The expense would otherwise be deductible.

Let's examine what all this means to you. If your spouse helps in marketing, computer work, or management of your business, it certainly would be important to take him or her to a convention where courses were given in these areas. If your spouse is your accountant, on the other hand, you would not be able to take him or her to the convention unless there were some programs relating to what he or she does, such as tax planning.

 Take your business car for family travel. Tax law allows you to deduct the cost of your business trip.[13] If you travel with nonbusiness family members, you are allowed to deduct the cost that you would have incurred had you taken the trip alone.[14] Since traveling with a full car costs no more than traveling alone, all of your business car expenses are deductible, even if you have nonbusiness passengers. What this means is that you could deduct your gas and tolls and increase your business mileage for your car.

Author's tip: For consultants and small business owners who normally don't have a lot of business mileage on their vehicles (such as medical or legal professionals), this point of taking your car to a convention or out-oftown seminars becomes crucial. This one trip could increase your business use to a significant extent, which would allow you to depreciate a large portion of your vehicle and deduct a larger portion of some big expenses, such as insurance and repairs. As we will discuss in Chapter 5, your deduction for various car expenses is a ratio of your business mileage to your total mileage. One out-of-town business trip could make a big difference.

Lodging and meal expenses. One common question I get concerns lodging and meals. If you take someone on the trip, your food costs will be more and your room costs may be more than what you would have spent had you gone alone. The rule is that you deduct all of your costs as if you had taken the trip alone.[15] Thus, if a motel costs $100 for one occupant and $120 for the family, you deduct $100. The $20 difference is a personal, nondeductible expense. What I recommend for documentation is either to ask the hotel what the single room rate would be or to remove the rate card from behind the door. (If you are ever in a room where the rate card is missing, I probably stayed in that room!)

Drive 300 miles a day toward your business destination. The federal government reimburses IRS employees a full day's per diem for each 300 miles of travel.[16] Take advantage of this rule. Plan your trips to cover 300 miles a day in direct route to your business destination. Each such day will count as a full business day and also allow you to deduct your on-the-road expenses for the day. This 300-mile rule also will determine the maximum amount of travel days that IRS will allow with your car. You would divide the amount of mileage for your trip by 300 and round up if there is a fraction. This will determine the maximum number of travel days allowed.

Example: Tom drives 800 miles to a convention in Orlando, Florida. He takes his time in seeing the sights and takes 14 days to go the 800 miles. The IRS will allow only three business days as travel days (800/300).

Take courses on U.S. cruise ships. There are a lot of organizations recently that are encouraging people to take courses on cruise ships with the promise of deductibility of those courses. Are all these claims true? The answer is clear-cut: it depends!

If you're looking for a vacation cruise ship subsidy, this is it—but only if you meet the four requirements below. You, and possibly your spouse, can deduct up to $2,000 each year for attending cruise ship conventions directly related to your business, provided:[17]

- The cruise ship is a registered U.S. vessel.
- All ports of call are in the United States or U.S. possessions.
- You submit two supporting statements with your tax return. One statement signed by you should give the days of transportation, number of hours of the trip, and the program of the scheduled business activity. In addition, you need a statement signed by an officer or official of the course or ship showing the number of hours of the business seminar and how many hours you attended.
- More than 50 percent of your total days should be spent on business. Thus, if the course is for one day but the cruise is for 14 days, you

would not get a deduction for the cruise. See the discussion below on transportation.

Make weekends deductible. How would you like to treat Saturday and Sunday as business days without ever working on the weekend? Believe it or not, you can treat weekends as business days—if you know what you are doing.

Generally, because it's so attractive, foreign travel has stricter rules than domestic travel.[18] If you meet these rules, you will satisfy any IRS challenge and lock in your travel deductions. I will, therefore, focus on the foreign rules for deducting travel expenses, since this will protect you when traveling both in the U.S. and abroad.

When you're traveling to a foreign destination, you may count as business days all weekends and legal holidays that fall between business meeting days.[19] Thus, you want to sandwich your weekend days and/or holidays between business days. This is important to you for two reasons:

- You deduct all the on-the-road expenses for the weekend and holidays.[20]
- You add these days for purposes of determining if your transportation expenses are deductible.

Example: Thelma leaves for a business meeting in Hawaii on Thursday with a business meeting on both Friday and Monday and returns home on the following Tuesday night. Saturday and Sunday would be considered business days since they are sandwiched in between business days (Friday and Monday).

Author's note: If Friday or Monday is a federal holiday, you can sandwich the weekend and the holiday between business days. Thus, if the holiday is on a Monday, you would set up meetings on Friday and Tuesday, thus sandwiching in three days without doing any work on those three days. They would all be deemed business days for the on-the-road expenses and for transportation. We really have some great tax laws; it's just that most people aren't aware of them!

A second approach to deducting weekends surprisingly comes from an unlikely source—the IRS! In a private ruling,[21] the IRS allowed Saturday and Sunday to be considered business days if the costs of staying over were less than the savings on airfare of traveling after Saturday, which is usually the case. The following example will illustrate this point.

Example: Thelma leaves for a convention in Hawaii on Sunday and would have returned home on Thursday, which would have cost her $1,200. If, however, she stays over in Hawaii Friday and Saturday and leaves on Sunday, her cost would be $400 (thus saving $800). As long as her food and lodging for Friday and Saturday and Sunday are less than $800, she may count Friday, Saturday, and Sunday as business days. She may also count as business days each convention day and each travel day.

Count travel days as business days. This is an idea most people often over-look. Days in transit are considered business days provided that the travel to your business destination is by reasonably direct route and does not involve substantial nonbusiness diversions.[22] Remember that when a day is classified as a business day, you can deduct all your on-the-road costs for that day and the day is counted toward satisfying the business trip test for transportation, which will be discussed later.

Example: Sam leaves New York for a convention in Vancouver, BC, on Thursday. He has a seminar on Friday and sets up referral meetings on Monday with various military base personnel. On Tuesday he leaves to return to New York; however, due to the time zone change, he doesn't arrive until Wednesday. Thursday is a business day (travel). Friday is a busi-ness day (seminar). Saturday and Sundays are business days because they were sandwiched between business days. Monday was a business day because it was a workday. Tuesday and Wednesday are business days due to being travel days.

Although you need to take a reasonably direct route, this requirement does not affect the mode of transportation that you use. Thus, you may take the trip by automobile, train, plane, or boat.[23] Thus, even if flying to your Hawaii destination would have cost only $400, you could take a boat to Hawaii that costs $1,400. The cost is not relevant.

There is, however, a special rule for luxury boats. The allowable deduc-tion for cruise ships may not exceed twice the highest amount generally allowable per day to a low-ranking White House employee traveling in the United States, multiplied by the number of days on the ship.[24] In addition, if you are simply using the cruise ship as a means of transportation to your business appointment or seminar, then it does not have to be a U.S. ship and you don't need any signed statements, as you would if you took a course on the ship.[25]

Author's note: It amazes me that someone would even bother to think about trivial guidelines like this. So much for tax simplification!

Example: You take a six-day cruise from New York City to London on the Queen Elizabeth II. Your deduction may not exceed twice the White House per diem rate. If the White House per diem rate is $215, your deduction for a six-day trip may not exceed $2,580 per person ($430 per day × six days).

Combine some fun with a business day without losing any deduction. If your presence is required at a particular place for a specific and bona fide business purpose, that day is counted as a business day, even if your presence is required for only part of the day.[26] This applies even if you spend more time sightseeing during normal working hours than participating in business activities.[27] Thus, if you were to deliver a document to a client in Washington, DC, or attend a meeting that lasted 30 minutes, you could spend the rest of the time having fun in Washington. The key is to set up in advance at least one business appointment.

Attend a convention or a seminar. If a convention or seminar has at least six hours of scheduled business activities during the day and you attend at least two-thirds of those activities, your day is considered a business day.[28] I call this the "four hour and one minute rule." Thus, if you spend the majority of the working hours (generally four hours and one minute) pursuing your trade or business by attending a convention or seminar, the day is counted as a business day.

When you are prevented from engaging in the conduct of your trade or business due to circumstances beyond your control, the day is still counted as a business day, even if you spend the day playing in the sand and enjoying the sun.[29]

Example: Todd was meeting a prospect in Hawaii with whom he had made an appointment in advance. If the prospect gets sick and cancels the meeting while Todd is in Hawaii, the entire day would still be deemed a business day. The same result would occur if Todd was expecting to fly home but the airline cancelled the flight due to mechanical difficulties and scheduled him to fly home the next day.

Caretake your rental property. Necessary travel to caretake your rental property is deductible.[30] The key is that it must be necessary, which is determined by the facts and circumstances. If you collect the rents and actively participate in the day-to-day operations of the rental property, you will obviously have to take some trips to make sure that the property is in good condition. You will also have to check on rents in the area, make repairs, and speak with certain vendors.

Even if you engage a management company to look after the property, you must check on their work. Are they maintaining the property? Is the rent reasonable? How do the tenants feel about the management company, and how does the company feel about the tenants? It could take several days to get the answers to all these questions and would certainly justify your trip. The key, again, is to document in your tax diary or tax organizer what you did and with whom you met.

If you spend any days repairing and maintaining the property on a fulltime basis, those days would be deemed business days and not personal days.[31] Moreover, even if people related to you use the property for recreation on the same day, the day is not a personal day.[32]

Visit colleagues and improve your skills and get referrals. The rationale is that you can learn new business skills from your colleagues. Therefore, you can design combined business and pleasure trips to make the rules work for you. Again, the key is to make appointments in advance and document them (with whom did you meet and for how long?). In addition, give a short description of the business discussion, such as " discussed sales or marketing techniques."

Example: You live in Washington, DC, and take a trip to Dallas, Phoenix, San Francisco, Denver, Minneapolis, and Pittsburgh. At each location, you spend a few days visiting with colleagues to learn new business skills or attempting to get referrals for any prospects who move to Washington, DC. You take the trip by automobile and drive at least 300 miles each or more each day toward the next visit. Assuming that you made no side trips for pleasure, all the days would be business days. You would deduct all of your on-the-road expenses and all days would be business days for the transportation deduction.

Get educated out of town. Most people mistakenly believe that if a course is offered in your hometown it would be unreasonable to take the same course elsewhere, such as Hawaii. The fact is that you are allowed deductions for travel to and from educational facilities, meetings, seminars, and conventions that improve your business—regardless of where the events are held.[33] Thus, if the exact same seminar is held both in your hometown and at a nice out-of-town resort, there is no requirement that you stay at home. At the Tax Reduction Institute, we always allow our participants to enroll in courses taken anywhere in the country or to transfer to any course and even encourage exotic locations. Famed speaker, Tony Robbins, takes this concept one step further: most of his courses and seminars are in Hawaii, Las Vegas, Florida, and Anaheim, California (where Disneyland is located). Nice planning, Tony!

Hunt for a job anywhere in the U.S. The IRS allows deductions for all expenses directly related to a search for employment in the same trade or business. It makes no difference if the search is successful or unsuccessful.[34]

Author's note: Do not take all your job-hunting trips to the same place every year! Also, to audit-proof a trip, you need documentation of your intention to search for a job *prior* to your trip. You should maintain in your files correspondence before the trip. In addition, you should maintain in your tax organizer or diary correspondence after the trip as to whom you met, when you met them, how long the meeting lasted, and a brief description of the discussion.

Maximize your deductions for travel in the U.S. As was discussed, you are allowed to deduct on-the-road expenses for each day that you are on "business travel status." Transportation, however, has a completely separate set of rules, as illustrated by the flowchart in Figure 3-1.

As I discuss the rules, I encourage you to follow along on the flowchart. Understanding this chart will enable you to determine exactly how many days must be business days for you to deduct all of your transportation.

It is essential that your primary purpose of the trip be for business.[35] Thus, you *must* have clear business intent before you leave for the trip. This is a crucial point that has caused a great deal of deductions to be lost without proper planning. You should document your intent by sending letters to confirm your appointments or keep copies of e-mails. You don't need to have all your appointments set up in advance, but at least a few must be prearranged.

Example: Connie is a network marketing consultant out of Sacramento, California. She wants to go to New York. She advertises for prospects in *The New York Times* and keeps a copy of the ad. She also sends confirming letters to her appointments, noting the day, time, and place for the meeting. This should be more than enough to satisfy the "intent" test.

For trips within the U.S., your primary purpose must be for business. Although the courts and the IRS have based this on "facts and circumstances,"[36] most cases interpret this to mean that you spend more than one-half your time attending to business and appointments.[37]

Example: Jim meets with some potential clients or distributors in Hawaii on Friday and Monday and returns home the following Friday. If he travels to Hawaii on Thursday, six days out of the nine would be business (Thursday and Friday for travel, Friday and Monday for work, and the weekend sandwiched between business days counts as business days). Since six out of nine is more than one-half, Jim may deduct all of his travel Hawaii. However, because he has only six business days, he may deduct only those six days of his on-the-road expenses.

Maximize your deductions for foreign travel. Like most things in tax law, there is very little simplification. Foreign travel has its own rules that make it different from domestic travel. The general rule is that when you

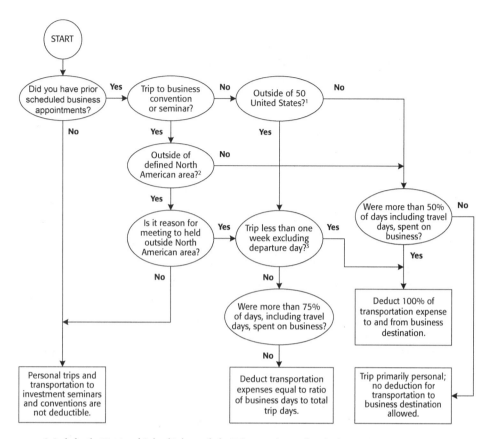

1. Includes the District of Columbia but excludes U.S. possessions and territories.
2. Trip outside Canada, Mexico, Jamaica, Barbados, Grenada, the U.S., its possessions, the Trust Territory of the Pacific, the Marshall Islands, the Federated States of Micronesia, Jarvis Island, Johnston Island, Kingman Reef, Costa Rica, Dominica, Dominican Republic, Guyana, Honduras, Saint Lucia, Trinidad, Tobago, and Palau. See Section 274(b)(3) and Rev. Rul. 87-95, 1987-2 C.B. 79 and Rul 94-56, 1994-36 IRB.
3. Assuming one deductible business day during the trip; Reg.§ 1.274-4(c).

Figure 3-1. Flowchart for deducting transportation expenses when trip combines business with pleasure

leave the U.S., you can deduct your transportation as a ratio of business days to total days.[38] Thus, if you take a 13-day trip of which eight were deemed business days, 8/13ths of your transportation would be deductible. There are, however, two notable exceptions to this rule where you would be able to deduct 100 percent of your transportation without spending 100 percent of your days on business.

The first exception is known as the one-week loophole.[39] You'll like this! Congress allows a 100 percent deduction for transportation even if you work on business only one or two days *if* you are back home within one week. Thus, if you have a meeting in London on Monday and you leave for that meeting the previous Sunday; you can deduct all of your transportation if you are back home by Saturday. If you leave on Saturday, you must be back home by Friday. Remember: this applies only to foreign trips and you must be home within one week to qualify for this exception.

The second exception to the general rule for foreign travel is if your total business days equal or exceed 75 percent of the total days away from home, you may deduct 100 percent of your transportation.[40]

Example: Sue has some distributors in Italy. She spends 12 days away from home and meets with her distributors or provides seminars for them or their customers for eight days. If she has two travel days, she may deduct 100 percent of her transportation under this exception because she spent 75 percent or more of her days on business (eight work days and two travel days).

Maximize your seminar and convention travel. The final type of trip that has its own rules is seminar and convention travel. As with the general rule for domestic travel, you can deduct a percentage of your transportation costs based on the ratio of business days to the total days.[41] However, if you travel outside of what is defined as "the North American area," the rules are a lot stricter. You must have a reasonable basis for being at those conventions,[42] which is a much tougher standard than for domestic conventions]or seminars or going within the North American area.

This North American area comprises the United States and its possessions, the Trust Territory of the Pacific Islands, Canada, and Mexico. Puerto Rico is considered a U.S. possession and thus is within the North American area.[43] In addition, the U.S., as a result of treaties, has added the Caribbean Basin countries to this area.[44] These countries are Barbados, Bermuda, Dominica, the Dominican Republic, Grenada, Guyana, Honduras, Jamaica, Trinidad and Tobago, Saint Lucia, and Costa Rica. (There must have been some members of Congress who wanted to visit these countries!)

Example: Carol and Nick attend a convention for U.S. makeup artists. If the convention is held in the defined North American area, it would be deductible; however, if held outside this area, it probably would not be deductible.

Author's note: If you are attending a convention or seminar outside of the defined North American area, you must have a strong reason for being there. Thus, for example, if you're a lawyer who deals in international law, you normally can't take a seminar or attend a convention in France. If, however, a seminar in France covers some specialized French law topic to which your practice relates and you can't get this training anywhere within the defined North American area, you could probably deduct the seminar in France.

Just to get you used to using the flowchart, we'll start off with the first question: "Was it a business trip?" If you didn't have business intent before you left for the trip, you would get no transportation deduction.

Let's use some examples to pull all these rules together and to get you to use the flowchart.

Example: Sam takes a 10-day trip to San Diego for a convention. The convention lasts five days, but he also has two travel (business) days. Thus, there are seven business days out of 10. It was a business trip. We proceed to the box, "Trip for business convention or seminar?" The answer would be yes. The next box asks, "Outside of the Defined North American Area." The answer would be no, since San Diego is within that area.

The next box asks, "Were more than 50 percent of the total days including travel days spent on business?" The answer would be yes (seven business days out of 10). Thus, Sam can deduct 100 percent of his transportation. In addition, because he has seven business days, he can deduct seven days of on-the-road expenses.

Author's note: If this trip were outside the area, such as France, he would have to have a good reason to be there for his business.

Example: Sam wants to set up a distributor network in Hawaii. He spends three days meeting with people and two travel days out of a 14-day trip. How much of his transportation can he deduct? Let's examine the flowchart. Was it a business trip? The answer would be yes. The next box asks, "Trip for business convention or seminar?" This would be no, since he's meeting prospects and not attending a seminar or convention. The next block asks, was the trip "Outside of the United States?" Last time I looked, Hawaii was clearly a state; thus, the answer would be no. The next block asks, "Were *more* than 50 percent of the days including travel days spent on business?" Is 5 out of 14 total days more than 50 percent? The answer would be no: Sam would get no deduction for transportation! He did, however, have five business days and would be able to deduct five days' worth of on-the-road expenses. Here is a good example of being able to deduct on-the-road expenses but not any transportation costs. He would have to have at least three more business days to deduct the whole transportation, with eight business days out of 14, which is more than half. I hope you finally understand how useful this flowchart is and hope that you can use it. Feel free to play around with it and try various types of trips.

Documentation and Audit-Proof Techniques

As I mentioned before, there is a great receipt rule: you do not need receipts for any travel expenses under $75 per expense.[45] Lodging, however, is an exception. If you pay for any lodging, you must get a receipt.[46] If you do not keep a good diary or tax organizer, you will need receipts for any travel expenses, even for those under $75. You may not simply make approximations while traveling.

Example: Janet stays in the Bates Motel, where the cost was only $22. (Apparently she hasn't seen the movie, *Psycho*.) She would need a receipt, since the expense is for lodging.

Author's note: Frequently, to save money on the trip, people stay with their friends or relatives. Unless you pay them for lodging, which isn't a bad idea, you wouldn't need a receipt, since you get no lodging deduction when you don't pay anything. You can, however, deduct on-the-road expenses that you incur. In addition, as I suggested, it might be wise to pay your relative a lodging fee. The IRS and Congress have a provision that anyone who receives less than two weeks of rent does not have to report this rent as income,[47] but you would still get a deduction for the rent.

Example: Sue attends a convention in Phoenix, but stays with her son while she is there. If she pays her son $100 per day for her week's stay, she can deduct the full $700 and her son does not report this $700 as income. What a great country!

The IRS allows self-employed taxpayers to use their per diem rates for meals and incidental expenses without having to keep receipts.[48] This amount varies generally between $30 and $46 per day, depending on location.[49] The IRS also has a per diem for lodging, but it can't be used for selfemployed individuals.[50]

Author's note: Although it may seem "nice" of the IRS to not require receipts for your meals and incidental expenses and give you a daily deduction of between $30 and $46, however, it really isn't recommended to use this method. Frankly, if you hear that something is the IRS method, would you think that it's good for you? You don't need receipts anyway, if the expense is under $75 per item! Thus, the IRS is, in effect, giving you "snow in the winter."

The travel expense documentation rules are easily summarized. Either write down the expense properly on the day it happens or lose it. Congress continually reemphasizes that the IRS is not to use or allow approximations of travel expenses.[51] In addition, when you have the right documentation in a daily log, diary, or tax organizer, the IRS spends much less time looking at your records.

You are to keep your on-the-road expenses separate from your transportation expenses. As a reminder, on-the-road expenses are deductible for a business day[52] and transportation expenses are deductible for a business trip.[53]

In addition, as explained above, in order to deduct 100 percent of transportation costs, your transportation must meet one of three tests:

- 51/49 test for U.S. trips, conventions, and seminars (more days business than personal)
- 76/24 test for foreign travel (more than 76 percent of your days for business)
- less than one week test for foreign travel

Thus, what type of documentation do you need to audit-proof your travel? To deduct your travel expenses, your records must prove all of the following:[54]

- The amount that you spend daily for such things as transportation, meals, and lodging

- The dates of your departure and return home from each trip and the number of days spent on business while away from home

- Where you traveled, described by name of city, town, or similar designation

- Why you traveled, including the business reason for your travel or the business benefit derived or expected to be gained (as specific as possible)

Author's note: Although not specifically required by the Internal Revenue Code, it would be important to also document preexisting business intent for the trip. You can solidify this proof with copies of correspondence sent to prospects, e-mails, and documented phone calls. The key is to have business intent by making appointments in advance of the trip. Simply knocking on doors and giving out your card won't work.

Keep a Good Diary

The Internal Revenue Code and IRS regulations both require that travel expenditures be recorded "at or near the time" that the expenses are incurred.[55] IRS agents are trained to require you to have contemporaneous records, since they have a "high degree of credibility" not present with respect to a subsequent statement when you generally lack adequate recall.[56]

In short, if you make your appointments in advance, have enough business days to satisfy the transportation tests noted on the flowchart found on page 35, and keep the right documentation with a tax diary or tax organizer, you will never have to fear an IRS audit on travel and will generate thousands of dollars in deductions that you probably weren't taking before you read this book.

Summary

- Know what the IRS considers "business travel." Use strategies to increase your travel deductions and add more fun:
  - Hire your spouse or significant friend.
  - Take your business car for family travel.
  - Track your lodging and meal expenses.
  - Drive 300 miles a day toward your business destination.
  - Take courses on U.S. cruise ships.
  - Make your weekends deductible.
  - Count travel days as business days.
  - Combine some fun with a business day without losing any deduction.
  - Attend a convention or a seminar.
  - Caretake your rental property.
  - Visit colleagues and improve your skills and get referrals.
  - Get educated out of town.
  - Hunt for a job anywhere in the U.S.
  - Maximize your deductions for travel in the U.S. and abroad.
  - Maximize your seminar and convention travel.
  - Know about documentation and audit-proof techniques.
  - Keep a good diary.

Notes

1. *U.S. v. Correll*, 389 U.S. 299 (1967); Revenue Ruling 54-407, 1954-2 CB 75, superseded in part by Revenue Ruling 75-432, 1975-2 CB 60; Revenue Ruling 75-170, 1975-1 C.B. 60.
2. *K. Waters*, 12 TC 414, Dec. 16,873; *C.M. Scott*, 110 F.Supp. 819.
3. Ibid.
4. Sections 162(a)(2) and 62(2)(B) of the IRC; section 1.162-2 of the ITR.
5. Ibid.
6. Ibid.
7. Section 1.162-2 of the ITR and IRS Pub 463. See also CCH Federal Tax Service Section G 8:41 and Revenue Ruling 63-145, 1963-2 C.B. 86.
8. Ibid.
9. Section 274(n)(1) of the IRC.
10. *Clarke Fashions, Inc. v. Commissioner*, 20 TCM 589, Dec. 24,812(M), T.C. Memo, 1961-121.
11. Sections 1.274-5© and 1.274-5T(c)(2)(iii) of ITR; IR 95-56, Notice 95-50, 1995-42 IRB.
12. *Giordano v. Commissioner*, 36 T.C.M. 430 (1977); *Howard vs. Commissioner*, 41 T.C. M. 1554 (1981). See also section 274(m) of the IRC.
13. Section 162(a)(2) of the IRC and section 1.162-1 of the ITR.
14. Revenue Ruling 56-168, 1956-1 C.B. 93; Section 1.162-2(c) of the ITR.
15. Ibid.

16. *IRS Manual*, Handbook HB 1763 314 (4).
17. Section 274(h)(2) of the IRC.
18. Sections 274(c)(1) and 274(c)(2) of the ITR; Section 1.274-4(d) and 1.162-2(b) of the ITR.
19. Section 1.274-4(d)(2)(v) of the ITR.
20. Section 1.162-2(a) and (b)(1) of the ITR.
21. Private Letter Ruling 9237014.
22. Section 1.274-4(d)(2)(i) of the ITR.
23. Ibid. and IRS Publication 463.
24. Section 274(m)(1)(A) of the IRC.
25. Ibid.
26. Section 1.274-2(d) of the ITR.
27. Ibid.
28. Sections 1.274-4(d)(2)(iii) and 1.162-2(b)(1) of the ITR.
29. Section 1.274-4(d)(2)(iv) of the ITR.
30. Section 162(a)(2) of the IRC. See also *J.S. Kopunek*, 54 TCM 239, Dec. 44,136(M), T.C. Memo 1987-417.
31. IRS Publication 17.
32. Ibid.
33. Section 274(h)(1) of the IRC.
34. Revenue Ruling 75-120 1975-1 CB 55.
35. *C. Harris*, 37 TCM 1370 (1978); *P.P. Irwin v. Commissioner*, 72 TCM 1148.
36. Section 1.162-2(b)(1) of the ITR.
37. Section 1.162-2(b)(2) of the ITR and *K.E. Fairey v. Commissioner*, 43 TCM 1169 (1982); *A.F. Habeeb v. Commissioner*, 35 TCM 1134 (1976).
38. Section 274(c)(1) of the IRC.
39. Section 274(c)(2)(A) of the IRC.
40. Section 274(c)(2)(B) of the IRC.
41. Section 1.162-2(d) of the ITR and Section 274(h) of the IRC.
42. Section 274(h) of the IRC.
43. Revenue Ruling 94-56, 1994-2 CB 37.
44. Sections 274(h)(3)(A), 274(h)(6)(B), and 274(h)(6)(A) and Ibid.
45. See footnote 11.
46. Section 274(d)(1) of the IRC.
47. IRS Publication 527.
48. Section 1.274-5(j)(1) of the ITR; Revenue Procedure 2000-39, 2000-41 IRB 340; Revenue Procedure 2001-3, 2001-1 IRB 11.
49. Ibid.
50. *J.L. Christian*, 80 TCM 902 (2000); *P.H. Duncan*, 80 TCM 283 (2000).
51. Section 274(d) of the IRC.
52. Section 1.162-2(a) of the ITR.
53. Ibid.
54. Section 274(d) of the IRC.
55. Section 1.274-5(c)(1) of the ITR.
56. Ibid.

4

Income Shifting and Income Splitting: One of the Greatest Single Wealth-Building Secrets

The only time that the average child is as good as gold is April 15.

—**Ivern Boyett**

There's nothing wrong with the younger generation that becoming taxpayers won't cure.

—**Dan Bennett**

This chapter is about income shifting. It's what the wealthy know that you don't. Who is going to benefit from this chapter? Anyone who is married or who is single with children, whether they are adult or small children, or who has friends will benefit. This should cover everyone.

Hire Your Spouse in Your Business and Save a Bundle!

Whenever you hire a spouse, you have to take out Social Security.[1] Thus the

42

key here is to pay your spouse minimum wage and give as many tax-free fringe benefits as possible. Thus let's discuss some of the tax-free fringe benefits. (There will be a much greater discussion in Chapter 13.)

The main benefit of hiring your spouse is to enable you to deduct medical expenses that ordinarily would not be deductible unless they exceeded a high threshold amount[2] of 7.5 percent of your adjusted gross income.[3] [*Adjusted gross income* means your salary, pensions, net rents (net of rental deductions), and net income from businesses minus certain deductions, such as moving and pension contributions.] Thus, if your adjusted gross income is $50,000, you can deduct only medical and dental expenses in excess of $3,750. If you're making $100,000, this figure would be $7,500. All this was a result of various tax reform and "tax simplification" bills.

Despite these rules, how would you like to be able to deduct all your medical expenses without any threshold?

Sadly, self-employed people normally are not allowed to be covered under this plan.[4] However, where there's a will, there's a lawyer. You can be an exception to the "normal rules" either by hiring your spouse or by forming a regular corporation and creating a self-insured medical plan in addition to your regular medical insurance. It will cover the holes that your policy doesn't cover, such as deductibles, coinsurance, braces, dental, mileage to and from the doctor, hearing aids, and nontraditional forms of medicine such as chiropractic and acupuncture.

> **How Self Employed Taxpayers Can Use the Medical Reimbursement Plan:**

The Internal Revenue Service (IRS) allows a medical reimbursement plan for even one employee.[5] In addition, the IRS was even more generous when it ruled that you could hire your wife and cover your family and yourself under the self-insured medical reimbursement plan.[6] Thus, if your only employee is your spouse, you still can qualify for a medical reimbursement plan.

You, as a sole proprietor, can pay for medical expenses that the insurance policy doesn't cover for your employees and their families if they *legitimately* work in the business. This would be in addition to any medical insurance that you would have and would cover expenses that are *not* covered by insurance.[7]

You even have full control of the design of this plan and can make it as broad or as narrow as you wish. For example, you can cover such expenses as deductibles, coinsurance, braces and dental, mileage to and from the doctor, preexisting conditions, routine physicals, psychiatric treatment, and nontraditional medicine such as acupuncture, chiropractic, etc. that are not covered by insurance. Your company would reimburse you and your family for all these out-of-pocket expenses.

You can get around this problem with hiring your spouse in your business and having him or her elect family coverage. In this way, you are deducting the medical expenses not as employee fringe benefits.

Here are the steps required to set up a self-insured medical reimbursement plan:

- If you're married and your business is a sole proprietorship or a limited-liability corporation, hire your spouse. If you're not married, form a regular corporation and have the corporation approve the plan in the board of directors' minutes.
- Have the self-insured medical reimbursement plan drafted.
- If you've hired your spouse, make him or her the primary insured on the plan, and elect family coverage, which means that you will be covering yourself and the kids.
- Either pay the doctor or dentist directly or reimburse the family member for any medical expense incurred. The bottom line is that you get a deduction, and your family gets the money tax-free!
- Keep the plan in existence for at least three years.
- Meet with your accountant to have a yearly per-employee maximum payout from the plan.

Author's note: If you're the sole stockholder in your corporation, you shouldn't have any problems getting this plan approved, should you? In addition, this tax strategy can be instituted for a sole proprietorship or a limited-liability corporation. However, if you own more than 2 percent of an S corporation's stock or are a partnership, you will not be able to benefit greatly from the self-insured medical reimbursement plan. Any reimbursements made to you will be included in your taxable income.[8] This also applies to partners in a partnership.[9]

In addition, the self-insured medical reimbursement plan is only for expenses incurred after implementation of the plan.[10]

Example: Ann incurred some medical and dental expenses in 2006. She also has some upcoming medical expenses in 2007. If she were to set up the plan in January 2007, she may benefit from the plan only for expenses incurred after the plan went into effect, which is 2007.

Author's note: S corporations get most of the benefits provided to sole proprietorships, which will be discussed in later chapters. Only owners of more than 2 percent of the S corporation's stock and partners in a partnership don't get the benefits of the medical reimbursements.

Discrimination Requirements for a Self-Insured Medical Reimbursement Plan

A self-insured medical reimbursement plan has one drawback: It must not discriminate in favor of the owners or highly compensated employees. In addition, you must cover all full-time employees.[11] Thus there are three key questions:

- What constitutes "discrimination"?
- Who are "highly compensated employees"?
- Who are "full-time employees"?

These are good questions and I am glad that you asked them.

The definition of discrimination seems complicated, but it's really easy to understand it and avoid discrimination. A plan is deemed discriminatory *unless*[12]

- it covers 70 percent or more of all employees, or
- 70 percent or more of all employees are eligible to participate and 80 percent of those eligible actually participate, or
- the IRS finds eligibility nondiscriminatory based on the facts and circumstances.

Example: David has 10 employees, but only 5 are full-time workers. To avoid discrimination, David must cover at least 7 of his workers or make at least 7 workers eligible.

Author's note: You can worry yourself and your accountant about all these statistics, or you can do what I did with my corporation, which is to cover all full-time employees. This eliminates any problems.

Example: Tom hires Carey, who is both his wife and only full-time worker, in his self-employed business. Tom sets up a medical reimbursement plan covering all full-time employees' medical expenses that aren't covered by insurance and elects family coverage. Tom may deduct all medical expenses covered by the plan for Carey and her family, who are Tom and the kids.

| Hot Tip |

The next question is, Who is considered "highly compensated"? Congress says that a highly compensated person is one of the five highest-paid stockholders or among the highest-paid 25 percent of all employees.[13] If there is discrimination, then the highly compensated people are taxed on the amount that is deemed discriminatory.[14] An example will explain this.

Example: Alan's corporation provides a self-employed reimbursement plan for those who aren't officers. If one of the officers receives $4,000 of the reimbursement, he or she would have to report $3,000 as taxable income, the amount in excess of what would be allowed those who aren't officers.

Author's note: It truly is amazing that there are people in Congress thinking of this stuff. Why they can't simply allow all owners to benefit without having to put in this complexity is beyond understanding.

Exceptions to the Rules

Now that I have informed you of all the discrimination rules, I should point out that the IRS and Congress have noted several groups of people who don't have to be covered. The following is a list of employees who are exempt[15]:

- Employees who are part time. This means employees who normally work less than 25 hours per week.
- Employees who have not reached age 25. (This exception seems very odd. As you probably know, age discrimination isn't allowed in this country, yet the IRS and Congress encourage us to hire people under age 25 without giving them this fringe benefit! You might wonder why this discrimination exists. The reason is that we don't have any tax policy in this country. Our policy is based on the short-term interests of those whom we elect to Congress.)
- Employees who are seasonal. This is defined as anyone who works for you less than nine months during the year. This exception was put in to encourage hiring college and high school children.
- Employees covered under a collective-bargaining agreement.
- Employees with less than three years of service. Thus you can make workers wait three years before they get these benefits—or you can fire them, which is another option (only kidding!).
- Employees who are nonresident aliens.

One further interesting allowable discrimination is for routine physicals.[16] You are allowed routine physicals and diagnostic procedures for officers or employees and highly compensated employees, and you can discriminate on providing this benefit. You just can't provide this to dependents of officers or employees without providing it to dependents of nonhighly compensated employees.

Example: Acme, Inc., provides a self-insured medical reimbursement plan for all its senior officers that provides reimbursement only for routine physicals and diagnostic procedures such as a complete MRI body scan. Even though only highly compensated people are getting this benefit, it would not be taxed to them because of this exception.

Hire Your Children and Deduct the Equivalent of Their Education and Weddings

If you were to send your kids to college, would the college tuition be deductible? The answer is no! You may get a little tax credit, but that's it.

If you pay for their room and board and provide a car, would that be deductible? The answer would be no. If you were to pay for your daughter's wedding, would that be deductible? No! But how would you like to be able to deduct the equivalent of all of this?

The answer is to hire your children in your business. Wages paid to an assistant are deductible. If your kids use this money to pay for college, room and board, and weddings, aren't you getting the equivalent of a deduction for all of these? Yes!

The tax rules on hiring kids are that wages paid from a parent to a child under the age of 18, if hired in either a self-employed business or a limited-liability corporation, are exempt from Social Security and unemployment taxes.[17] This exemption does not apply to incorporated businesses, which must take out Social Security and unemployment tax on everyone. You also can hire kids who are 18 or older, but it doesn't work as well unless you are in a fairly high tax bracket. The reason is that once the kids reach age 18, you must take out Social Security and federal unemployment tax.

In 2007, the first $5,350 of earned income (i.e., wages) is tax-free because your children receive a standard deduction of this amount on their own tax return.[18] You would, in addition, obtain the standard $3,400 exemption per child on your tax return. In addition, your child will be able to take the standard deduction on his or her return.[19] Now we're talking! If you pay your kids more than $5,350, they would pay some income tax, but only at the 10 percent bracket on the first $7,825 earned above this exemption.[20]

Example: You pay your child $5,350 in wages for the year in your self-employed business. You deduct the $5,350 in wages on your Schedule C (Schedule E if hired in conjunction with rental property), assuming that the wages were reasonable for the time and services performed. You pay no Social Security or unemployment taxes. Your child reports the $5,350 as income from wages on IRS Form 1040 and then deducts the $5,350 as his or her standard deduction. If you're in the 35 percent tax bracket, the $5,350 produces a tax refund of $1,872 from federal taxes alone, plus a potential savings of $155 from the Medicare surcharge in addition to any state tax savings. Above the $5,350 in wages, you would save at the 25 percent rate (35 percent minus 10 percent bracket of the child).

In addition, your child could put away $3,400 per year of his or her earnings into a Roth IRA that would allow the interest and appreciation to be tax-free to the child if used for college. In effect, by hiring your children, Uncle Sam underwrites the education, weddings, and other uses to which the children put their money.

A common question I get at seminars is, "At what age can I hire my children?" There is a tax court case that held that you could hire a child who is at least age 7. The IRS, which had fought the case, acquiesced (agreed to follow the case), effectively approving the employment of 7-year-olds.[21] This legitimates hiring children who are at least age 7. The problem is what happens if you want to hire your children who are under age 7. Some tax planners are urging people to put their child's picture on their business cards and pay a modeling fee, even if the child is under age 7. Will this work? Unfortunately, no one knows for sure. We do know that a child can be hired at age 7. If you hire a child under age 7, you are taking a risk. If you wish to be a trailblazer, maybe we can have a case named after you.

Unlike hiring a spouse, who is subject to Social Security, children under age 18 are exempt if hired in a self-employed business. Thus you want to pay them as much as possible. However, there's one major issue when you hire family members: The wages must be reasonable for the hours and work that they perform.[22] It certainly would be unreasonable to pay a child $40,000 to answer phones occasionally!

Although there has been lots of litigation on this issue,[23] it really isn't that hard to do it right. A salary is considered reasonable if an unrelated employer would pay the same employee under the same circumstances and preferably in the same business.[24] When setting a salary, be sure to allow for the experience or inexperience and ability of your child. The more experience and ability, the more you can pay per hour. Also consider the nine factors that the IRS uses to examine wages for reasonableness[25]:

- Duties performed
- Volume of work
- Type and amount of responsibility
- Complexity of work
- Amount of time required for work
- General cost of living in the area
- Ability and achievements of the employee
- Comparison of amount of salary with amount of business income
- Pay history of the employee

Author's note: In order to make your life easier, what I recommend at my seminars is to find out what you would pay to a comparable agency that does the type of work that you need and then pay your child less per hour than that agency. Thus, if you want your 12-year-old son to do some filing and bookkeeping, call a temporary agency such as Kelly Girl or Manpower and find out what they charge per hour. If the charge is $15 per hour, you would pay your child $12, and this should be deemed reasonable. If you want to have your 24-year-old daughter mow the lawns on your rental properties, you would call a landscape service and get a quote. You also would need to document what hourly rate you were quoted. It would be ideal to get this documentation in writing in the form of a written quotation from the organization.

Documentation Strategies Necessary When Hiring Any Relative

Be honest! If you were an IRS auditor, would you believe that your child or spouse was a bona fide employee? You would only if you saw adequate proof. In most cases, it's absolutely essential that your relatives fill out time sheets or a tax diary at the end of each week. To get your deductions for wages, you must be able to prove what work actually was performed.[26] Each day that the relative works, the time sheet or diary should show

- The date worked
- A description of the tasks performed
- The hours worked

Month July		Child's Name I. M. Child	
Day of Week (Mon, Tues, etc.)	Date	Description of Tasks Performed	Hours Worked
Mon.	7	Sorted files & made 3x5 cards	4
Tues.	8	Cleaned office & emptied trash	2
Thurs.	10	Addressed brochures	2
Sat.	12	Arranged business trip files	2
Sat.	12	Typed business letters	2
Total Hours Worked			12
X Hourly Rate			5
Total Wages Paid with Check No. 164			60

Figure 4-1. Dependent child's business services and wage sheet.

At the end of each day or week, you should approve the time sheet or diary for payment. Payment to either your spouse or your children always should be made by check. Even if your child is too young to have a checking account, you should pay by check. In this circumstance, establish a custodial checking account at your local bank. This would require your signature for the child to withdraw any money! The check completes the audit trail by establishing two things: that you paid the relative and that the relative actually received the payment. The time sheet establishes the validity and reasonableness of the payment. Together you will be audit-proof from the IRS.

In addition, have your attorney draft up an employment contract noting the pay rate, duties, benefits, etc. The pay should be based on the hours worked.[27]

Finally, you want to file the appropriate IRS forms required for hiring any employee. The first step in hiring—relatives or others—is to obtain a taxpayer ID number from the IRS and from your state. Next, you want to complete the necessary payroll paperwork. There's paperwork even on your child under age 18, who, as an employee of his or her parents, is exempt from Social Security and unemployment taxes.[28] However, even if no taxes are due, you must complete the following federal paperwork:

- **IRS Form W-4.** This simple form must be completed by your employee and stored in your files.[29]
- **IRS Form W-2.** If you pay your spouse or child $600 or more, you must give your employee a copy of IRS Form W-2 and file it along with IRS Form W-3 with both the IRS and the Social Security Administration.[30]
- **IRS Form 941.** Use this form to report on a quarterly basis withheld income taxes and to make a deposit.[31]
- **IRS Form 940.** Although you are not liable for unemployment taxes on wages paid to your child if he or she is a dependent and under age 21, you must file IRS Form 940 anyway at the end of the year.[32] If your child is your only employee, you simply enter your child's wages as "exempt" from unemployment tax and return the form to the IRS.[33]

The bottom line is this: Stop paying allowances, tuition costs, and wedding costs. Instead, hire your children in your business, and pay them a reasonable wage. Let them use the money for their tuition, room and board, and weddings.

Miscellaneous Income-Shifting Strategies

Gift and Shift-the-Tax Technique

Here's one strategy that you will *really* like. In fact, the good news is that if everyone in the United States understood this strategy, we could legally reduce all taxes paid into the IRS by over $2 trillion! The bad news is that the IRS has nothing to worry about because over 99.9 percent of taxpayers in this country have never heard about it. However, it clearly is one of the most powerful techniques available.

With this strategy, you gift property rather than cash to a person in a lower tax bracket. The test on who would qualify for this is simple. Take a mirror, and put it in your freezer overnight. The following day, take the mirror out of the freezer and place it under the nose of anyone with whom you wish to use this technique. If the mirror fogs, the person passes the test. You can use this strategy with virtually anyone—your kids, grandchildren, nephews, nieces, parents, or even significant friends who are not related to you.

You simply give away the property to these relatives who are in a lower tax-bracket than you, and then they sell the property one day later and pay the tax at their bracket.[34] This must be done without a prearranged resale.[35] Thus you must do this before any contract for the sale of the property occurs. The result is that both you (the donor) and the person to whom you give the property (the donee) have more cash to spend because the IRS took less tax from the person in the lower tax bracket.

Think about how this works. Here is a great example from someone I met on an airplane. He was a successful lawyer, and he also was successful in the stock market. He had three kids, and he was paying $20,000 a year for each of his kids to go to college. A smart person was doing a dumb thing. He ought to have been giving each of his kids stock. They then could sell their stock and be taxed on the gain at their brackets and pay their own tuition. Now this lawyer was easily in the 50 percent tax bracket (counting federal taxes, state taxes, and Medicare taxes), and his kids were in the 10 to 15 percent tax bracket. He could have cut his taxes by 70 percent (35 percent savings divided by 50 percent)! This can be done with any-thing–stocks, bonds, valuable collectibles, or real estate. As you can see, the savings from this one strategy alone can be massive.

Interestingly, there are no income-tax consequences to making a gift (although there are gift-tax consequences that we will discuss shortly). This means that any recipient doesn't pay income taxes on the gift (and you get no deduction for it).[36] The donee takes the same basis and holding period that you had, increased by any gift tax paid.[37] I should note that this discussion applies to gifts and not if you inherit property as a result of death. With inheritances, you get a fair-market-value basis as of the date of death, and the holding period begins on the date of death.[38]

Example: Jackie receives some stock from her parents as a gift. The parents bought the stock two years ago for $20 per share, and it's worth $50 when they give it to her. (I wish this happened to me!) Jackie would get a $20 basis, the same basis as her parents had, and the same two-year holding period. (In contrast, if Jackie inherited the stock and it was worth $50 at the time of her parent's death, her basis would be $50, the fair market value.)

Author's note: I have assumed that the basis of the gift is less than the fair market value. If, however, the fair market value is less than the basis paid, the recipient won't be able to get a loss when he or she sells the property. The basis is always either the basis when the property was purchased or the fair market value as of the date of the gift, whichever is lower! Thus no loss would be allowed if you sell the property shortly thereafter.

Congress wants part of our profits but as little as possible of our losses. This is illustrative of the "Golden Rule": He who has the gold makes the rules.

The key is to never use this technique with property that would produce a loss. Use only with appreciated property.

As mentioned earlier, there are gift-tax consequences in making a gift. If you're single, you can give away up to $12,000 per person per year gift-tax-free.[39] If you're married, you can give double this, which is $22,000 per person per year, free of gift tax, by consenting to treat one-half the gift as made by each spouse.[40] This may not seem fair, but there are two people involved instead of just one. In addition, you get a lifetime exemption from gift taxes of $1 million in 2007.[41] Thus you can give away a lot of gifts without paying any tax. An example will illustrate how financially rewarding this strategy can be.

Example: Melissa owns some real estate that is worth $200,000 and has appreciated $90,000 since she purchased it. If she sells the real estate, she will pay at least $18,000 in capital gains tax plus any state income tax. This also doesn't take into account any depreciation that she took, which would be taxed as ordinary income. If she transfers this property to her three children, who, in turn, sell the property shortly thereafter, Melissa would owe no gift tax owing to the annual exclusions and lifetime exclusion. The children each would pay tax on one-third of the gain, $3,000 each (10 percent bracket times $30,000 of gain to each child). Thus Melissa would have saved 50 percent of the tax, or $9,000! This savings alone could almost pay for the tuition for one child.

Beware of the Kiddie Tax

Congress was aware of how powerful this gift-tax technique could be, even though it is not used by most Americans. Congress thus tried to kill off or at least limit its benefits with what is now known as the "kiddie tax." Children under age 18 by December 31, which is the measuring date for each year, must pay tax on investment income over $1,700 at the highest earnings of the parent's tax rate.[42] If the parents are not married or are divorced, the income used is that of the custodial parent.[43] Now, you may be thinking, what if you're married filing separately? Sharp thinking! Unfortunately, Congress has already thought of this. In that case, you are to use the tax bracket of the parent who has the higher income.[44] As mentioned, the kiddie tax applies only to investment income, such as dividends, capital gains, rents, royalties, etc., but not wages.[45]

Author's elaboration: Using prepaid tuition plans and section 529 plans to save for your kid's college tuition is now even more important than putting money in their names. All interest and gains in these plans are tax-free to the extent the funds are used for college tuition.

Double-Deduct All Your Equipment Plus Protect It from Judgments!

How would you like to double-deduct all the equipment that you use in any business or real estate venture and make your assets lawyer-proof from judgments? Sounds too good to be true, doesn't it? Well, you can, and it isn't that hard to accomplish. This is far and away one of the top financial planning strategies in the country, especially for physicians.

You start by giving away property that you are using in business, preferably after it has been depreciated, either to your relatives or to an irrevocable trust set up for your relatives. You then would lease it back from them in trust and pay monthly lease payments. You've already depreciated the equipment, and now you're deducting the monthly lease payments, which, in effect, gives you a double deduction for the equipment. Moreover, if you're sued thereafter, you have no business assets in your name and thus have liability-proofed your assets. This strategy is known as the *gift-leaseback technique.*

The gift-leaseback involves several steps:

- *Give away property that you own.* To put the gift-leaseback strategy to work, you first must own the asset. You as an individual would give away the asset to your children or to any other person who passes the "mirror test" described earlier.[46] If you have a corporation, however, your corporation may not make such gifts.[47]

- *Give away property that you've depreciated.* Fully depreciated property produces the maximum deductions for the gift-leaseback strategy. By using fully depreciated assets in a gift-leaseback, you actually create new deductions. Fully depreciated property produces no depreciation deductions. However, the gift-leaseback technique creates a rent deduction from the fully depreciated equipment.

Example: You own and use in your business a Cadillac. The car is fully depreciated. It has a retail value of $10,000, as published by the National Automobile Dealers Association in its *Official Used Car Guide*, which is available on the Internet (www.nadaguides.com). According to the IRS Annual Lease Value Table, the annual rent on the Cadillac is $3,100 for the next four years.[48] Thus you set up an irrevocable trust for your 14-year-old daughter, give the Cadillac to the trust, and then lease it back.

The result is that you get a yearly tax deduction for the $3,100 of rent that you pay to the trust, which will own the property.[49] Assuming that you're in the 45 percent federal and state tax bracket, your taxes are reduced by $1,395. Your daughter receives $3,100 from the trust and pays a tax of roughly $235. The family unit—you and your daughter or son—receive a net benefit of $1,160 from a car that otherwise would have produced no tax benefit. Remember, however: Do not give away property that would produce a deductible loss if you sold it.

- *Give the property to an irrevocable trust rather than directly to your son or daughter, and use an independent trustee.* Although you may be able to give the property directly to your son or daughter if they are not minors, some cases, and especially if you live in the fifth circuit (Louisiana, Texas, and Mississippi), require you to use a trust and have an independent trustee.[50] In addition, if your kids or grandkids get sued, the creditors can't touch the property held in trust if the trust document is drafted correctly. Finally, if your children are minors, they can't own a car or real estate directly; thus a trust becomes mandatory. In short, regardless of where you live, I would advise setting up a trust for this technique. It will greatly protect you in a wide variety of ways.

- *Pay a reasonable rent.* All cases in the area require a reasonable rental for the property used. With cars, you can use IRS Publication 15-B, Annual Lease Value Table. Just plug in your vehicle's fair market value, and this publication will tell you how much a reasonable rental would be. If you want to lease equipment other than vehicles, you have several ways of tracking down what a reasonable lease payment would be. One method would be to get a quotation from an equipment leasing company for similar equipment. The IRS also has taken in its litigation the position that you can charge 40 percent of the fair market value of the property as of the beginning of a three-year lease.

Example: Mary has a 1-GHz laptop computer with 512 MB of RAM and a 30-GB hard drive. (When it comes to computers, I have no idea what I'm talking about, but it certainly sounds right.) If the computer is worth $2,000 today, she could lease it back from her son or daughter's trust for 40 percent of its value, or $800 per year, for the next three years.

Author's note: Go to your local newspaper and clip out an ad that looks similar to your equipment. This would establish a fair market value. (By the way, you can't be the one who places the ad in the newspaper!)

- *Document your nontax business reason.* Another requirement of some courts is to have a nontax reason for the gift-leaseback or sale-leaseback (which will be discussed below).[51]

With what property can you use this technique? It will work for any tangible property, such as computers, printers, desks, file cabinets, chairs, cars, copiers, and shredders. (In Washington, DC, we have a lot of shredders.) Moreover, you can do this with anyone who passes the mirror test. Thus anyone is eligible. Get a letter from your lawyer outlining a nontax reason for the gift-leaseback. (See my discussion of the sale-leaseback below.)

Deduct 100 Percent of Your Real Estate—Even the Land

One interesting twist with this technique is with real estate. Buildings are depreciable, but land is not. You thus have to make some allocation of the purchase price for any rental property between land and buildings. If you don't, the IRS will make the allocation for you, which you will not like.

How would you like to make your rental properties 100 percent deductible—even the portion allocated to the land? You can by using this technique. When you purchase a property, you would divide the title between the land and the building. The building would be in your name, but the land would be in the name of a trust for your children. You would then lease back the property from the trust. The result is that you can depreciate the building *and* can get a deduction for the land in the form of ground rent. Thus you are now effectively able to deduct 100 percent of your purchase price. Isn't this a great strategy?

Even if you already own some rental property, you can accomplish this. Just have your lawyer transfer the title to the underlying land to a trust set up for your children or relatives. (Get an appraisal on the land.) You then would pay ground rent to the trust.

easeback Technique

way to shift income is with the sale-leaseback technique. This
e has been around for many years. It puts the friend or relative in
ng business but allows you to select the asset. It has the same
ents and steps necessary for the gift-leaseback, but this is a sale
a gift. You would use this technique when you want to cash out or
you want to help your children or grandchildren with some great risk-free
estate planning. A great example of how this works follows.

Example: Sam lives in his home, which is completely paid off; he gets few
tax benefits from the home because there's no interest and no depreciation
since it is his home. Although Sam paid $130,000 for his house 20 years
ago, it's worth $380,000 based on an appraisal. Sam now sells the home to
his three children for the full fair market value but gives them great terms:
$3,000 down, and he finances the rest of the purchase price with an install-
ment note for the remaining $377,000 at 7 percent interest. Subsequent to
the sale, Sam's children rent the house back to Sam at fair market rent. The
results are startling:

- Sam has no capital gain because his total gain is under $250,000.
  (As you will learn in Chapter 6, a principal residence can be sold
  with no capital gain consequences if the gain is less than $500,000
  for a married couple and $250,000 for a single person.)
- There is a relatively even cash flow because the mortgage payment
  is just a little more than the rent payment.
- Sam's children now can depreciate the home because it is rental
  property.
- Sam's children can deduct any repair costs because it is rental
  property.
- If the house appreciates before Sam dies, all appreciation is out of
  Sam's estate because his kids own the house.
- Finally, the children can visit Sam and the property once a year and
  deduct their trip as a caretaking expense.

This is one technique for which you will need a good lawyer because it
must be done correctly.[52] The lease should be relatively short term and not
exceed the seller's life expectancy. The rent and sale price should be at fair
market value; there can be no "deal" given. An independent appraisal for
both the sale price and the rent should be obtained. All payments should
be made to the appropriate parties. No forgiveness of any payment should
occur, especially in the first two years. In addition, the mortgage payments
should not exactly equal the rent. Make one of the payments more than
the other.[53]

Finally, as with the gift-leaseback, you will need a legitimate nontax reason for this transaction.[54] Get a letter from a lawyer stating that this transaction is recommended:

- To protect from creditors such as nursing homes
- To avoid any ethical conflicts
- To provide professional management of the property
- To avoid probate fees and to save on estate taxes

Summary

- Hire your spouse and save a bundle deducting medical expenses.
- Hire your son or daughter and deduct the equivalent of their education and weddings.
- Have the right documentation when hiring any relative.
- Use the gift-push and shift-tax technique. It could save you an enormous amount of taxes.
- Beware of the kiddie tax.
- Use the gift-leaseback technique to double-deduct all your equipment.
- Use the sale-leaseback technique to give benefits to your children, cash out, and get some great risk-free estate planning.
- Use the sale-leaseback technique to deduct land.

Notes

1. Sections 3121(b)(3)(A) and 3306(C)(5) of the IRC. See IRS Publication Circular E.
2. Section 213(a) of the IRC.
3. Ibid.
4. Section 105(g) of the IRC.
5. Section 1.105-5 of the ITR.
6. IRS Letter Ruling 9409006, ISP Coordinated Issue Paper (UIC-162.35.22); See also Revenue Ruling 71-588, 1971-2 CB 91.
7. Section 105 of the IRC.
8. Sections 1372 and 105(g) of the IRC.
9. Section 707 of the IRC.
10. *W. W. Wollenburg v. U.S.*, 2000-1 USTC 50,156.
11. Section 105(h) of the IRC.
12. Section 105(h)(2) of the IRC.
13. Section 105(h)(5) of the IRC.
14. Section 1.105-11(c) of the ITR.
15. Section 105(h)(3)(B) of the IRC.
16. Section 1.105-11(g) of the ITR.
17. Section 3121(b)(3)(A) and 3306(c)(5); Revenue Ruling 2000-45, IRB 2000-41.
18. Revenue Procedure 2001-59, 2001 FED 46,742.
19. Ibid.

20. 2001 *Tax Weekly*, No. 37 (Sept. 20, 2001). See also section 1(j) of the IRC.

21. *Eller v. Commissioner*, 77 TC 934; *acq.* 1984-2 CB 1.

22. Section 162(a)(1) of the IRC.

23. *Mayson Manufacturing Co. v. Commissioner*, 178 F.2d 115 (6th Cir.); *Ridgewood Provisions, Inc. v. Commissioner*, 6 TC 87 (1946) *(acq.)*; *Ken Miller Supply v. Commissioner*, 37 TCM 974 (1978) et al.

24. Section 1.167-7(b)(3) of the ITR; *Automotive Investment Development, Inc. v. Commissioner*, 66 TCM 57 (1993); *Giles Industries, Inc. v. United States*, 496 F.2d 566 (Ct. Cl. 1974).

25. IRS Publication 535, Chapter 2 (2001 Edition).

26. Section 1.162-7(a) of the ITR.

27. *R. Haeder v. Commissioner*, 81 TCM 987 (2001).

28. Sections 3121(b)(3)(A) and 3306(c)(5) of the IRC.

29. Section 31.3402(n)-1(b) of the ITR.

30. IRS Instructions for Preparing Forms W-2 and W-3.

31. Section 31.3402(n)-1 of the ITR. See also IRS Instructions for Form 941.

32. IRS Instructions for Form 940.

33. Section 31.3402(n)(1) of the ITR. See also IRS Instructions for Form 941.

34. Section 1015 of the IRC. See also *Taft v. Bowers*, 278 U.S. 470 (1929).

35. Ibid.

36. Sections 102(a) and 2503(b) of the IRC and Section 262 of the IRC. See also *R. Wright v. Commissioner*, 26 TCM 425 (1967) and *J. R. Howard*, 41 TCM 1554 (1981).

37. Sections 1223(1) and 1223(2) of the IRC. See also Section 1.1223-1(b) of the ITR.

38. Sections 2033-2036 of the IRC.

39. Revenue Procedure 2001-59, 2001-52 I.R.B. 623. See also Section 2513(a) of the IRC.

40. Ibid. See also Section 6019 of the IRC and Section 25.2513-1(c) of the ITR.

41. Section 2010(c) of the IRC.

42. Sections 1(i) and 1(g) of the IRC.

43. Section 1(g)(5)(A) of the IRC.

44. Section 1(g)(5)(B) of the IRC.

45. IRS Form 8615, Tax for Children Under Age 14 with Investment Income of More than 1,500 (2001 edition). Revenue Procedure 2001-59, 2001-52 I.R.B.

46. Section 2503(b) of the IRC.

47. For example, *Epstein v. Commissioner*, 53 TC 459 (1969), *acq.* 1970-2 C.B. 19.

48. Sections 1.61-2T(d)(2) and 1.61-21(d)(2) of the ITR. See also IRS Publication 15B.

49. Section 162(a)(3) of the IRC.

50. For example, *J. Wiles v. Commissioner*, 59 TC 289, *acq.* by IRS and *aff'd* 74-1 USTC 9379 (5th Cir. 1974); *H. L Brown v. Commissioner*, 11 TC 744, *aff'd* 180 F.2d 946 (5th Cir. 1950).

51. For example, *Matthews v. Commissioner*, 61 TC 12 (1973), *rev'd* 75-2 USTC Par 967 (5th Cir. 1975); *Frank Lyon Co. v. Commissioner*, 435 U.S. 561 (S. Ct. 1978).

52. *Estate of Maxwell*, 98 TC 39 (1992).

53. Ibid.

54. See note 52.

5

How to Turn Your Car into a Tax-Deductible Goldmine

This is the season of the year when we discover that we owe most of our success to Uncle Sam.
—Wall Street Journal (referring to the period from January to April)

I am often asked at my seminars, "What is the number one business expense that gets audited by the Internal Revenue Service (IRS)?" Most people think that it is entertainment or home office. The answer is your vehicle expense. The reason is that a car is a big-ticket item and is the most used and abused. My purpose in this chapter is not only to increase your automotive deductions significantly but also to lock them in with proper documentation tactics.

Business Use

If you drive only one car for business, what's the maximum business-use

> **Chapter Overview**
> - Find out why using two or more cars in business will maximize your deductions.
> - Learn why the IRS method of deducting car expenses is generally a bad deal (with one exception).
> - Learn when buying or leasing a car is best.
> - Know which vehicles can give as much as eight times the normal automobile deduction.
> - Learn about some frequently overlooked automotive deductions.
> - Learn when it is best to either sell a car or to trade one in.
> - Understand why donating a business car is a tax disaster and should almost never occur.
> - Know how to maximize your business mileage and some little known rules that even most accountants don't know.

percentage that you can achieve? 100 percent. If you drive two cars for business, could you drive one car 100 percent for business and another car 100 percent for business? Yes![1] Your business use is based on business miles driven. You calculate your business use

Chapter Overview (Cont.)
- Take advantage of the one secret to audit-proofing your automobile from any auditor: a tax diary.
- Learn a nice, simple, "no hassle" way to prove your business use.

by dividing business miles by the total miles driven during the year.[2] You do this for each car driven for business.[3]

Example: Jeremy drives his car 20,000 total miles during the year. If he puts on 15,000 miles for business, he may deduct three-fourths of any automobile-related expenses or three-fourths of his total mileage at the IRS standard mileage rate.

Use Multiple Cars for Business and Increase Your Spendable Cash

The two-car strategy puts extra money in your pocket only when you're converting an otherwise personal asset to business use. In other words, if you have two cars in your family, make them both deductible. But don't buy a second car simply to implement this strategy. See the comparison in Figure 5-1.

In addition, some cases have required you to have some business purpose for using more than one car.[4] This is very easy to establish, however. Can you use one car for rainy days and one for sunny days? Can you use one car for "high sale" prospects and one to look a bit "poorer"? There are lots of reasons for using different cars.

Author's note: I have a friend who is a successful life insurance salesman. He uses his Mercedes when he meets with multimillionaire estate-planning prospects and his older Lexus for nursing home care insurance sales.

You will notice that by using two cars and switching off between them, you are able to get an extra $2,069 in new deductions each year. Moreover, I based my analysis on cars that cost $16,000. More expensive cars will generate more tax savings.

There's one disadvantage to using the two-car strategy, however: you must keep track of your business mileage during the year on a daily basis. Simplified record keeping using a statistical approach, which will be discussed later, won't work.[5]

Now that you realize that you should use your second car in business, too, the next question becomes, "What basis do I use for depreciation?" Although tax law mandates that you depreciate your car's basis, which is usually your purchase price,[6] there's a slightly different rule if you used the car for personal use first. When you convert your car to business, your

	One Car	Two Cars	
		Car 1	Car 2
Business/Personal Use			
Total Miles for Business	22,000	18,000	4,000
Total Miles for Year	24,000	20,000	7,800
Business Percentage Use	**92%**	**90%**	**51%**
Deduction Calculations			
Gas and Oil	$2,880	$2,400	$480
Insurance	800	800	600
Repairs and Maintenance	800	800	800
Tags and Licenses	100	100	80
Wash and Wax	230	230	202
Other	50	50	50
Total Operating Expense	**$4,860**	**$4,380**	**$2,212**
Business Use Percentage	**x 92%**	**x 90%**	**x 51%**
Business Total	**$4,471**	**$3,942**	**$1,128**
Depreciation	**$2,760**	**$2,700**	**$1,530**
Total Deductions	**$7,231**	**$6,642**	**$2,658**
Extra Deductions		**$2,069**	

Note: The two cars in this example cost $22,000 each.
Note: Interest, state, and local taxes are also deductible under both the IRS and Actual Methods to the extent the automobile is used for business. Rev Proc. 2006-49.

Figure 5-1 How the two-car strategy produces extra deductions.

basis for depreciation becomes the lower of the cost or the market value of the car on the date it is first used in business (which is usually the lower basis).[7] We accountants call this the *lower of cost or market-value rule*. Although many people do not know this rule, it's applicable to all sorts of property. Thus, if you convert your home to a rental property, the same rule applies.

As used here, *cost* is what you paid for the car plus any capital improvements, such as amounts spent to rebuild an engine.[8] *Market value* is the fair market value of the vehicle on the day that you convert it to business use.[9]

Author's note: Generally, you can determine market value using the Blue Book, *The National Automobile Dealer's Association Official Used Car Guide,* which lists two values for used cars: retail and wholesale.

You want the higher number, which is the retail value. In addition, there are many Web sites that list this information, such as my site, www.taxreductioninstitute.com.

Example: Assume that you purchased your personal car several years ago for $20,000 and today that car has a retail value of $10,000. (You should be that lucky!) Your basis for purposes of computing depreciation is $5,000, which is the lower of cost or market value.

Deduct the Larger of the Actual Expense or the Optional IRS Standard Rate

Unlike corporations, individuals such as employees and the self-employed have a choice of methods to write off their vehicle expenses.[10] You can use either the IRS optional standard mileage rates or the actual expenses. The actual method allows you to deduct all car expenses based on your business use.[11] This means that you can deduct part of your gas, wash, wax, depreciation, insurance, repairs, tolls, interest, taxes, and other costs related to your car.[12] As an alternative, you could use the IRS standard mileage rates in lieu of all this. Even if you're using the IRS method, however, you can deduct the business use's share of interest, taxes, and tolls.[13]

Author's note: Many people miss this one deduction. Interest and taxes are deductible to the extent a car is used for business. Sadly, many people, including some accountants, don't know this. They've thus taken out home-equity loans in order to deduct the interest on their car payments, which they didn't need to do, and taken a risk if they didn't pay off the loans. Many people are still making this bad mistake owing to a lack of knowledge.

In 2007, the IRS gives you 48.5 cents per business mile, 19 cents of which is depreciation, and 14 cents per mile for charitable use and 20 cents for medical mileage and moving.[14]

Example: In prior years, you deducted 52,000 miles using the optional IRS standard mileage rate. This year you put on 20,000 miles for business. You may deduct $9,700 (48.5 cents per mile times 20,000 miles).

Interestingly, the IRS method allows the same 48.5 cents per mile regardless of the cost of the car, regardless of its prior mileage and condition, and regardless of age. Thus the older and more "doglike" the car, the better the method becomes. Consequently, the IRS method is best for cars that cost less than $20,000 and where you accrue at least 15,000 miles per year.

Author's note: I called a firm that specializes in car costs and helps to develop the numbers for the IRS.[15] According to one of the company specialists, the IRS method assumes that you purchase one of the cheapest cars made in the United States (normally a Ford Escort LX), which costs about $16,000. It assumes that you have no options on the car. It assumes that you drive 20,000 miles per year for three years. Thus, if you have a vehicle that meets these criteria, you may be better off with the IRS method; otherwise, using actual expenses (i.e., gas, oil, depreciation, repairs, insurance, etc.) would be the better deal.

There are some limitations to the IRS method that you should know about. First, as noted earlier, it can only be used by employees, people who are self-employed, and limited-liability corporations, not corporations.[16] Second, it can't be used in a fleet operation, such as using two cars at once. You can switch cars and you can use the cars in different businesses simultaneously, but you just can't use the cars simultaneously in the same business.[17] You also can't use the IRS method if you took any accelerated depreciation on the car.

Now that you've probably used the wrong method, can you switch? The IRS allows you to switch to the method of actual expenses anytime, with no hassle and no audit.[18] However, going from actual expenses to the IRS method is much tougher. If you used the slower straight-line method of depreciation and not the faster accelerated method of depreciation, you can switch to the IRS method.[19] In addition, if you sell your car and get another car in business, you can start using any method.

Author's note: You might be wondering why the IRS allows you to switch easily from the IRS method to actual expenses but makes it more difficult to go from actual expenses to the IRS method. I don't have the slightest idea why this occurs. This is just one of the quirky rules in tax law.

Depreciating an Automobile

My goal here is not to make you an accountant; thus I am not going to delve into the intricacies of depreciation. However, there are some tax-planning tips and traps that you should know about.

Depreciation is nothing more than a cost-allocation method; therefore, pick the method that gives you the biggest deductions each year.

There are two basic depreciation methods for business vehicles: straight line, the slower method that allows you to deduct in equal amounts, and accelerated, which allows for faster deductions up front. As a result of the "tax simplification" law placing limits on depreciating luxury cars, this is further complicated.[20] The accelerated-depreciation rates (modified accelerated cost recovery system, or MACRS), the straight-line rates, and the luxury limits for passenger cars placed in service in 2006 are listed in Figure 5-2.

In addition, tax law requires you generally to treat your car as having been purchased during the middle of the year of purchase.[21] Thus, if you buy your car in January, for depreciation purposes, you're deemed to buy the car on July 1. The same would be true if you purchased the car in

Year	MACRS	Straight Line	Luxury Limit
1	20.00%	10.00%	$2,960
2	32.00%	20.00%	$4,900
3	19.20%	20.00%	$2,950
4	11.52%	20.00%	$1,775
5	11.42%	20.00%	$1,775
6	5.76%	10.00%	$1,775

Figure 5-2 Depreciation rates—after year 6, 5.75% and $1,775.

September. This is important: Because it's considered to be purchased on July 1, you don't get a whole year's depreciation in the first year.

Thus you would think that you should buy your business vehicle in December, get a half-year depreciation, and probably get a better deal from the dealer too. However, there's a congressional "gotcha." (Someone actually thought of this.)

If you buy over 40 percent of all depreciable equipment for the year during the last three months of the year, then you must treat the purchase as if you made it in the middle of the last quarter of the year, or on November 15. The effect of this is to cut back on your first year's depreciation.[22]

Author's note: This is a great example of needless complexity in our tax laws. The result of this needless complexity is a deferral of your depreciation until a later year. The bottom line is that you should buy most of your vehicles before October 1, unless you can elect to expense the vehicle, which will be discussed below.

In addition, as you can see from Chart 1, you're subject to yearly depreciation limits—and you don't even get these if you use your car less than 100 percent for business. An example will illustrate this.

Example: You purchase a $20,000 car and use it 75 percent for business. The personal use reduces your deductions.[23] The depreciation options that you would have are as follows (see Chart 1):

- $3,000 under MACRS ($20,000 × 20 percent × 75 percent business use)
- $1,500 under straight line ($20,000 × 10 percent × 75 percent business use)
- $2,220 under the luxury limits ($2,960 × 75 percent business use) (using the higher of the MACRS and straight-line amounts)

The maximum depreciation you can claim is $3,000 because of the luxury limits.

Buy "Heavy Metal" Vehicles and Get Fast Write-offs

There are some exceptions to these luxury limits that you should know. First, if you have an electric vehicle, you get three times the yearly luxury limits.[24] You may not be able to go more than 100 miles in these vehicles, but you do get more in depreciation. Thus, if the luxury limits for the first year are $2,960 (based on Chart 1), you would get up to three times the yearly limit, or $8,880, in the first year and three times the luxury limits for each succeeding year.

Second, you should note that all the luxury limits apply only to passenger automobiles. If you can come outside the definition of *passenger automobile,* you have no luxury limits and can write off the entire business use of the car over five years or even less with the expense election. So what is a *passenger automobile?*

Congress defines a *passenger automobile* as a four-wheeled vehicle that is manufactured primarily for use on public streets and highways and has an unloaded gross vehicle weight of 6,000 pounds or less.[25] However, if a vehicle is a truck or a van or has a truck base, as most sports utility vehicles do, then the test changes to having a loaded gross vehicle weight based on manufacturer's suggested carrying weight.[26] I should note that certain commercial vehicles, such as ambulances, hearses, taxicabs, and limousines, are not deemed passenger cars if they're used for commercial purposes.[27]

Example: Sam drives a sports utility vehicle that has a manufacturer's suggested carrying weight of 7,500 pounds. This is not deemed to be a passenger vehicle, so the yearly luxury limits on depreciation do not apply.

Author's note: You might be wondering how you can tell what the manufacturer's suggested carrying weight of a vehicle is. You can either call your dealer or look on the door jam of the driver's side. There is a metal plate that notes your manufacturer's suggested carrying weight.

Even better (you're going to like this—and hate your accountant), if your vehicle is not deemed to be a passenger automobile and you purchased this vehicle after October 22, 2004, you can elect to write off the business use of the vehicle up to $25,000 of its cost and depreciate any excess as long as your business use is at least 50 percent or more.[28] This may be one reason you see lots of sports utility vehicles and vans on the road.

Example: You purchase a new van for $40,000 in September 2006 and use it 90 percent for business; thus your business-use cost allocation would be $36,000 (90 percent of $40,000). If the van has a loaded manufacturer's carrying weight of over 6,000 pounds, you could elect to deduct all this cost this year and up to $25,000, and you can depreciate the difference of $11,000 over six years. I'd bet that you didn't know this and never heard about this from your accountant! Thus, the bottom line is to buy "heavy metal" vehicles and elect to write them off up to $25,000 of the cost in the year that you buy them.

Author's note: I should note that if your business use drops below the business-use percentage during any of the succeeding five years, you will have to recapture or pay back some of the depreciation that you claimed. Thus try to keep the vehicle in your business for at least five years for the same business use. Also, one extra perk that I bet you didn't know: The IRS allows you to deduct the business use of any chauffeur cost.[29] Thus, if you pay a chauffeur $40,000 to drive you everywhere and use the vehicle 80 percent for business, 80 percent of this cost would be deductible.

Tax Credits for Automobiles

There are a host of new tax credits available to hybrid cars and those that use alternative fuels. The rules used to figure out these credits are very complicated and beyond the scope of this book. However, if you buy a hybrid car, you may be eligible for a variety of tax credits:

- *Qualified fuel-cell motor vehicle credit.* If your car uses fuel cells that combine oxygen with hydrogen fuel and has a gross vehicle weight of at least 8,500 pounds, you may qualitfy for a tax credit that varies from $8,000 to $40,000 depending on the weight of the vehicle; the heavier the gross weight, the greater is the credit. However, most hybrid vehicles don't use hydrogen fuel; thus you probably won't get this credit.
- *New advanced lean-burning technology credit.* If you have a vehicle that achieves at least 125 percent of a 2002 model year city fuel economy and has a gross vehicle weight of 6,000 pounds or less, you may be eligible for a credit that ranges from $400 to as much as $2,400 depending on the fuel economy.[30]
- *Lifetime fuel savings credit.* In addition, hybrid cars may be eligible for a lifetime fuel savings credit of between $250 and $1,000.[31] I should note that this credit phases out based on each manufacturer producing 60,000 vehicles. Thus you need to speak to your automobile dealer to ascertain whether you qualify for the credit.
- *New qualified hybrid motor vehicle credit.* This involves several credits that require a certificate of conformity with the Clean Air Act, meet California emissions standards, and other complicated rules. You would get total credits for passenger automobiles of between $650 and $3,150.

Because the credit rules are complicated to figure out, the IRS has published a list of cars that qualify for these credits and the amount of the credit available. For example:

Car	Credit
2006 Ford Escape hybrid front WD	$2,600
2007 Ford Escape hybrid front WD	$2,600
2006 Ford Escape hybrid 4WD	$1,950
2007 Ford Escape hybrid 4WD	$1,950
2006 Mercury Mariner hybrid 4WD	$1,950
2007 Mercury Mariner hybrid 4WD	$1,950
2005 Toyota Prius	$3,150
2006 Toyota Prius	$3,150
2007 Toyota Camry Hybrid	$2,600
2006 Toyota Highlander hybrid 4WD	$2,600
2006 Toyota Highlander hybrid 2WD	$2,600
2006 Lexus RX400h 2WD	$2,200
2006 Lexus RX400h 4WD	$2,200
2007 Lexus GS450h	$1,550
2005 Honda Civic hybrid (SULEV) MT	$1,700
2005 Honda Civic hybrid (SULEV) CVT	$1,700
2006 Honda Civic hybrid CVT	$2,100
2005 Honda Insight CVT	$1,450
2006 Honda Insight CVT	$1,450
2005 Honda Accord hybrid AT	$650
2006 Honda Accord hybrid AT	$1,300
2006 Honda Accord hybrid AT (without updated control calibration)	$650
2006 GMC Sierra 4WD hybrid pickup truck	$650
2007 GMC Sierra 4WD hybrid pickup truck	$650
2006 GMC Sierra 2WD hybrid pickup truck	$250
2007 GMC Sierra 2WD hybrid pickup truck	$250
2006 Chevrolet Silverado 4WD hybrid pickup truck	$650
2007 Chevrolet Silverado 4WD hybrid pickup truck	$650
2006 Chevrolet Silverado 2WD hybrid pickup truck	$250
2007 Chevrolet Silverado 2WD hybrid pickup truck	$250
2007 Saturn Vue Green Line	$650

It's Usually Better to Buy than Lease a Vehicle

2007 Update: Most Toyota and Honda cars get 50 percent of the above noted credits.

Author's Note: These credits are available for the first 60,000 models of each car sold. Check with your dealer to see if your model still qualifies for the credit.

Since Congress put some severe limits on depreciation, you would think that leasing would be the better deal; however, Congress thought of this too. Congress made the IRS come up with killer tables that approximate the benefits of what you would have gotten had you purchased the vehicle. You actually would add back some income on your tax return, which is the same as eliminating some lease deductions. Figure 5-3 shows this table. To use it, add back the dollar amounts under "Tax Year During Lease" to your income on your tax return, based on the fair market value of the car and how old the lease is. In later years of the lease, the "add back" to your income is higher; the higher the car value, the greater is the "add back." (Add-back amounts are for automobiles—other than electric automobiles—with a lease term beginning in calendar year 2002.)

If you examine the table, you will see that the more expensive the car, the worse the leasing deal becomes, and the longer the lease, the worse the deal is. Thus four-year leases are worse than three-year leases, which are worse than two-year leases.

After doing a lot of computer analysis, I have found that the best treatment for a business vehicle is to buy it and keep it at least four or more years, with 10 years being ideal. However, there are a few other times when buying is better than leasing, as follows[30]:

- You get great finance terms, such as 0 percent interest.
- The vehicle is not deemed a passenger automobile.
- You put on more than 15,000 miles per year.
- You can't buy a car with decent terms owing to a bad credit rating.

Leasing generally becomes better if

- You can't get good financing.
- You put on less then 15,000 miles per year.
- Your car is a passenger automobile.

Fair Market of Automobile		Tax Year During Lease				
Over	Not Over	1st	2nd	3rd	4th	5th and later
18,000	18,500	14	30	44	53	61
18,500	19,000	16	35	52	62	72
19,000	19,500	18	40	60	71	82
19,500	20,000	21	45	67	80	93
20,000	20,500	23	50	75	89	103
20,500	21,000	25	56	82	98	114
21,000	21,500	28	60	90	108	123
21,500	22,000	30	66	97	117	134
22,000	23,000	33	74	108	130	150
23,000	24,000	38	84	123	149	171
24,000	25,000	43	94	139	166	192

Figure 5-3 Lease "add back" table.

Fair Market of Automobile		Tax Year During Lease				
Over	Not Over	1st	2nd	3rd	4th	5th and later
25,000	26,000	47	104	154	185	213
26,000	27,000	52	114	169	203	234
27,000	28,000	57	124	185	220	255
28,000	29,000	61	135	199	239	276
29,000	30,000	66	145	214	258	296
30,000	31,000	71	155	230	275	318
31,000	32,000	75	165	245	294	338
32,000	33,000	80	175	260	312	360
33,000	34,000	85	185	276	329	381
34,000	35,000	89	196	290	348	402
35,000	36,000	94	206	305	367	422
36,000	37,000	99	216	321	384	443
37,000	38,000	103	226	336	403	464
38,000	39,000	108	236	351	421	485
39,000	40,000	112	247	366	439	506
40,000	41,000	117	257	381	457	527
41,000	42,000	122	267	396	475	549
42,000	43,000	126	278	411	493	570
43,000	44,000	131	288	426	512	590
44,000	45,000	136	298	441	530	611
45,000	46,000	140	308	457	548	632
46,000	47,000	145	318	472	566	653
47,000	48,000	150	328	487	584	674
48,000	49,000	154	339	502	602	695
49,000	50,000	159	349	517	620	717
50,000	51,000	164	359	532	639	737
51,000	52,000	168	369	548	657	758
52,000	53,000	173	379	563	675	779
53,000	54,000	177	390	578	693	800
54,000	55,000	182	400	593	711	821
55,000	56,000	187	410	608	729	842
56,000	57,000	191	420	624	747	863
57,000	58,000	196	430	639	766	883
58,000	59,000	201	440	654	784	905
59,000	60,000	205	451	669	802	925
60,000	62,000	212	466	692	829	957
62,000	64,000	222	486	722	866	999
64,000	66,000	231	507	752	902	1,041
66,000	68,000	240	527	783	938	1,083
68,000	70,000	250	547	813	974	1,125
70,000	72,000	259	568	843	1,011	1,166
72,000	74,000	268	589	873	1,047	1,208
74,000	76,000	277	609	904	1,083	1,250
76,000	78,000	287	629	934	1,120	1.292
78,000	80,000	296	650	964	1,156	1,334

Figure 5-3 Lease "add back" table. (continued)

This book assumes that you or your spouse have a small business or consulting practice or are considering going into business. If you're solely an employee, the rules are different and, as mentioned, more restrictive. Employees cannot deduct interest and taxes on cars, but they can deduct the business-use portion of their lease payment. Thus, if you are an employee, either pay all cash for the car or lease the car.

Author's note: Considering that a lease payment includes the interest that someone is paying, I find it strange that employees can't deduct interest but can deduct the entire amount of the lease payment based on the business use of the vehicle. This is another example of incongruous tax treatment between employees and small business owners.

Deduct Supplies and Equipment Used to Maintain Your Business Car

If you use the actual method of deducting your car expenses (i.e., gas, repairs, depreciation, etc.), you may be missing a bunch of automotive deductions. Go through your garage and basement or wherever you store tools and cleaning supplies. Make a list of the items that you use on your car. You'll probably find a battery charger, battery cables and tester, shimmies, wax and wash cans, a pump, a vise, a tire inflator (that plugs into a lighter), sander, small tools, and a car repair manual. (My wife, Lori, fixes my car.) You should have found a number of items that you'd overlooked. Generally, you can deduct the cost of nonequipment items (i.e., shimmies, wax cans, and water cans) if they're expected to last less than a year.[31] Most equipment, such as compressors, tools, and tire inflators, must be capitalized and depreciated unless they're considered to be of de minimis value.[32]

Author's note: From my experience with IRS audits, generally an item that is worth under $100 might be allowed as an expense rather than being capitalized and depreciated over time. Since you'll be backtracking through past acquisitions, it's likely you won't have receipts. Take photographs that can represent reasonable substitute evidence and conservatively estimate the value of the items if sold today. This will be less than cost, but it will be better than no deduction.

When to Sell and When to Trade: That Is the Question

There are two ways in which you can dispose of your vehicle: Sell it or trade it. Some people think that donating a business car to a charity after completely writing it off is a good deal. Sadly, this is a tax disaster.

Most people know only half the charitable deduction rules; that is, if you donate an item such as stock or a car to a qualified charity, you can deduct the fair market value of your donation. Thus, if your car is worth

$6,000 today, you would get a $6,000 deduction. Now for the rest of the story.

You must deduct from this fair market value any amount of gain that would not be a long-term gain.[33] What this means is that you must subtract any depreciation taken on your vehicle. Thus, if your vehicle was worth $6,000 and the depreciation taken was $6,000 or more, you would get *zero* deduction—nothing, nada, zip. This is why, from a tax standpoint, you should rarely donate a car or other depreciated property to a charity.

Author's note: I heard in my seminars about two other methods for disposing of a vehicle. One was to park your vehicle in certain shopping malls near Los Angeles where there's a high probability of car theft. The other method was from a New York student who suggested abandoning the vehicle on the highway. Needless to say, these methods aren't legitimate.

Now that you understand some of the basics, let's go over the flowchart shown in Figure 5-4.

As you can see, the first question that you need to answer is whether there will be a gain or a loss on the disposal of your vehicle. To do this, you would first need to know your adjusted basis. This is your cost plus any major improvements, such as a new engine, minus any depreciation taken.[34] Thus, if you paid $20,000 for a car and got $10,000 in depreciation deductions, your adjusted basis would be $10,000. What this means to you is simple: If you sell the car for more than your basis, $10,000 in this example, you would have a gain, but if you sell the car for less than your basis, you would have a loss.[35] It's really that simple.

Author's note: If you don't know how much depreciation you've taken on your vehicle, you could either ask your accountant or look on your latest tax return. In addition, even if you used the IRS method, depreciation is built into the numbers, with the depreciation portion changing each year. The following are the depreciation amounts that were built into the IRS method from 1992 through 2007[36]:

- For 2006 and 2007, 19 cents per business mile
- For 2005 and 2006, 19 cents per business mile
- For 2003 and 2004, 16 cents per business mile
- For 2001 and 2002, 14 cents per business mile
- From 1994 through1999, 12 cents per business mile
- For 1992 and 1993, 11.5 cents per business mile

Example: In 2006 you drove your car 20,000 miles for business. You would reduce your basis by 17 cents per business mile, or $3,800 (20,000 business miles × $0.19 for 2007). Once you know your basis, you need to know what your car will sell for. You can go to my Web site at www.taxreductioninstitute.com, which has an appraisal button, or you can go to your classified adds or check out other Web sites. Now, follow the arrows in Figure 5-4. If a loss would result, which is normally the case, you should sell your car and take a deductible loss. Thus, if you used your car 80 percent for business over the last three years and the estimate is that you will have a loss, you can deduct 80 percent of that loss in the year you sell the vehicle!

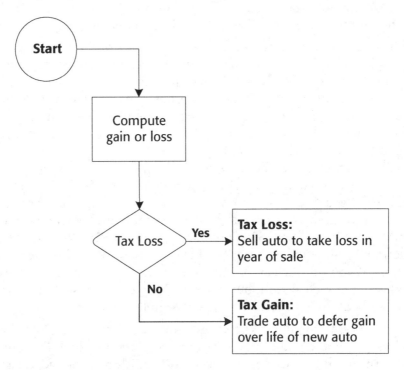

Figure 5-4 Disposing of the automobile, decision flowchart.

Example: You have a car that cost you $24,000, and you've taken $8,000 of depreciation. Thus your adjusted basis is $16,000 ($24,000 cost minus $8,000 depreciation). If this vehicle is worth only $10,000 when you sell it, your loss would be $4,800 ($6,000 total loss × 80 percent business usage).

However, if you were to have a gain, then the flowchart recommends that you trade the vehicle and not sell it. The reason is that there are no losses or gains allowed on trade-ins.[37] Thus, if you have a gain, you pay no tax.

Unfortunately, an estimated 80 percent of all people who use their car in business don't know this information, so they've made tremendous mistakes. If you trade in the car, which happens many times, the loss is not allowed.

I had a physician in my audience who bought a new Cadillac every three years and then traded it in. He did this for all of his 20-plus years of practice. When I ran the numbers, I figured out that he had lost about $16,000 of loss deductions every three years for the full 20 years of practice. That's about $96,000 of lost deductions! How's that for an expensive mistake that an inexpensive book like this could have eliminated?

Interestingly, the $96,000 of losses that the physician would have received are not eliminated; they're deferred to the next car, and the next, and so forth. Thus, when he sells his current vehicle and stops his cycle of trading, he can deduct all the deferred $96,000.

Author's note: When I told the physician that all he had to do was sell his current car to deduct the $96,000 of deferred losses, he ran out of the room as if he was running for the goal line. I never saw anyone move so quickly! I guarantee that he got rid of his current car even if he had to blow it up. If you've been trading in business vehicles, this idea could be an enormous tax windfall to you.

What Counts as "Miles Driven for Business"?

After speaking to over 200,000 people over the last 17 years, it still amazes me how little most people know about what trips constitute business mileage and about the documentation needed for the IRS. In fact, I would estimate that well over 95 percent of my students aren't aware of this information. Obviously, both the IRS and accountants aren't doing a good job in disseminating this crucial information, as you'll soon see.

So what are the rules for business mileage? The IRS requires you to separate business use from personal use.[38] Your business-use percentage determines your business automobile deductions.[39]

Example: You drive your car 30,000 miles per year, but only 20,000 of these miles are for business. Thus two-thirds of your car expenses—such as depreciation, wash, wax, interest, repairs, and insurance—would be deductible.

If your corporation provides a car to you or your employees[40] or if you're self-employed and you provide a car to your employees, the personal-use percentage determines additional employee compensation. The compensation to your employees can be based on one of three methods:

- *The annual lease table rule,*[41] for which you would use the IRS lease tables. Essentially, you would determine the fair market value of the vehicle on the date of first use and find that number on the IRS Lease Valuation Table in Appendix B. The correct lease amount will be noted. You then would multiply this amount by the personal use.

Example: Your corporation buys a car for $20,000 and provides the car for your use. If you use it 50 percent for business, 50 percent of the lease valuation amount would be taxable to you ($5,600 × 50 percent = $2,800). This is an easy method but very expensive. Although there are other, cheaper methods, they have limited availability, as you'll see.

- *The cents-per-mile rule,* in which you would be taxed a flat 48.5 cents per mile on your personal mileage in 2007. A good tax diary would be essential for you to distinguish between personal and business mileage. As I've said before, the golden rule—"He who has the gold makes the rules"—applies here. The cents-per-mile method works only with a vehicle whose fair market value is under $16,000 and if employees drive it at least 10,000 miles per year.
- *The commuting valuation rule,*[42] which is (as you would guess) for commuting use only. The good news is that this is a great method that probably provides the lowest cost to the employee or to you if you're incorporated. However, it's also the most limited. There are three conditions.

First, you would need a written policy requiring the employee to commute to work. Second, you would need a written policy noting that the car cannot be used for personal purposes other than for commuting. Third, you can't use this for a "control employee." This is the IRS "gotcha." A *control employee* is either a board member or an officer who makes $50,000 a year or more, a director, any employee who makes at least $100,000 a year, or a 1 percent or more stockholder or equity owner.

Author's note: As you can see, the commuting valuation method won't work for you as the owner of your corporation. Also, as a reminder, all these methods apply only if you provide a vehicle to your employees or your corporation provides you a company-owned vehicle. If you're self-employed or a limited-liability corporation (which is treated like being self-employed anyway), you don't need to worry about this.

When Is the Mileage Business and When Is It Personal?

Before I discuss what constitutes business versus personal mileage, you need to know the difference between a temporary business trip and a regular business stop or trip. A *temporary business stop* is one where you're expected to be for less than a year.[43] A *regular business stop* is one where you're expected to be for more than a year or where your stay will be indeterminate. Thus, if you're going to the bank from your home or to the post office, this would be a regular business stop because you will be going to the bank on a regular basis and not less than a year; on the other hand, if you visit a client or attend a seminar, that would be a temporary business stop.

Most people know that when they go to a business stop from their office, the mileage is business. Thus, going to a client, the bank, or the printer from your office is all business mileage. The real question and confusion arises when you go to a business stop from your home. The IRS says that there are three types of situations that will determine whether your mileage from your home is business or personal.

Situation one: Your home is your principal place of business. If your home is your principal place of business, as defined in Chapter 6, all business stops from your home are deemed to be business mileage, with the exception of a direct commute from your home to your main office where you might have a job.[44] Thus home-based business owners and consultants who make their home their principal office come out ahead here.

Example: Tom is a consultant who works primarily out of his home. He goes to the bank from his home to make deposits on Monday and visits clients Tuesday through Friday. All mileage would be deemed business mileage because his home is his principal place of business.

Situation two: *Your home is not your principal place of business, but your business trip takes you outside your "normal geographic area of work."* If you're traveling outside the geographic area where you normally conduct business, then all round-trip mileage to these business stops constitutes business mileage, as long as you will not be there more than one year.[45]

Example: You live in Detroit but attend a one-day seminar in Grand Rapids. All round-trip business mileage would be deductible. If, however, you were stationed in Grand Rapids for a project that's expected to last more than a year, this mileage would not be deductible because it wouldn't be a temporary business stop.

Situation three: *You travel within your normal geographic area.* If your home is not your principal place of business, your business mileage to your office and/or back home would be deductible *if* you went to a temporary business stop on the way to the office or on the way home.[46] All business stops after the temporary business stop also would be deemed business mileage.

Example: You go from your home, which is not your principal office, to meet a prospect for business. You then go to Stops A, B, and C and then to your office. All stops would be deemed business mileage.[47]

Example: Instead of the preceding stops, you first go to the post office and then to business stops A, B, and C and then to the office. Your trip to the post office would not be deductible because it's a regular business stop and not a temporary business stop. However, all mileage thereafter would be deductible.[48]

In case you don't remember all these situations and rules, I provide a great flowchart in Figure 5-5. Just read it over. I think that you will find it amazingly simple yet thorough.

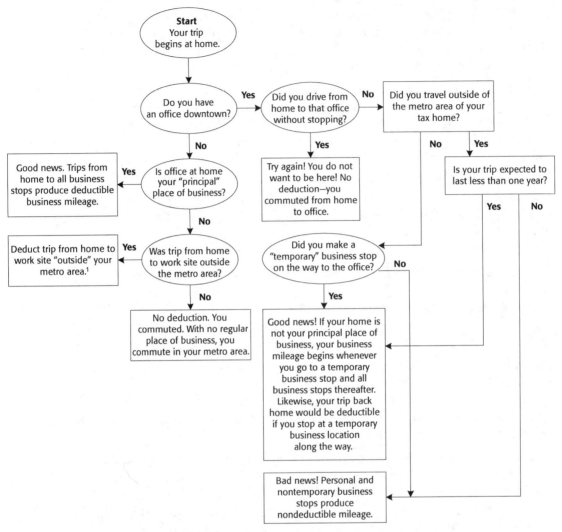

1. A recent case noted that 35 miles away from your normal work area was outside your geographic area.

Figure 5-5 Flowchart for determining business mileage (home business owners should be able to deduct all trips from home to any business stop).

Make Your Records Bulletproof from the IRS

When you file your tax return, you or your corporation will have to answer specific questions regarding business vehicles and about having appropriate documentation in writing. The questions are part of your tax return, and you must answer all questions under penalties of perjury.[49]

One question you will have to answer is, "Do you have evidence to support business use?"[50] Another question is, "Is the evidence written?"[51]

To sustain your business deductions and not be hit with severe penalties, you must be in a position to answer "Yes" to both questions.

Author's note: I should note that it is IRS policy to allow electronic documentation.[52] However, based on my audit experience and that of other accountants whom I've interviewed, IRS agents are much more willing to accept paper documentation over electronic documentation.

There are four other dreaded questions that also must be answered regarding the miles driven during the year. In your tax return, you must report miles driven during the year broken down in the following four categories[53]:

- Total miles
- Total business miles
- Total commuting miles
- Other personal miles (noncommuting)

Author's note: Many people are surprised that the IRS asks for "other personal miles" and are curious what this entails. Other personal miles, other than commuting, are trips to a doctor, a place of worship, charitable functions, and driving children to various activities, such as karate, music or dance lessons, etc.

Your records also must be adequate to support business use.[54] An adequate record[55] is one made at or near the time of business use.[56] *Other sufficient evidence* is acceptable only if you have direct corroborative evidence (such as statements from witnesses) or other documentary evidence.[57] I should note that you don't need to keep your records daily or contemporaneously with each trip, but the log should be completed near or at the time of each event.[58] A weekly log of what you did during the week would be acceptable.[59]

Author's note: What this all means to you is that the IRS clearly states that the log need not be daily. A log of your weekly activities made at the end of the week would suffice. However, I have found (and other accountants concur) that if you don't have something "triggering" you to record your mileage, expenses, tips, and other items daily, you'll probably forget about these expenses and thus lose the deduction. It's crucial to have a good tax organizer or diary. I've developed one that has all the IRS questions and is color coded for simplicity. Check out my Web site, www.taxreductioninstitute.com, for an example.

One other point is that although the IRS allows for other evidence such as statements by witnesses, I wouldn't depend on this if I were you. People forget quickly, and having to call in witnesses is a pain. Just keep a good tax diary or organizer and you will simplify your life. If you use the IRS method, you still need adequate records of your business mileage; you just don't need to keep receipts.[60] The IRS standard mileage method eliminates the need to keep gas and oil receipts but, most important, does not eliminate the need for mileage records to be broken down into business, personal, and commuting categories.

Author's note: I should add that a careful reading of the IRS regulations seems to indicate that you do not need to keep receipts for automobile expenses such as gas, oil, or tolls that are under $75 per expense.[61]

If you fail to keep the required records, such as a tax diary or organizer, this will expose you to huge penalties. Moreover, Congress wants the IRS to start asking for fraud penalties when taxpayers don't have good records of automobile business use.[62]

Types of Mileage Logs That the IRS Will Accept

The good news is that you have your choice of several types of methods that are acceptable to the IRS. The bad news is that I'll bet that you haven't been doing it right all these years.

The first choice, which is the IRS's favorite method, is the "perfect one-day log." An example of this is shown in Figure 5-6.

You would list all your appointments, both business and personal, in a tax diary or tax organizer. When you use the car to get to an appointment, you would list the mileage next to the appointment. At the end of the day, you would record your final odometer reading. Finally, you would tally your business, personal, and commuting miles and reconcile those numbers with your beginning and ending odometer readings. The important point is that you would record your business and personal mileage daily for each stop and for each trip. This is clearly the most complicated of all the allowable methods.

The second option is the 90-day log. IRS regulations allow a mileage record for a representative portion of the year to substantiate business use for the entire year.[63] In the first example used by the IRS, it's noted that you can keep detailed daily records of your business and personal mileage, somewhat akin to the "perfect-use one-day log method," but for the first three months of the year, to substantiate the entire year, if your business use of the vehicle follows the same pattern for the remaining nine months of the year.[64]

Example: You would keep track of your business and personal mileage for three consecutive months. If your business mileage for the three sample months is 6,000 miles and your personal mileage is 2,000 miles, you may deduct three-fourths of your car expenses for the year, or you may take three-fourths of your total year's mileage and use the IRS standard mileage rate on this amount.

| **1** | MONTH _____ | | | |
| | DAY OF THE WEEK   S   M   T   W   T   F   S | | | |

APPOINTMENTS DAILY	**BUSINESS**	**COMMUTE**	**PERSONAL**
7:00 AM			
7:30			
8:00			
8:30			
9:00			
9:30			
10:00			
10:30			
11:00			
11:30			
12:00 PM			
12:30			
1:00			
1:30			
2:00			
2:30			
3:00			
3:30			
4:00			
4:30			
5:00			
5:30			
6:00			
TOTAL MILES			
BEG. ODOMETER			
END ODOMETER			
CIRCLE VEHICLE	**1 2**		

TRI   © Sanford C. Botkin

Figure 5-6 The perfect one-day car log.

Author's note: Although the IRS regulations use the first three months of the year as an example, you probably can use any normal three consecutive months. They can be January through March, March through May, or (if you've nothing for the year yet) October through December. This method is available only if you use your car on a relatively even basis from month to month. The IRS will want to see that you're not picking your busiest three months. They would check your tax diary or appointment book to see if you had relatively the same number of appointments during the other nine months.

I also should note that this method assumes that you drive the same car in business during the year. If you switch off cars in the same business, you may not be able to use any statistical approach and may be limited to the "perfect one-day log."

The third approach, which is also a sampling type of approach, is called the *first-week rule*. Here, the IRS assumes that you keep an automobile log for the first week of each month and then can prove by adequate records that your business use for the remainder of each month was consistent with that of the first week.[65]

The key to all the sample approaches listed here is to enter all appointments in your appointment book, tax organizer, or diary—this proves consistent business use. As you can see, these methods are fine but a bit complicated. How would you like a much easier method? I call the fourth approach the *no-hassle approach*.

This method was started by Mr. Frankel.[66] He was told by his accountant to keep track of his automobile using the perfect one-day log. He did this for one month and wrote down over 600 appointments. He realized that he probably was losing money on all the time spent on documentation. He thus came out with a brilliant approach. He decided to keep track of only his personal and commuting mileage, which was a lot less involved.

This method is somewhat similar to the 90-day log. If you list your daily appointments in your diary or tax organizer, here's how you can make your 90-day test:

- Document your beginning and ending 90-day odometer readings and the odometer readings on January 1 and December 31.
- Record personal miles each day during the 90-day test.
- Record your commuting mileage during the 90-day test.
- Apply the percentages to the test to determine the actual mileage.

Example: For 90 days you would keep track of your personal mileage only and your beginning and ending odometer readings for the test period. Thus you might say, "To office, three miles and to home, three miles," and record all your business appointments without noting the business mileage. If your total mileage for the three-month test is 8,000 miles, of which 2,000 were personal miles, then 6,000 miles were for business. Thus, in this example, you could deduct three-fourths of your car expenses for the year.

Author's note: As a reminder, this method works only if appointments are recorded and they substantiate the business mileage. In addition, you must keep track of your appointments to show that the time period chosen truly represents the business activities for the entire year.[67] Also, as noted earlier, you can't use any sampling method if you use a second car during the year.[68]

If Your Records Were Lost or Destroyed, Use the Reconstruction Approach

What do you do if you have no records for the prior year? I have a method for you. It's called the *desperation* or *reconstruction approach.* Here you would backdate a tax diary based on your appointment book and, in effect, create the records.

The IRS allows you to reconstruct your records if they were lost owing to circumstances beyond your control.[69] Examples of circumstances beyond your control would be flood, fire, earthquake, theft, or other casualty.[70] You theoretically cannot reconstruct records if they were lost through your own carelessness or negligence.[71]

Author's note: Practically speaking, most IRS agents on audits will let you reconstruct your records if you use a reasonable basis for the reconstruction. You just can't pull the numbers out of thin air. For example, if you keep a diary of your appointment, you probably could write down the estimated mileage next to the appointments.

However, don't use what IRS agents call the *finger in the wind approach.* This is where you estimate your business mileage without a log or some backup support. You'll be hit with substantial penalties for trying to pull the wool over IRS eyes.

At many seminars I get asked about what is a reasonable percentage for business mileage for various professions. I thus did some research and, based on actual cases, and found the following information on various professions and the amount of business mileage allowed for that profession by the court:

Anesthesiologist	39 percent[72]
Attorney	30 percent[73]
Auto dealer	70 percent[74]
Cemetery plot sales representative	80 percent[75]

Dentist (who directed clinics and made outside calls)	80 percent[76]
Doctor	75 percent[77]
Income tax preparer	15 percent[78]
Rental real estate owner	20 percent[79]
Structural engineer	70 percent[80]
Traveling sales representative	80 percent[81]
Wholesale grocer	50 percent[82]

Author's note: These statistics are based on actual cases of people showing the business use allowed for their professions. Certainly, with the right documentation, you may be able to claim much more than was given. You can't, however, use these statistics in lieu of documentation. I offer them here to give you a feel for what was allowed by the courts.

Summary

- Use two or more cars in business and generate a lot more in deductions.
- Deduct the larger of the actual method for your car expenses or the IRS standard rates. Generally, the actual method produces more deductions.
- Buy heavy cars (weighing over 6,000 pounds) and get a fast write-off.
- Buy your car, rather than lease it, and hold onto it for at least four years.
- Identify and deduct supplies and equipment used to maintain your car.
- Sell cars that produce a deductible loss, but trade cars that produce a taxable profit.
- Generally sell cars if you've used the IRS method of deducting vehicle expenses.
- Rarely donate a car that has been depreciated. You probably won't get any deduction.
- Make your car into a tax-deductible goldmine either by making your home the principal office for your business or by having a temporary business stop on the way to the office and/or on the way home.
- Keep a 90-day daily log of car use, preferably using the no-hassle approach.

Notes

1. Sections 1.162-1(a) and 1.162-2 of the ITR. See also *Commissioner v. Griner*, 71-2 USTC Par. 9714 (N.D. Fla. 1971) and *Commissioner v. Cavender*, 71-2 USTC Par. 9723 (S.D. W. Va. 1971).
2. Sections 1.274-6T, 1.274-5T(b)(6), and 1.274-5T(c) of the ITR. See also *Reems v. Commissioner*, 67 TCM 3050 (1994) and IRS Publication 17 (2001).
3. See note 1.
4. *On-RI-GA-Medical Professional Association*, T.C. memo 1978-183.
5. Section 1.274-5T(c)(3) of the ITR.

6. Sections 1001, 1012, and 1016 of the IRC.
7. Section 1.167(g)-1 of the ITR.
8. Sections 1011 and 1012 of the IRC.
9. See note 7.
10. Revenue Procedure 2001-54, 2001-48 IRB 530.
11. Sections 1.162-1 and 1.162-6 of the ITR.
12. Ibid. and Revenue Procedure 2001-54, supra.
13. Ibid.
14. Ibid.
15. Runzheimer International.
16. Revenue Procedure 2001-54, supra.
17. Ibid.
18. Ibid. and IRS Publication 463.
19. Ibid.
20. Section 280F(a)(2)(A) of the IRC; Revenue Procedure 2002-14, 2002-5 IRB 450.
21. Section 168(d)(3)(A) of the IRC and Section 1.168(d)-1(a) of the ITR.
22. Ibid.
23. Section 280F(d)(2) of the IRC and Section 1.280F-2T(i) of the ITR.
24. Section 280F(a)(1)(C) of the IRC.
25. Section 280F(d)(5)(A) of the IRC and Section 1.280F-6T of the ITR.
26. Ibid. and Section 280F(a)(1)(C) of the IRC.
27. Section 1.280F-6T(c) of the ITR.
28. Sections 179 and 280F of the IRC.
29. *Rodgers Dairy Co.*, 14 TC 66 (1950), *acq.*
30. Research Recommendations, Vol. 54, No. 25, p. 4 (12/3/2001).
31. Section 1.263(a)-1(b) of the ITR. *Cincinnati, New Orleans, and Texas Pacific Railway Co. v. United States,* 424 F.2d 563 (Ct. Cl. 1970); *Metrocorp, Inc. v. Commissioner,* 116 TC 211 (2001).
32. Ibid.
33. Section 170(e)(1)(a) of the IRC.
34. Sections 1001(a)-(c), 1012, and 1016 of the IRC.
35. Section 1001 of the IRC.
36. Revenue Procedure 2001-54; see note 10; and CCH Exp 2002 FED Par. 14,417.043, *Substantiation Requirements and Per Diem Rules.*
37. Section 1031 of the IRC and *Schmidt v. Commissioner,* 28 TCM 481 (1969).
38. Section 1.274-5t(b)(6) and (d) of the ITR.
39. Sections 274(d)(4) and 280F(d)(4)(A) of the IRC. See also Sections 1.274-5T(d) and 6T(d) of the ITR.
40. Technically speaking, personal use determines the amount of the fringe benefit reportable by your corporation and includable in your income if either the vehicle cents-per-mile or commuting valuation methods are used for valuing the fringe benefits. See section 1.61-2T(d)-(f) of the ITR.
41. Section 1.61-2T(d) of the ITR.
42. Section 1.61-2T(f) of the ITR.
43. Revenue Ruling 99-7, 1999-5, I.R.B. See also PLR 199948019 (12/7/99) and IRS Publication 463, pp. 13-15 (2001).
44. Revenue Ruling 90-23, I.R.B. 1990-11. Modified and superseded by Revenue Ruling 99-7, 1999-5 I.R.B. See also *Curphey v. Commissioner,* 73 TC 766 (1980). Interestingly, the IRS made a mistake in superseding Revenue Ruling 90-23. This ruling was more encompassing and had most of the rules spelled out clearly and

simply. Although Revenue Ruling 99-7 was supposed to clarify some ambiguities in Revenue Ruling 99-23, the IRS obsoleted the ruling instead of simply amplifying it (elaborating on the ruling). This has made this whole area very confusing and unclear.

45. Revenue Ruling 99-7, supra.
46. Ibid.
47. Ibid. and IRS Publication 463, pp. 13-15 (2001).
48. IRS Publication 463, pp. 13-15 (2001).
49. IRS Form 1040 and see declaration immediately above the signature line on IRS Form 1040 (U.S. Individual Tax Return) and Form 1120 (U.S. Corporation Tax Return). See IRS Form 2106 and Section 1.274-5T(d)(2)(1) of the ITR.
50. IRS Form 2106. See also section 1.274-5T(d)(2)(1) of the ITR.
51. Ibid. See also Form 4562 and the instructions thereunder.
52. Revenue Procedure 91-59, 1991-2 C.B. 841.
53. See notes 48 and 49.
54. Section 274(d) of the IRC.
55. Section 274(d) of the IRC and Section 1.274-5T (a) of the ITR.
56. Section 1.274-5T(c)(1) and 1.274-5T(c)(2)(ii)(A) of the ITR.
57. Section 1.274-5T(c)(3) of the ITR.
58. Section 1.274-5T(c)(2) of the ITR.
59. Ibid.
60. Revenue Ruling 2001-54, 2001-48 I.R.B. 530. See also IRS Publication 463.
61. Section 1.274-5T(c)(2)(iii)(A) of the ITR.
62. Conference Committee Report on P.L. 99-44, as found in 8A Standard Federal Tax Report [CCH 5528.034 (1988)].
63. Section 1.274-5T(c)(3) of the ITR.
64. Section 1.274-5T(c)(3)(ii) of the ITR.
65. Ibid. and see IRS Publication 463.
66. *J. E. Frankel v. Commissioner*, 27 TCM 817 (1968) and *B. W. Moretz*, 36 T.C.M. 1341 (1977).
67. Section 1.274-5T(c)(3)(ii) of the ITR.
68. Section 1.274-5T(c)(3)(ii)(B) of the ITR.
69. Section 1.274-5T(c)(5) of the ITR.
70. *I. A. Murray v. Commissioner*, 41 TCM 337 (1980).
71. *P. L. Luben v. Commissioner*, 37 TCM 550 (1978).
72. *Edilberto Beltran*, T.C. Memo 1982-153.
73. *Glenn Strother*, T.C. Memo 1957-102.
74. *Harry Canelo*, 41 BTA 713 (1940), *acq.*
75. *Doris Jones*, 11 TCM 529 (1952).
76. *Floyd Bickel II*, T.C. Memo 1966-202 (1966).
77. *T.K. Lewis*, 9 TCM 32 (1950).
78. *Frank Thomas*, T.C. Memo 1969-108 (1969).
79. *Nickolas Barnes*, T.C. Memo 1981-539 (1981).
80. *William Schmidt and Comp.*, 25 A.F.T.R. 2d 70-1353 (7th Cir. 1970).
81. *Reems v. Commissioner*, 67 TCM 3050 (1994).
82. *Harriet Wagner v. Lucus*, 38 F.2d 391 (CA Dist. 1930).

6

Home Office: The Misunderstood Key to Saving $15,000 Every Five Years

Tax reform is taking the taxes off things that have been taxed in the past and putting taxes on things that haven't been taxed before.

—Art Buchwald

Is a home office really worth it? Be honest. Do you believe or have you heard from your accountant that taking a home office deduction isn't worth the risk or hassle? I'll bet your answer to this question is yes!

Without question, the home office area has more myths than any other topic. People have told me that they'd heard that they can't claim a home office because their home is not zoned commercially. The truth is that the Internal Revenue Service (IRS) couldn't care less about your local zoning. I also have heard with more frequency than I would have believed that "you can't claim a home office deduction unless

Chapter Overview

This will be one of the best and most comprehensive chapters on this subject that you'll ever read. I'll be covering the following:

- Learn why it's worth taking a home office deduction.
- Learn how to qualify for a home office deduction using your home as a principal residence.
- Learn how to qualify for the home office deduction by using the "meet and greet" test.
- Learn how to qualify for the home office deduction by having a separate structure apart from the home as an office.
- Learn how to qualify for the home office deduction by storing inventory and product samples.
- Learn how to qualify for the home office deduction by having a day-care business in the home.

you have a back entrance." I'm not sure what business these people are in!

A home office deduction is like having a bunch of pregnant dollar bills—they give birth to many more dollars. If you look at the example for the individual named Snyder, you will see that, based on a $200,000 home, a home office can generate over $14,000 in cash *every five years* (see Figure 6-1).

This is based on that fact that you get some new deductions. You can deduct some of your property taxes and mortgage interest as a business expense. You also can increase your business mileage because travel from a

> **Chapter Overview (Cont.)**
> - Learn about the little-known IRS strategies needed to audit-proof a home office deduction.
> - Learn how to avoid most taxes on the sale of a home where the home office deduction was claimed.
> - Take the one deduction that normally gets missed—even if you never claim a home office.
> - Understand the rules for the wonderful expensing of assets that could increase your depreciation deductions by over $20,000 per year.

qualified home office to a business stop is all business.[1] Finally, you get additional deductions that you aren't normally eligible to get, such as depreciation, some repairs on the home, utilities, and some house cleaning.[2] I also have factored in something that most people never think of: interest. I assumed that you could earn a conservative long-term interest rate of 6 percent on your tax savings. My question now is simple: "Assuming that you would qualify for the home office deduction, would an extra $14,000 or more every five years be worth the slight increase in documentation?"

Home Office Rules

The general rule is that you can't deduct your home or dwelling unit insofar as it is used as a residence.[3] However, if you meet the home office rules, you can deduct some expenses related to your residence. The law states that a home office deduction is available only to the extent that a portion of the dwelling unit (your home) is used exclusively on a regular basis as one of the following[4]:

- Your principal place of business
- A place of business that you use to meet and deal with patients, clients, or customers in the normal course of your trade or business
- A separate structure that is not attached to the dwelling unit (residence)
- Part of a day-care business

First-Year Tax Refund

	Total	Home Office Percentage	Home Office Deduction	Tax Benefit Rate	Tax Refund
Mortgage Interest	$10,401	15.84%	$1,648	13.02%	$215
Real Estate Taxes	947	15.84%	150	13.02%[1]	20
Utilities	1,704	15.84%	270	54.02%[2]	146
Homeowner's Insurance	310	15.84%	49	54.02%	26
General Repairs	600	15.84%	95	54.02%	51
Pest Control	400	15.84%	63	54.02%	34
Repairs to Office	200	100%	200	54.02%	108
Depreciation – Furniture	1,886	100%	1,886	54.02%	1,019
Depreciation – Home	2,545	15.84%	403	54.02%	218
Snyder's cash-in-pocket from home-office deduction					**$1,837**

Economic Results	
Cash from home-office deducation	$1,837
Cash from extra business mileage	582[3]
Total first-year cash	2,419
6% annuity due factor for 5 years	x5.9753
Net cash after 5 years	$14,454

1. Self-employment tax rate.
2. Self-employment tax rate plus 31% federal tax rate plus 10% state tax rate.
3. Snyder's home business allows him to reduce his personal mileage and increase his business auto expense by $1,077. Thus $582 is refunded by the tax collectors ($1,077 x 54.02%).

Facts: Snyder files a joint tax return with his wife. The Snyders earn $198,000 in taxable income. This puts them in the 33 percent federal and 8 percent state income tax brackets. Mrs. Snyder earns $98,000 from her job as an employee in town. Mr. Snyder works out of his home and earns net taxable income of $100,000, which is reported on Schedule C of Form 1040.

Figure 6-1. How Snyder benefits from the home office deduction

In addition, in the case of an employee, the home office deduction is allowed only if the exclusive use is for the convenience of the employer.[5] Although this is a factual issue, if you are an employee, the courts generally feel that this test is met if "you are required by the employer to have a home office or to work out of your home." Let's examine these tests.

Qualify by Making Your Home Your Principal Place of Business

What constitutes a principal place of business has been the subject of a great deal of litigation and controversy. The good news is that this issue went all the way up to the Supreme Court to decide.[6] The bad news is that the Supreme Court should never take a tax case because the justices rarely understand what they're doing in this area.

The court provided two tests for determining whether your home is a principal office.

The first and most important test is, "Where are the most important functions conducted for your business?" For most businesses, it's where you would see customers or patients or where you render your services.

Example: Doctor Soliman was an anesthesiologist. He rendered his services in the hospital but billed his patients and kept his books from home. The hospital is where he performs his important services.

The second test is a time test. If you work over 50 percent of your total working hours out of your home, then your home will qualify as a principal place of business.

This is important to you because the IRS requires all businesses first to examine where they do their most important functions for their business. If there's a clear answer, this is the test that is used, and you never resort to the time test.[7] Some examples of major factors that the IRS uses would be where you meet your customers, where you render your services, where contracts are signed, etc. Some examples will illustrate the application of the *Soliman* decision very clearly.

Example: A sales representative spends 30 hours per week taking orders from clients in various stores and spends 12 hours per week working at home on administration for his business. Visiting with clients and taking orders will be deemed the most important functions for his business, and he would not be eligible for the home office deduction under *Soliman.* Yuck!

Example: Same facts as above, but the orders are placed over the phone, and the sales representative spends 30 hours a week working from his home and 12 hours seeing customers. He would be allowed a home office deduction because the most important business functions occurred at home (selling products and taking orders), and if there was any confusion, he met the 50 percent time test.[8]

Those adversely affected by *Soliman* will be people who really perform most administrative duties out of their home and/or put in over 50 percent of their working hours outside the home. Realtors, insurance professionals, financial planners, and many consultants probably will have their home office deductions disallowed because of where they see clients and where they usually perform most of their working activities. The same would be true for most plumbers, carpenters, electricians, etc.

Thus who can take a home office deduction under the *Soliman* case? Anyone who truly works out of his or her home and performs his or her most important functions at home. This would include network marketers, freelance writers, musicians who do most of their practicing out of their homes, and consultants who do most of their important work out of their homes.

Because the *Soliman* case eliminated the deduction for many people, Congress passed a great exception to the *Soliman* case. If you meet this exception, you don't need to worry about the *Soliman* requirements. If you don't meet this exception, you're back to trying to fit within the *Soliman* factors.

Exception to *Soliman*

Starting in 1999, Congress passed a new exception to *Soliman* that will help many small-business and home-based business owners. Your home office qualifies as a principal place of business if [9]

- The office is used to conduct administrative or management activities of your trade or business, and
- There is no other office where you conduct substantial administrative activities.

Thus, if you do your logs, contact patients or customers, listen to educational tapes, read business materials, and prepare bills for customers, you're rendering administrative activities.

Example: John, a self-employed plumber, spends most of his time in homes repairing and installing plumbing. He has an office at home that he uses exclusively and regularly for his administrative and management activities, such as billing customers, making appointments, and ordering supplies. His home qualifies as a principal office for the home office deduction.[10]

Example: Eddie, an independent contractor of clothing, meets with clothing store owners in their stores. He shows his new lines and takes the initial orders, which he completes in his home. His home is where he conducts his administrative activities for billing customers, keeping his books and records, ordering supplies, and forwarding orders and reports to his company. Assuming that Eddie uses a room exclusively and regularly for his business, his home office is deemed to be his principal place of business for the home office deduction.

The real congressional "gotcha" is found in the second part of the exception. You can't have another office where you render any significant administrative or management activities.[11] This means that you can have another office, but you just can't do any substantial administrative services there.[12] In fact, even if an office is provided you, you still may claim a home office deduction if you opt to work out of your home and perform all your administrative and management activities out of your home. Thus, if you do some minimal paperwork elsewhere, this won't disqualify you from the home office deduction.[13] This is especially true if you render some administrative or management services at a location that isn't a fixed office or fixed place, such as a hotel while traveling or a car.[14]

Example: Edith is a traveling saleswoman. She occasionally writes up orders and sets appointments from the hotel room during business travel. She has no fixed location for performing her administrative or management activities other than in a set spot in her home. She does all her other administrative activities in her home, including finishing the sales paperwork, preparing reports to her company, keeping her books and records, and billing customers whenever credit was declined or a check bounced. Her home qualifies as the principal office for purposes of the home office deduction.

Author's note: This is a very different result from that of the *Soliman* case, where both Edith and Eddie would have been deemed to perform their most important functions away from the home. Thus this exception has saved their deduction, as it will save the home office deduction for many small-business owners.

I also should note here that the key is that your administrative and management activities must occur out of your home. Other activities can occur from other locations. Thus, if you meet with clients or customers or you render services such as medical, legal, and plumbing away from the home, these services will not disqualify you from the home office exception.[15] The key to the *Soliman* exception is that your administrative or management activities must occur out of a set spot in your home.

One final point that should be noted is that you can have other companies do some administration for you, and this won't disqualify you from the exception.[16] Thus, if you have a billing company bill your customers, this *won't* disallow the deduction.

Qualify by Meeting and Greeting Clients or Customers in Your Home

If you do not use your home office as your principal place of business, another way to qualify for the deduction is to use the home office as a place to meet or deal with clients, patients, and prospects in the normal course of your business.[17] However, this exception applies only if the use of the home office by your clientele is substantial and integral to conducting your b usiness.[18] Occasional meetings are insufficient to make this exception applicable.[19]

Example: A lawyer meets with clients in her office three days a week and in her home two days a week. She qualifies for the exception.

This "meet or greet" test requires a physical presence in your home. You can't just make phone calls, no matter how extensive or frequent the conversations.[20]

Author's note: If you want to use the "meet and greet" exception, I recommend at my seminars that you have your clients, customers, or prospects sign a guest log whenever they come to your home. This log should show who the guest was, the date that he or she visited you, and the reason for the visit. More on this will be discussed below in the section on audit-proofing your home office.

Qualify by Using a Separate Structure

You may qualify for a home office deduction if, in connection with your trade or business, you use a separate structure not attached to your dwelling unit.[21] The separate structure must be used exclusively and on a regular basis for your business.[22] (These requirements will be discussed further below.) It need not, however, be your principal place of business or a place where you meet customers or prospects.[23] Examples of structures that meet the "separate structure" requirement would be an artist's studio, a florist's greenhouse, and a carpenter's workshop.[24]

Qualify by Storing Inventory or Product Samples

A deduction is allowed when you use your home on a regular basis to store either inventory or product samples if you are in the business of selling products at retail or wholesale and if your residence is your fixed location for that business.[25] This exception is available to you even if you sell your products at no fixed locations, such as craft shows, flea markets, or a customer's business premises.

On reading this, you might be tempted to place all your product samples along your hallways and in your bathrooms in order to inflate the deduction (as some tax books and even some companies have recommended). However, the IRS has thought of this trick. The storage of your inventory or product samples must be in a separately identifiable area suitable for storage.[26] Moreover, only this separately identifiable storage area would qualify for the deduction.

Example: Jane runs her network marketing business out of her home, where she sells vitamin supplements. She stores her inventory and product samples in a set part of her basement. She may claim a deduction for the space used to store product samples and inventory.

The space used doesn't have to be used exclusively for storing inventory. It just has to be in a set, identifiable area. Thus, even though Jane uses her basement for occasional personal use, her deduction wouldn't be denied.[27]

Finally, this exception applies only to inventory or product samples and not to other business assets. Thus it doesn't apply to old records,[28] law or business books,[29] or client or business files.[30]

Qualify by Running a Day-Care Center in Your Home

Without question, day care is in big demand and is very encouraged by companies and the government as well. In fact, in terms of deducting home office expenses, day-care business gets slightly better treatment than other small businesses.

The general rule is that a day-care business can deduct a portion of a home that is used regularly in the trade or business of day care for children and adults who are age 65 or older or who are mentally or physically incapable of caring for themselves. The key is that the day care must have applied for or have been granted a state license or be exempt from having a license.[31]

Author's note: If you want to claim a home office deduction for a day-care facility, you must comply with state law requirements.

The nice fact about day-care facilities is that you don't need to use a room or part of a room exclusively for the business.[32] In fact, you can use a room for day care during the day and use it for your family or for personal reasons at night and still get a home office deduction. However, the IRS has developed a formula for prorating your business use among the available hours.[33]

The formula uses two fractions. The first fraction is the square footage used by the day-care facility out of the home's total square footage. The second fraction would be the total hours in the year that the day care uses the home divided by the total hours in the year, which is 8,760 for a normal year and 8,784 for a leap year. Hours used to prepare for the day care or to clean up after the care is over also get treated as day-care hours.[34] Thus it would appear as follows:

$$\frac{\text{Square feet used by day care}}{\text{Total square feet of the home}} \times \frac{\text{total hours in the year for day care}}{\text{hours in a year(8,760)}}$$

This fraction is the portion of home expenses such as interest, taxes, utilities, repairs, and depreciation that can be deducted on the tax return for the day-care business.

Example: Mary runs a day care out of her home for 12 hours a day, 5 days a week, 50 weeks a year. (Thus she runs the day care for 3,000 hours a year.) She uses 1,200 square feet of the home's 1,600 square feet for the day care.[35] Assuming that her total housing expenses for taxes, interest, depreciation, utilities, garbage, etc. totaled $10,000, the following would be her home office deduction:

$$\frac{1{,}200 \text{ sq ft}}{1{,}600 \text{ sq ft}} \times \frac{3{,}000 \text{ hour}}{8{,}760 \text{ total hours}} \times \$10{,}000 \text{ expenses} = \$2{,}569$$

You Must Use Your Home Office for Business Regularly

In addition to one of the business uses that I noted earlier, you must use your home regularly for business. Interestingly, the Internal Revenue Code does not define *regular use.* However, some courts indicate that *regular use* means using your home three to four days a week for 10 to 12 hours a week.[36] Thus, if you use your home for business less than this, such as four hours per week, your use may not be deemed regular, so your deduction may be disallowed.

You Must Use Your Home Office for Business Exclusively

With the exception of storing inventory or product samples or running a day-care facility in your home, you can qualify for the home office deduction only for the parts of your home used exclusively for business. This is a difficult requirement for many people. The term *exclusive use* means just that.[37] No personal or other nonqualifying work may occur in the home office area.[38] A portion of a room can qualify as a home office, but all business items must be located in the same contiguous area, and there should be some physical separation of the business area from the personal area.[39] You must get all personal items out of the home office area other than purely de minimis items such as a radio for music while you're working, etc.

Author's note: I constantly get asked whether the IRS actually will come over to your home and check out whether you're using a portion of the home exclusively for business. The answer is yes, an agent may pay a visit. Get any personal items out of the home office area. Get all nonbusiness books out of the bookshelf in the home office, and don't play games on the computer. An IRS agent that I know was involved in an audit where the taxpayer kept a convertible couch in his home office. When questioned, the taxpayer admitted that his parents sometimes slept there on occasional visits. His entire home office deduction was disallowed.

What Deductions Are Available with a Home Office?

In claiming deductions for a home office, you need to break them into three categories:

1. *Expenses that are directly related to the home office portion.*[40] Examples of these types of deductions are painting of the home office or repairing a water leak in the home office. These would be deductible in full.
2. *Expenses that don't benefit the home office either directly or indirectly.* These expenses are *not* deductible because they are clearly not related to the home office in any way. Some examples of these expenses are repairs or painting in another room, plumbing repairs in an unrelated bathroom, and according to the IRS, lawn care if you don't meet and greet people in your home.[41] These expenses are not deductible at all.

Author's note: Many people believe that in order to take the deduction, you must own your home. This is incorrect. You can deduct the portion of the rent that's attributable to your home office square feet.

3. *Indirect expenses related to the home in general.* These include depreciation, costs for a home security system and for monitoring, utilities, repairs and painting to the outside of the house, etc. These expenses get allocated using one of three methods noted below.

Methods for Allocating Indirect Expenses

There are three methods that you can use to calculate the amount of indirect expenses that you can deduct.

Method one is based on the amount of home office square feet out of the total usable square footage of the house.[42] Interestingly, only the *usable square feet* count, not the total square footage.[43] You also can ignore square feet outside the house, such as a deck (see Figure 6-2).

Example: You have 1,675 square feet in your home, and your home office is 221 square feet. The allocation of your indirect expenses would be 221/1,675 = 13.19 percent.

The second method is known as the *number-of-rooms method.* You would take the room used for the home office and divide by the number of rooms in the house.[44] Thus, if you have eight rooms, and you use one room as an office, you may deduct $\frac{1}{8}$, 12.50 percent, of the indirect costs. There's a catch with this method, however. The IRS allows this method only if your rooms are approximately equal in size and you don't use a room that's much smaller than the other rooms.[45]

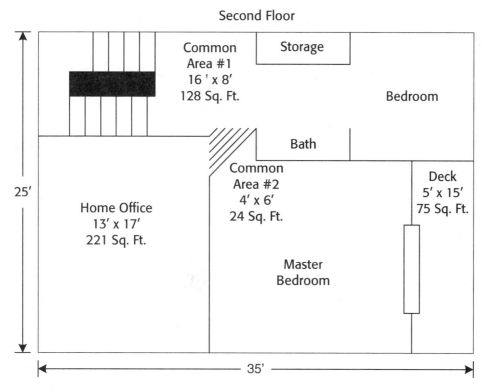

Three Choices
1. Number of rooms office occupies, divided by total rooms in house.
2. Total square feet office occupies as a percentage of total square feet in house.
3. Net square feet applicable to office use.

Computation of Net Square Feet

Total square feet 25' x 35' x 2 floors		1,750

Deduct

Common area:		
First floor entry and stairway	128	
Second floor stairway and landing	128	
Second floor common area	24	
Deck (not a living area)	75	355
Net square feet base		1,395

Analysis of Choices Based on:
1. Number of rooms 1/8 – 12.50%
2. Total square feet 221/1,675 (1,750 – 75 for deck) = 13.19%
3. Net square feet 221/1,395 = 15.84%

Figure 6-2. Maximizing home office square footage.

The final method, which may be the best method of all, is called the *net-square-footage method.*[46] This is similar to the square footage method, but you subtract from your total square feet of common areas, such as hallways, entranceways, landings, and stairways. In the preceding example, you would have 221 square feet in your home office divided by your net square feet, which would be 1,395. This would result in a deduction of 15.84 percent of your indirect expenses.

Author's note: I've discussed these methods in order to alert you and your accountant to take the approach that results in the biggest deduction. As you can see, in our example, the amount of the deduction will vary from 12.50 percent using the number-of-rooms method to 15.84 percent using the net-square-footage method. This could result in thousands of dollars of extra deductions over your duration of use of a home office.

Audit-Proofing Your Home Office

Take a Picture

Take a yearly, dated picture of your home office to establish that it was used exclusively for business. It's easy to say that you qualified for the home office deduction. However, if you get audited for it, you'll need some planning to prove that you were eligible in the past. Thus one important bit of documentation that you should have is a yearly photograph of your office to prove that it actually existed and that there were no personal items in the office that would disqualify the deduction. It's best to use a digital camera because the date of the photo usually is recorded on the picture.

Author's note: Do *not* send the photo to the IRS with your tax return. One person did this—and in the photo made some "undesirable" hand and arm gestures! Personally, I thought that it was quite amusing, but the IRS higher management didn't, and the person got audited.

Keep Records of the Square Footage

Keep blueprints or other documentation showing the square footage of your home office and the square footage of your home. If blueprints aren't available, make a drawing of your home office showing the relationship of the home office's square footage to the total square footage of the home.

Display Your Address and Phone Number

Use your home office phone number and address on business cards, stationery, and advertising as proof that you actually operated a business from your home. If economically feasible, install a separate business phone in your home. The business phone should be listed in the business's name in both the White and the Yellow Pages.[47] You should have business stationery with your home address on it.[48] If you have two business addresses, they should have equal prominence on the stationary.[49] You also should use your home address on your business cards.[50] If two addresses appear, they should have equal prominence.[51] If you have two phone numbers, they should have equal prominence too.[52]

Author's note: You would be wise to put in a second business line anyway because tax law allows no deduction for the first telephone line into your personal residence regardless of use.[53] Local charges are deductible only if you install a second phone line in your home. Welcome to tax simplification!

I should note that long-distance charges made for business reasons are deductible and should be documented on your bill.

Have Your Business Visitors Sign a Logbook

If you claim a home office deduction because you use the office in the normal course of business to meet and deal with clients, patients, or prospects, have your business visitors sign a guest book each time they come to your office. The guest book need not be formal, just a record of business contacts who meet with you in your home office. It should contain the name of the guest, the date of the visit, and the purpose. Remember: The burden of proof is on you. If you claim use of your home office to see clients and customers, you must be able to prove that clients, patients, prospects, or colleagues were physically present in your home office.

Keep a Work-Activity Log for Time Spent in Your Office

Showing how much time you spent working in the home office is important because it establishes that you put in your substantial administrative time and worked in the office regularly (at least 10 hours per week). Thus a work-activity log, which could be a meticulously annotated daily diary or tax organizer, constitutes an excellent supporting document to establish where you spent your work time. This does not need to be elaborate. You already have a daily diary. Simply use it as an activity log. If you are working in your home office, you simply could write "home office" (or some abbreviation) and note the time spent there.

Author's note: I've also found that some details that indicate the specific type of work you are doing at home help immensely. See the example in Figure 6-3.

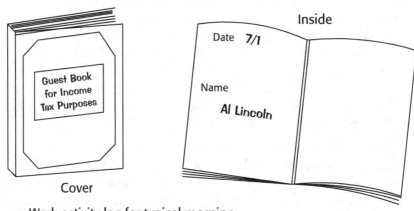

Work activity log for typical morning

1			BUSINESS	COMMUTE	PERSONAL
MONTH _____ May _____					
DAY OF THE WEEK S (M) T W T F S					
APPOINTMENTS DAILY			**BUSINESS**	**COMMUTE**	**PERSONAL**
7:00 AM					
7:30					
8:00	Study HTSA Program	HO			
8:30					
9:00	Prospect calls				
9:30	Al Lincoln contract				
10:00					
10:30					
11:00					
11:30	Wendy Wilson	OO			
12:00 PM					
12:30					
1:00					
1:30					
2:00					
2:30					

HO = Home Office, OO = Other Office

Figure 6-3. Guest book and work-activity log for a typical morning.

Problems with Claiming a Home Office

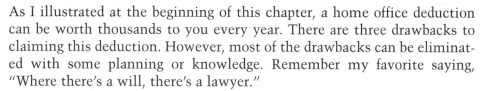

As I illustrated at the beginning of this chapter, a home office deduction can be worth thousands to you every year. There are three drawbacks to claiming this deduction. However, most of the drawbacks can be eliminated with some planning or knowledge. Remember my favorite saying, "Where there's a will, there's a lawyer."

1. The Home Office Deduction Has a Gross Income Limitation

Your home office deduction is the only business deduction that is limited to the net income from the business that is attributable to your home office.[54]

Example: Alan conducts a home-based business for which he claims a home office deduction. He grosses $6,000 from his business and has $5,000 of business expenses other than for his home office. His home office expenses for his share of the taxes, utilities, interest, depreciation, security monitoring, and garbage collection costs amount to $2,500. He may deduct only $1,000 of these costs because his net income from the home-based business is $1,000 ($6,000 less $5,000 of business expenses). This is the bad news.

The good news is that you don't lose the excess deductions from the home office because you get to carry them over forever.[55] What this means is that you can use the excess deduction against future income from your home business.

Example: In the preceding example, if Alan makes a net profit of $4,000 next year, he may use the unused $1,500 deduction to offset this $4,000 net profit and thus pay tax on only $2,500 in the next year.

2. You Will Have to Pay Tax on Any Depreciation at the 25 Percent Rate

If you claim a home office deduction, you will be depreciating a portion of your home. This means that you take the home office portion of your residence and deduct the cost over 39 years.[56]

Example: You paid $200,000 for your home. If you use 10 percent for your home office, then you deduct $20,000 over 39 years at the rate of approximately $513 per year. Thus, if you were in the 35 percent federal tax bracket over all the 39 years, this would save you $7,000.

If you sell your home, you cannot exclude the entire amount of gain on the sale. As a result of the tax simplification law, Congress makes you pick up this depreciation taken after May 6, 1977, as income and taxes you on it at your normal tax rate, but up to a maximum 25 percent rate.[57]

Example: Karen claims a home office in 1998 and thereafter. If she claims $4,000 in depreciation as a result of the home office, she'll have to report the first $4,000 of gain on the sale of her home at the 25 percent rate of tax, which means that she would pay back $1,000 on the depreciation taken.

Author's note: This may sound bad to you, but it isn't. If you are in the 31, 36, or 38 percent bracket when you take the depreciation but have to pay it back at only the maximum rate of 25 percent, you're certainly coming out ahead!

An Employee Can Claim a Home Office Deduction Only if the Office Is for the Convenience of the Employer

As I mentioned earlier, employees don't get the same benefits from the tax law that self-employed people get. If you're an employee, your home office not only must meet all the rules noted earlier but also must be used for the convenience of the employer.[59] Thus the home has to be more than just helpful and appropriate for you.[60] This means[61] that

- Your company must require you to maintain your home office as a condition of your employment, or
- The home office is necessary for the functioning of your employer's business, or
- The home office is necessary for you to perform your duties.

What all this means is that if your employer provides you with a perfectly good office, you probably can't claim a home office deduction as an employee. If, however, the office is inadequate for you to perform your functions (if there's too much noise, if there's not enough privacy for sensitive work, or if you're a musician and practice is mandatory), then you can claim a home office.

Author's note: Frankly, it's much better for an employee to have a side business and work this business out of the home. However, if you choose not to have a business, at least get a letter from your boss mandating that you work at home and giving the reasons for this directive. Remember: If the IRS feels that the office is for your convenience and not that of the firm, you won't get the deduction.

Depreciate Furniture and Equipment That You Use for Business

A major misunderstanding is that the home office deduction applies to all business equipment, too. This is not true. The deduction applies only to the real estate and related deductions, such as interest, taxes, depreciation, utilities, rent, and maintenance.[62] Furniture and equipment are depreciable to the extent you use these items for business. You do *not* need to claim a home office deduction in order to deduct your furniture.[63]

Example: You work in an office in your home but do not qualify for the home office deduction because the office is not used exclusively for business. Your work adds up to 80 percent of the use. The result is that you may depreciate the furniture and equipment such as the desk, the chair, the computer, the carpeting under the desk, and the lamp lighting up the desk.

Author's note: This applies even if you're an employee taking work home. If you use a desk 80 percent for business, you may depreciate that desk.

Now that you are aware that you can depreciate furniture such as desks, chairs, file cabinets, and computers, the question becomes, "What do you depreciate?" The answer is that if you purchased the desk, the chair, the file cabinet, and the computer several years ago, you may start to depreciate those items under what is known as the *lower of cost or fair market value rule.*[64]

Example: You have an antique desk that you purchased three years ago. It cost you $500 but has a current fair market value of $600. (Antiques tend to appreciate.) If you use the desk 80 percent for business, you may depreciate 80 percent of the original cost of $500, which is the lower of the cost or fair market value.

Required Record Keeping

You'll need to have some reasonable method for determining your business use. With bookcases and file cabinets, it's easy to determine business use. If you have three file drawers, of which you use two strictly for business files and one for personal files, then you can depreciate two-thirds of the file cabinet. Similarly, if you have a bookcase with four shelves, of which three are for business books and one for fiction, then you can depreciate three-fourths of the bookcase.

With desks, chairs, and computers, it becomes tougher. You want to keep records of use for three consecutive months, as you would do with your automobile, by documenting what you or your family members do when using the furniture.[65] The following is an illustration of what I would do for some sample days out of the three months.

On Monday, no one uses the room, so you write down nothing. On Tuesday, you made client calls from 6 to 9 p.m., so you note in your log "made client calls 6 to 9 p.m." On Wednesday, your son plays the game EverQuest from 3 to 7 p.m., so you log "game or personal use 3 to 7 p.m."

Keeping this log will show what percentage you can deduct your desk, your chair, your computer, your rug, and your lamps. Thus, if you use this furniture 150 hours for business out of 200 hours during the three-month test, you could depreciate three-fourths of these items.

Expense New Equipment Instead of Depreciating

There are, in effect, three methods of depreciation. Yes, you read that correctly! You can depreciate computers and monitors over five years and furniture over seven years. The second method, which is known as a *Section 179 expense election* (named after the code section that allows this), allows you to deduct the cost of the equipment immediately, rather than depreciate, up to $112,000 in 2007 and $25,000 for sport utility vehicles (SUVs) used in business.[66] The same rule applies to the Section 179 method as to the 30 percent method: The equipment must be new to you.

Example: You buy a new computer, monitor, and printer for $2,500 and a used shredder for $1,000. (Shredders are popular in Washington and Houston.) You may depreciate the computer equipment over five years and the shredder over seven years, or you may elect to write off the entire $3,500 purchase in the year that you buy the equipment.

Author's note: You may make this election on most items of business equipment but not equipment used for investment purposes. Some examples of equipment used in business include desks, computers, printers, faxes, shredders, lamps, chairs, throw rugs, cell phones and phone systems, etc.

Warning: If you expense an asset but your business use drops to under 50 percent or less during years that it would have taken to depreciate the asset, you must recalculate the original expense amount as if you had claimed the straight-line depreciation and then report the difference as taxable income.[67] Thus, for computers, you must keep the business use above 50 percent for five years, and for other office equipment, you must keep the business use above 50 percent for seven years.

What if You Purchase over $112,000 Worth of Equipment?

Let's say that you want to purchase $145,000 worth of equipment in 2007. You can elect to write off up to $112,000 and depreciate the difference.

Author's note: I would buy only $112,000 worth of equipment in one year and buy the rest in the next year. In this way, you could deduct the equipment over two years by making this election.

One final point that I want to make regarding the expense election is that you actually must elect on your tax return to expense rather than depreciate. You actually would check off a box on your tax return noting that you make an election to deduct up to $112,000 of equipment. You just don't take the deduction without the election. Many people make this mistake—to their dismay when the IRS finds out.

Summary

- A home office deduction is a tax-deductible gold mine. If you're eligible, you should clearly take the deduction. Earning over $14,000 every five years should convince you that it's worth the trouble.
- The best ways to ensure a home office deduction are to use your home as a principal place of business or where you meet and greet customers in the normal course of business, have a separate structure that isn't attached to your home (such as a greenhouse or an art studio), use your home to store inventory or product samples, or run a day-care center.
- Audit-proof your home office by taking yearly pictures, keeping blueprints of the home that clearly show your home office square footage, and having business cards, stationery, and Yellow Pages listings of your home office address and/or phone number.
- Deduct all expenses for equipment that you use in your home for business, even if you never claim a home office deduction.

Notes

1. See Chapter 5 for this discussion and for the footnotes.
2. See IRS MSSP, *Child Care Providers* (3/2000).
3. Section 280(A)(a) of the IRC.
4. Section 280(A)(c)(1) of the IRC.
5. Section 280(A)(c) of the IRC.
6. *Commissioner v. Soliman*, 506 U.S. 168 (1993).
7. Revenue Ruling 94-24, 1994-1 CB 87 and IRS Publication 587 (2001).
8. IRS Publication 587 (1998).
9. Section 280(A)(c)(1) of the IRC.
10. IRS Publication 587 (2001).
11. Section 280(A)(c)(1) of the IRC.
12. Section 280(A)(c)(1) of the IRC and IRS Publication 587 (2001).
13. H. Rept.105-148 (PL 105-34), p. 407.
14. IRS Publication 587 (2001).
15. H. Rept. 105-148 (PL 105-34), p. 407, and IRS Publication 587 (2001).
16. Ibid.
17. Section 280A(c)(1)(B) of the IRC and Section 1.280A-2(c) of the ITR.
18. Section 1.280A-2(c) of the ITR.
19. Section 1.280A-2(c) of the ITR. See also IRS Publication 587 (2001), p. 6.

20. Ibid. See also *Green v. Commissioner*, 707 F.2d 404 (9th Cir. 1983).
21. Section 280A(c)(1)(c) of the IRC and Section 1.180A-2 (d) of the ITR. See also IRS Publication 587 (2001), p. 6.
22. Ibid.
23. Ibid.
24. IRS Publication 587 (2001).
25. Sections 280A(c)(1)(c) and 280A(c)(2) of the IRC.
26. Section 1.280A-2(e)(2) of the ITR.
27. IRS Publication 911 (2000), p. 5, and IRS Publication 587 (2001).
28. *Lloyd Pearson*, T.C. Memo 1980-459.
29. *James Druker*, 77 T.C. 867 (1981).
30. *Thomas L. Borom*, T.C. Memo 1980-459.
31. Section 280A(c)(4)(B) of the IRC.
32. S. Report No. 95-66 (P.L. 95-30), p. 91.
33. Section 280A(c)(4)(c) of the IRC; IRS Publication 587, p. 10. See also Revenue Ruling 92-3, 1992-1 C.B. 141.
34. IRS MSSP, *Child Care Providers* (3/2000), p. 12.
35. This example was taken from Revenue Ruling 92-3, 1992-1 C.B. 141.
36. *Green v. Commissioner*, 78 T.C. 428 (1982) *rev'd* on another issue, 83-1 USTC Par. 9387 (9th Cir. 1983).
37. Section 280A(c)(1) of the IRC.
38. *Hamacher v. Commissioner*, 94 T.C. 348 (1990). See also Section 1.280A-2g(1) of the ITR.
39. *Gomez v. Commissioner*, 41 T.C.M. 585 (1980); Section 1.280A-2(g) of the ITR.
40. Section 1.280A-2(i)(5) of the ITR.
41. IRS Publication 587 (2001).
42. Section 1.280A-2(i) of the ITR and IRS Publication 587 (2001).
43. *Ronald Culp*, T.C. Memo 1993-270.
44. Section 1.280A-2(i)(3) of the ITR. See also *Gene Moretti*, T.C. Memo 1982-552.
45. IRS Publication 587 (2001).
46. Ibid.
47. *Jackson v. Commissioner*, 76 TC 696 (1981); *Heuer v. Commissioner*, 32 TC 947 (1959).
48. Ibid.
49. Ibid.
50. Ibid.
51. Ibid.
52. Ibid.
53. Section 262(b) of the IRC.
54. Section 280A(c)(5) of the IRC.
55. Ibid.
56. Section 168(c).
57. Section 121(d)(6) of the IRC.
58. Section 121 of the IRC.
59. Section 280A(c)(1) of the IRC and IRS Publication 587 (2001).
60. IRS Publication 587 (2001).
61. *Hamacher v. Commissioner*, 94 T.C. 348 (1990).
62. IRS Publication 587 (2001), p. 2.
63. Section 280 of the IRC and *Mulne v. Commissioner*, T.C. Memo 1996-320.

64. Section 1.167(g)-1 of the ITR. See also IRS Publication 551 (1992).
65. Section 1.274-5T(c) of the ITR.
66. Sections 168 and 179 of the IRC.
67. Section 280F(d)(1) of the IRC and IRS Publication 587 (2001).

7

Beating the Dreaded IRS Audit

We do not have, and never had, and could not have a "voluntary" tax system.
—**Donald C. Alexander, former IRS commissioner**

Chapter Overview
- Most taxpayers should be as aggressive as possible.
- Learn your rights on audit. (Yes, you do have some significant rights.)
- Learn the nine ways to reduce your chances of an IRS audit.
- Know the 15 steps that you should take if you are audited. (Going to Mexico for a long vacation is *not* one of the steps.)
- Learn how to collect money from the IRS by ratting on someone. This could be a lucrative opportunity.
- Avoid the scam artists who try to convince you that a tax return need not be filed or that taxes need not be paid.

If there is anything that you learn from this book, it is that you should be as aggressive as possible but not cheat!

Did you ever notice that most Internal Revenue Service (IRS) stories about people being jailed usually are announced on television and radio from January 1 to April 15? What are you thinking about during this period? *Taxes!*

My favorite story involves Leona Helmsley. She was convicted of 33 counts of tax evasion August 30, 1989—but not sent to a federal prison until more than two and a half years later, on the morning of tax day, April 15, 1992, the busiest filing day. This was *not* a coincidence. The IRS wants you to feel intimidated. The question is whether you should be intimidated or be aggressive with your deductions. The answer, for a number of reasons, is to be aggressive.

Author's note: By *aggressive,* I do *not* mean cheating. I simply mean that you take any deduction that you're reasonably entitled to.

The first reason for you to be aggressive is because of the IRS person that you may encounter. Here's what I mean.

The person who's lowest on the IRS totem pole is called the *taxpayer service representative.* These are the people who answer questions on the telephone. Although they're usually quite courteous, they're usually the dumbest thing on two legs. They're dumber than sheep, cattle, or plant life. I conducted my own survey consisting of 27 yes/no answers several years ago, and taxpayer service reps answered 6 questions correctly. You have a better shot asking your friends. At least they have a 50-50 chance of getting the right answer. These representatives aren't even lucky.

Normally, when the IRS hires them, they must have at least two years of college in any field; there's no requirement for any accounting or tax course. They get training, but it's very limited. As of several years ago, the IRS provided 20 days' worth of training for the people who answer the phones. In many cases these people never worked for the IRS as auditors. Moreover, you take a risk in accepting any answers they give you because the IRS is not bound by their answers. You are just stuck and must pay the proper tax plus interest and penalties.

Author's note: Based on my experience and based on some conversations with IRS appeals officers, you may be able to get the IRS to waive penalties if you relied on a bad answer from these people. However, you must record in a log the following:

- The name of the person
- The badge number of the person
- The date of the call
- The time of the call
- The question asked
- The answer given

If you record all these items in a log, the IRS ordinarily will waive penalties.

Author's note: I have found that the taxpayer service representatives will give you their badge number for identification, but they say it very quickly. I usually ask them to repeat it slowly because I'm getting older.

The next person on the totem pole is an IRS tax auditor. If you're going down to the IRS office to present your information, you will in all likelihood be visiting a tax auditor. To qualify, a tax auditor must have a four-year college degree—in anything. Tax auditors generally start at a salary of

$18,000 to $20,000 and can advance to $40,000-plus. Before advancing to a salary of about $27,000, a tax auditor must have completed at least six semester hours of accounting courses.

The auditors generally are not required to interpret guidelines or engage in research. They're told what to audit, how to audit, and almost what to think. The issues in contention are clearly defined by a classifier before the returns are assigned to individual examiners. The group manager must approve any expansion beyond that.

The next rung on the ladder is the revenue agent. Revenue agents must have a four-year college degree and a minimum of 24 semester hours of accounting. Experience can be substituted for the 24 hours of accounting. The IRS does not recruit many "A" students; they're usually snapped up by the better-paying, big accounting firms. Sadly, many of the revenue agents squeak through college with "C" averages. In fact, one unnamed manager said that some of the people that the IRS was hiring don't understand the tax law; thus the IRS is giving remedial reading courses to some of these people. The bottom line is that, for many audits, you will get a less competent person than found in many accounting firms.

The second reason to be aggressive in your deductions is based on how IRS agents get promoted. Revenue agents are expected to be good soldiers. This is important. For the IRS system to work, revenue agents must believe that it's their IRS, right or wrong. They learn tax law the way the IRS teaches it, as the IRS wants them to see it. Revenue agents go through extensive initial and yearly training to learn the way the IRS wants things done. They can handle some complex returns that require full use of their accounting skills. Unlike a tax auditor, the revenue agent sets the entire scope of the examination. The starting salary, however, lags seriously behind that of most accounting firms and way behind that of the major accounting firms.

The key to the importance of all this is that both revenue agents and tax auditors get promoted based on the number of cases closed and not on the money collected. You might wonder why this is the case. The reason is that about 1 percent of national revenue is obtained through audits. Thus 99 percent of the revenue is gotten through "voluntary" compliance from people who have not been audited. Therefore, the more audits the IRS conducts, the greater the fear is for people who have *not* been audited. So there really is some logic in government.

If you came to my seminar, you would find that because of the need for all agents to close their cases quickly, over 90 percent of students who have been audited in the past either got a refund or no change on an audit, or if they paid anything, there usually was a compromise or settlement. This doesn't always happen, but it certainly happens enough to justify a lot of aggressive treatment of your deductions.

The final reason for being audited is based on what we CPAs call the "audit lottery." The following are the IRS statistics showing your chances of being audited in 2005 based on the type of return and the type of income[1]:

Income Range Percent Audited

Tax Returns for Employees with No Businesses (TPI = total positive income, which is gross income before any deductions):

- TPI of $25,000 to 50,000—0.60 percent
- TPI of $50,001 to $100,000—0.57 percent
- TPI of $100,001 to $200,000—1.41 percent

Tax Returns for Small Businesses That File Schedule C (TGR = total gross receipts before any deductions):

- TGR of less than $25,000—3.68 percent
- TGR of $25,001 to $100,000—2.21 percent
- TGR $100,001 or more—3.65 percent

S Corporations: 30 percent

Regular Corporations:

- Assets between $5 million and $10 million—2.67 percent
- Assets between $10 million and $50 million—12.31 percent

Several conclusions can be drawn from these audit statistics. First, if your deductions go up by $5,000, $10,000, or more, you will not increase your chance of an audit. However, if your income suddenly skyrockets or triples, you might increase your chance of an audit. Second, your actual chance of an audit are about once every 30 years. The bottom line is to be as aggressive as possible.

Author's note: I want to note that when I say that you should be aggressive, I do *not* mean cheat! An aggressive taxpayer is one who has some basis in tax law for the deductions that he or she takes and has the documentation to support those deductions.

Taxpayer Rights

You have significant rights as a taxpayer, and you need to be aware of those rights. As you may have seen in the Senate hearings, the IRS can exercise significant power.

A good example happened about 10 years ago. A couple ordered my Tax Strategy Program and tax organizer. About half an hour after my seminar was over and after they had gone home, they came back to the seminar to cancel their order. The wife was crying. What happened was that when they got home, they received a notice that the IRS had seized their bank accounts, and all their outstanding checks were bouncing. Now, without any funds left, they had to find an accountant to represent them. Good luck!

Because of problems such as this, Congress passed several laws that protect taxpayers. These laws provide for the following:

- If you get audited, or if the IRS wants any money out of you, you must receive a copy of all your appeal rights from the examination to the collection (IRS Publication 1, "Your Rights as a Taxpayer").
- You now have the right to be treated fairly, professionally, promptly, and courteously by IRS employees. This is why you may find a slightly "friendlier" IRS. However, don't be fooled by the friendly manner: The IRS still has just as much power as in the past.

You now can appeal to the Taxpayer Advocate Service (TAS). This is an independent oversight group that can overturn anything that the IRS does with a Taxpayer Assistance Order (TAO). The TAS can get back money taken, lift a lien, follow up on a refund claim, and much more. The phone number for your local TAS office must be published in the phone directory and is also usually found in both the White Pages and the Yellow Pages.

To apply to the TAS, you'll need to send a statement of the facts and problem with a special IRS form, "Application for Taxpayer Assistance Order." (You'll love the number of this "emergency" form: It's Form 911.)

To take advantage of a TAO, you must try to resolve your dispute with the IRS through normal channels first, or you must show that you will suffer a significant hardship if a TAO is not issued.[2] A significant hardship includes any of the following conditions[3]:

- There's an immediate threat of adverse action.
- There's been a delay of more than 30 days in resolving the problem.
- You'll be incurring significant costs and fees if relief isn't granted.
- If relief isn't granted, you'll suffer irreparable injury or a long-term impact.

What all this means is that you must try to deal with the IRS, but either the IRS isn't communicating with you or you're about to suffer a major irreparable injury such as loss of a business, inability to hire a professional to represent you because all funds are frozen, or a lien that's destroying your credit and drastically harming your ability to function in business or in life.

Author's note: All this sounds great, but the IRS and the Taxpayer Advocate Service have put into practice some strict policies before you can use the taxpayer advocate. First, you need to contact the IRS and try to get it to act appropriately if the agency is wrong. You generally must write to the IRS three times, and you can't have received within the last 30 days a notice that agents are working on your problem. Also, you should show that the IRS clearly acted improperly or that you have a very winnable case or that an irreparable injury will occur, as noted earlier. The following is an actual case.

Example: A couple called me who had sold their business to their ex-partner. Subsequently, the partner never paid the IRS any withholding taxes. The IRS seized the couple's bank accounts and garnished their wages, leaving them with $150 per week on which to live. They hired a lawyer who charged $5,000 and accomplished nothing. They then called me out of desperation. I recommended that they contact the Taxpayer Advocate Service with a cover letter noting that they had previously sold their business and include a copy of the sales agreement, garnishment notice, and bank seizure notice. Several months later, I received a bouquet of roses with a letter of thanks: They had got back all their money, and the seizure had been lifted. This whole unfortunate situation cost them $5,035—$5,000 for the lawyer, $10 for the Federal Express notice to the Taxpayer Advocate Service, and $25 for the roses to me. Had they known about the TAS, they would have saved a lot of money and suffered a lot less frustration and stress.

Here are some other rights in an audit:

- You have the right to have your personal and financial information kept confidential and the right to know why the IRS is asking for the information, how any information will be used, and what might happen if you don't provide the information.
- You clearly have the right to plan your business and personal finances in such a way that you will pay the least tax that is due under the law.[4] Thus the IRS states that you can plan your transactions to try to reduce your taxes. Tax planning is fully accepted by the IRS as long as you are using legitimate techniques.
- You also have the right to tape-record the audit. You must bring the tapes and give the IRS at least 10 days' notice of your desire to record the audit. The IRS can record you as well.

Author's note: I do not ordinarily recommend taping the audit. The reason is that audits are negotiating sessions, so taping makes the auditor nervous. The IRS is putting more auditors on cases that involved taped audits, and settlements tend to be fewer. I would, however, record an audit if you get a bad auditor, such as someone who appears to want to "nail" you or disallows a lot more in deductions than you think is warranted. You can stop the audit and request a postponement to get a recorder and some tapes, to obtain some representation, or to consult with an advisor.

- You can ask that the examination take place at a reasonable time and in a place that is convenient to both you and the IRS.

- You can request that the IRS not examine your return for the same items it examined in either of the two previous years if no change in your liability was proposed. Thus you can effectively end harassment on the same issue(s).

- You also can recover some litigation expenses (currently up to $150 per hour) if you substantially prevail in the dispute and the IRS does not show that its position was justified.[5]

- You have the right to enter into an installment agreement, which means paying your taxes over a period of months or years, if you don't have the money to pay the tax at present.

- You also have the right to claim Innocent Spouse Tax Relief if the IRS goes after you for something that arose from your ex-spouse if you filed a joint return. If you file jointly with your spouse, you are jointly and separately liable for the taxes due. Frequently, couples get divorced, yet the IRS goes after one ex-spouse for a tax problem resulting from the other. Now you can elect Innocent Spouse Tax Relief, which is your right to be taxed on your share of the income and deductions and not be taxed on your spouse's problems. You also can elect this relief if you can prove that you were an abused spouse and were forced into signing a joint return.

Author's note: This sounds great, but in practice, there are some problems. You can't have known or should not have known about the potential problems of your spouse. The following examples will illustrate this point.

Example: Unknown to you, your spouse was a drug dealer. Despite having a nice state government job, you lived in a million-dollar home and drove a Mercedes. The IRS probably will hold that you should have known something was amiss and will not allow Innocent Spouse Tax Relief.

Example: You knew that your spouse had a part-time business that you were told made $10,000. However, your spouse really made $100,000 and placed the money into a separate account. You probably will be able to elect Innocent Spouse Tax Relief on all the earnings above the $10,000 that you knew about.

Nine Ways to Reduce Your Chances of an IRS Audit

Before I begin this discussion, you should know what happens to your tax return when you send it to the IRS. First, it goes to the local service center, where it's scanned and checked for math errors and with all Form 1099s to see if you underreported income. Your return is then sent to the Martinsburg,

West Virginia, center, where it's given a score using a computer program known as the *Discriminant Function System* (DIF). The higher the score, the better is the chance that your return will be examined immediately for problems. However, if you've attached schedules and statements explaining the problem in more detail, the examiner may put your return back into the hopper, and you may totally avoid an audit. Although this program is the best-kept secret in government (better kept, in fact, than the making of the atomic bomb), there are some things that we know about this program that you can use to reduce the risk of an audit.

1. Mail your return either by registered mail, return receipt requested, or by Federal Express. If the IRS regional service center fails to receive your tax return, your chances of being audited increase automatically. To make sure that you're not taking unnecessary chances, send your tax return by registered mail, return receipt requested, or by Federal Express Priority Overnight or Second Day service, DHL Same Day and Overnight Worldwide Express, or Airborne Express (either overnight or next-day service).[6]

2. Send all changes of address to the IRS by filing Form 8822, "Change of Address," whenever you move. As reported in *USA Today* several years ago, the IRS wants to send out $78 million in refunds, but the people have moved, and it can't find them. (Maybe I'm crazy, but if the situation were reversed and the IRS wanted money from you, don't you think that it would find you?) The IRS likes to know where you are and appreciates being notified of any change of address. This certainly will benefit you if the IRS needs to notify you. If you move, you may be liable to the IRS without knowing it because you didn't provide a change of address. Its only responsibility is to send you all notices to your last known address.

3. Use the IRS's preaddressed label to speed up the processing of your tax return.

Author's note: There are rumors to the effect that the IRS label contains information that will be detrimental to you. To the best of my knowledge, this is not the case. This label is only used to expedite processing.

4. Make sure that your tax return is neat. I met a taxpayer who thought that if the IRS couldn't read the return, it wouldn't audit him. This is absolutely false! Although your tax return doesn't have to be typed, it must be neat and easy to read. Legible tax returns create an impression of attention to detail. In addition, you don't want your return to stand out in any way.

5. File all elections that you're entitled to. There are certain tax breaks and options that require the filing of an election, such as expensing $24,000 of equipment instead of depreciating equipment (as discussed in Chapter 6). Sometimes the filing can be done merely by picking a method of reporting.

It's generally better to attach separate statements for all elections made in a tax return or to check all required boxes on the return. This further supports the impression of attention to detail and shows an understanding of the tax law.

Author's note: Again, the key is to have your return look professional and complete. You don't want it to stand out for any reason or have something clearly amiss that would cause increased IRS scrutiny.

6. Report all of your income. The IRS has implemented various audit programs for unreported income. Make sure that your tax return reports all income you earned and identifies the income by source. If you receive a Form 1099 for consulting services, for example, report the income on a supporting schedule, and include the taxpayer ID number from the Form 1099. Since the IRS already has the information from the 1099, you'll reduce your chances of being selected for an audit by enabling the IRS to match the Form 1099 information with your tax return.

Author's note: In addition, if you're incorporated, be sure that the Form 1099s match the entity that earns the income. Many people never notice that income earned by their corporation has their Social Security Number on the Form 1099, and vice versa. If you receive an incorrect Form 1099, immediately notify the sender to give you an amended Form 1099. If you can't get this, attach a schedule explaining that there's a difference between what was reported and what is shown on the Form 1099.

7. Have your return prepared by a competent tax preparer. Most people are not aware that if they do their own returns, they increase their chances of an audit because the IRS perceives that they don't know as much as an accountant who prepare hundreds of returns. Moreover, accountants who prepare lots of returns use sophisticated software that ensures fewer errors. If you really want to save money on the cost of the preparation of your return, use Turbo Tax or some tax-preparation software, and then give your return to an accountant to get his or her name on it as the preparer. You may cut the costs of preparation—and the accountant may find things that you missed.

In addition, I would recommend a CPA, an enrolled agent, or an attorney to prepare or review the return. This will help to minimize your chances of an audit examination.

8. Break your income and large expenses into small segments. Income reported to the IRS on Form 1099s should be separated from other income. The separation will help to determine that you've indeed reported all income earned. Also break down expenses as far as possible to explain to the IRS examiners exactly what was involved in the expenses. If, for example, you had promotional expenses of $10,000 and that's all that appeared on your tax return, your chances of audit would be significant.

However, should your promotion be broken down into travel, advertising, and entertainment expenses, you may reduce your chances of audit. I should note that certain big-ticket items need not be broken down because the IRS understands that these particular items are inherently large. An example of this type of large item would be medical malpractice premiums for doctors.

9. Keep records of expert advice. If you relied on the advice of your accountant or lawyer, keep records as to the nature and date of the advice. There are cases in which penalties have been waived for a good-faith reliance on an independent expert.[7]

15 Steps for Preparing for an IRS Audit

Let's assume that you follow to the letter everything that is written in this book, but you still get a notice from the IRS that invites you down for a "chat." Don't panic or go on an extended vacation. Here are 15 steps that will help you greatly in the audit process.

1. Assume that you will be audited whenever you prepare your tax return. The time to get ready for an IRS audit is while you're preparing your tax return. This is the only time that you have all your tax information in front of you. Reference your support to the return so that you can find it later, if you should need it. Questionable items, if any, should be supported by tax memorandums or other information from your tax advisor.

2. Don't panic. An audit notice doesn't indicate that anything is wrong with your tax return. It's simply a request by the IRS to find out if your tax return was prepared properly and to determine the proper amount of tax— no more and no less. Generally, you'll be notified of the audit by mail, although you could be telephoned. If you're notified by mail, you'll be asked to telephone the examiner.

3. Try to limit the scope of the audit. There are a number of suggestions here. In an IRS office audit, the IRS tells you what's being examined and sets the scope of the audit. In addition, the IRS generally has three years from the date you file your return to audit it. Many times, an audit occurs in the last year allowed or the audit takes longer than usual, and the time limit may run out. In these cases, IRS agents usually ask taxpayers to extend the statute by a year so that it can continue the audit. Your first reaction may be to deny this request, but the IRS simply will disallow many deductions, and you'll be stuck in IRS appeals or, even worse, in court. The best thing that you can do is to negotiate an extension, but only regarding specific items on your return, such as for travel or for entertainment. The reason for limiting the scope of the extension is that if the IRS finds anything after the time limit for the audit expires, it can't assess anything against you except for those items that you agreed to extend.

4. Understand that the burden of proof is on you. Tax law requires you to prove that your deductions are valid and that you have paid the proper amount of tax. The IRS need prove nothing. When going through your records and getting ready for the audit, make sure that you keep in mind that the burden is on you. None of that "innocent until proven guilty" business applies to a tax audit, unless there's a potential criminal investigation.

5. Dress normally for the audit. Do not make a special trip to Goodwill Industries to buy clothes for your audit. Don't wear expensive clothes or jewelry such as Rolex watches. IRS examiners dislike people who look like they make more money than the examiners. Dress and act normally during the entire audit. Do not plead poverty or stupidity. Excuses don't work.

6. Be on time for the audit. Put an asterisk here, and burn this point into your head. IRS examiners are graded on efficiency. If you are late for your appointment and cause the auditor to be inefficient or to take a longer time on the audit than he or she should, you start the audit in an antagonistic environment. Moreover, IRS examiners start examining your return to see what the problems are about a half hour before the audit is scheduled to begin. If you're late for the appointment, you give the auditor extra time to scrutinize your records before the audit begins. Thus the bottom line is that if you're late, you irritate the auditor and allow more time to find problems. *The best bet: Be early.*

7. Bring organized information. Make sure that you're prepared to answer questions and deliver documents to the auditor. If you receive notification from the IRS about the documents that you need for the audit, make sure that they are organized so that you not only can answer the questions but also can deliver the supporting documents quickly. This helps the examiner to complete the audit more efficiently, get a better rating from his or her superiors, and bring the whole unpleasant task to a quick conclusion.

8. Don't volunteer information. Although I recommend that your accountant show up for the audit without you, sometimes your presence is necessary. If you attend the audit, there are only four statements that you should make. They are "Yes," "No," "I don't know," and finally, my favorite—"It's my accountant's fault." (Enron managers learned this technique very well.) Never say, "I've always done it that way." Don't elaborate; answer only questions asked. Be concise. If the question does not appear relevant, ask why it is being asked. Bring only the documents requested in the IRS's "invitation" letter. Do not volunteer any information during the audit process. Finally, be very careful what you say to an IRS agent. This information can be used in a criminal trial.[8]

9. Don't leave any ends dangling. I had a student who was being audited and found that she didn't have $500 worth of receipts for certain deductions. She asked me if she should point this out to the auditor before the audit begins. The answer? Absolutely not! If the examiner gets money out of you very easily, he or she may decide to dig deeper, and you'll end up losing your tail. Thus, if it's easy to find something wrong, the immediate conclusion is that there must be lots of other things wrong in your return.

10. Ask for tax law references. If you think that you're right, ask the auditor or agent for the legal references. Don't accept vague statements or interpretations of the law. Make your tax advisor the goat by saying, "My accountant told me that this deduction was proper. Can you give me something that shows he's wrong?"

11. Don't give in too quickly. Most people feel that if you give in quickly, the IRS audit will go faster, and the agent will like you. Nothing could be further from the truth. The IRS manual states, "Hasty agreement to adjustments and undue concern about immediate closing of the case may indicate that more thorough examination is needed." If you appear to be a soft touch, the IRS will look for larger contributions from you.

12. Never be alone with a Special Agent. Special Agents are not special. Their job is to investigate criminal actions. If there are ever two agents to see you, ask whether either of them is a Special Agent. If so, terminate the meeting, and seek out a good criminal tax lawyer.

Author's note: You've probably learned that "if you are nice to people, they are nice to you." This isn't true for Special Agents. They're promoted based on indictments. Thus, unlike a regular IRS examiner, do not be nice or accommodating to Special Agents.

I also should note that there's no privilege protecting your communications with your accountant.[9] Accordingly, never hire an accountant to represent you in criminal matters. In addition, you should terminate your relationship with your accountant for a while because the IRS in a criminal investigation can obtain any communications to the accountant. If you need to deal and communicate with the accountant, have the attorney hire the accountant so that any future conversation is protected under the attorney-client privilege.

13. Don't *ever* tamper with the evidence. No backdating of documents or intimidating of witnesses should ever occur. More people get indicted for these items than for the original offense because they are easier to prove. To be safe, don't contact any witnesses for the government; let your lawyer do it.

14. Never, ever die. The IRS audits approximately 68 percent of all final returns. The only good thing about dying is that you may not have to show up at the audit.

15. Be careful of the "rat fee." The IRS pays a 10 percent commission for people to rat on you. If you want to make a living reporting tax cheats, get Publication 733, "Rewards for Information Given to the Internal Revenue Service."

Taxes Are Not Voluntary and Are Very Constitutional

In recent years, charlatans have gotten a lot of attention by claiming that taxes are unconstitutional and can be avoided with *pure trusts* or *foreign trusts*. You may have heard a well-dressed speaker declare that there have been many cases to this effect and that he or she has personally beaten the IRS in court on several occasions.

Who wouldn't want to avoid all federal and state taxes? However, before you invest your hard-earned money to create various recommended trusts, not to mention your life savings in a foreign or pure trust (otherwise known as a *constitutional trust*), *stop and reconsider!* Here's the real story. Here you'll find out what companies that promote these concepts are not telling you.

The only bit of truth to all these claims happened in the year 1895. In that year, the U.S. Supreme Court, in *Pollock v. Farmers' Loan & Trust Company*,[10] held that the Income Tax Act at the time was unconstitutional. However, what is not revealed by many seminar speakers on this subject is that in 1913 the country ratified the 16th Amendment to the Constitution to correct this problem and specifically overruled *Pollock*.[11] This amendment gave Congress the power "to lay and collect taxes on incomes, from whatever source derived" and allowed passage of the Income Tax Act of 1913, which was the predecessor to the current Internal Revenue Code.[12]

Since that time, there have been numerous attempts to get the courts to hold that the Internal Revenue Code is unconstitutional.[13] Some of the arguments have been that the 16th Amendment was ratified incorrectly.[14] Taxpayers even have tried to avoid paying tax on religious grounds.[15] What is important to know is that all taxpayer attempts have failed!

In fact, the courts are so tired of hearing these frivolous arguments that they are now assessing the government's legal fees against the taxpayers who claim this, as well as upholding the IRS's imposition of a special frivolous return penalty.[16] In fact, even the penalty for filing a frivolous return was held to be constitutional.[17] The bottom line is that the Income Tax Act and the Internal Revenue Code are quite constitutional, and Congress can enact almost any tax law as long as there's a rational basis.

The next major argument by many of these "tax protest" speakers is that you can avoid income tax by maintaining all assets and income in either a pure trust (otherwise known as a *family estate trust*) or a foreign trust. These types of trusts usually involve the transfer of your assets to a trust in a foreign jurisdiction with a corresponding assignment of lifetime services to the trust. These trusts usually pay fees and living expenses such as your rent and make other distributions of income.

Sadly, this has been at best a waste of thousands of dollars to set up and at worst a dangerous loss of all assets placed in trust. As many of these speakers note, these types of trusts are not subject to income tax. In fact, this is true! What they neglect to say is that all the income of the trust is taxed to the grantor (you) who set up the trust[18] if you meet any of the following conditions:

- You can revoke the trust.
- You can derive income from the trust.
- You can control the trust.

Thus, if you keep any control whatsoever, you are taxed on the income. In addition, even if you were willing to give up the requisite control, income from trusts reaches the higher tax brackets faster than individual income. You actually could be increasing your taxes. Moreover, if you place your assets out of the United States, you will not be subject to any U.S. legal protections if the assets are embezzled, which happens all too often.

The bottom line is simple: Whenever you hear someone tell you, "Psst! Taxes are unconstitutional and can be avoided with some trust," *run* away as fast as you can! Always remember that the difference between tax *avoidance* and tax *evasion* is five years!

Summary

- Be as aggressive with your deductions as possible.
- Understand and use your taxpayer rights when audited.
- Learn the nine ways to reduce your chances of being audited.
- Understand the 15 steps that you should apply if you get audited.
- Study IRS Publication 733 if you want to collect the "rat fee" from the IRS.
- Avoid all scam artists or tax protesters with various devices and claims that taxes need not be paid or that taxes are unconstitutional.

Notes

1. Commissioner's Advisory Group Report (2001).
2. Report on the IRS National Taxpayer Advocate's Fiscal Year 2001 Objectives.
3. Section 7811(a)(2) of the IRC.

4. IRS Publication 1.

5. Section 7430 of the IRC.

6. IRS Notice 2001-62, 2001-40 IRB 307.

7. *George S. Mauerman*, T.C. Memo 1993-23.

8. Section 7207 of the IRC and 18 U.S.C. 1001.

9. *Couch v. United States*, 409 U.S. 322 (1973).

10. *Pollock v. Farmers' Loan & Trust Company*, 157 U.S. 429 (S. Ct. 1895).

11. The Constitution of the United States: Analysis and Interpretation, S. Doc. No. 16, p. 1839 (1982).

12. *Brushaber v. Union Pacific Railroad*, 240 U.S. 1 (1915).

13. Ibid.

14. *United States v. Foster*, 789 F.2d 457 (7th Cir. 1986).

15. *Adams v. Commissioner*, 110 T.C. 137 (1998).

16. *Gerald Funk*, T.C. Memo 1981-506, *aff'd.*

17. *Heitman v. United States*, 753 F.2d 33 (6th Cir. 1984).

18. Sections 671-677 of the IRC. See also Revenue Ruling 75-257, 1975-2 CB 251.

8

How to Shield Yourself from the IRS Weapon of Classifying a Business as a Hobby

I have trouble reconciling my net income with my gross habits.

—Errol Flynn, actor

This is a crucial chapter. In fact, for many readers, this one chapter will pay for this book numerous times. The reason is that classifying an activity as a hobby instead of a business is the Internal Revenue Service's (IRS's) favorite weapon because it yields such nice results for the IRS. If you have a network marketing business or you are conducting a side business, you should read this chapter several times and apply every suggestion made.

Chapter Overview
- Understand the huge benefits of business losses.
- Learn why the favorite IRS weapon against taxpayers is to classify an activity as a hobby rather than a business.
- Learn when the IRS is required to presume that you are in business.
- Learn about the election that requires the IRS to postpone any determination.
- Learn about the criteria to be deemed a business and not a hobby.
- Learn how to bulletproof your activities from being classified as a hobby. (This one concept will pay for this book alone.)

Huge Benefits in Business Losses

Being in business is the last great tax-reduction opportunity. If your business produces a loss, you generally may deduct that loss against any form of income.[1] This loss can be used against your interest, dividends, rents, retirement income, and even your spouse's income if you file a joint return.

Author's note: This should ensure that you never get divorced. However, what happens if your losses exceed your total family income for the year? You'll like this. If your losses exceed your income for the year, you may carry back the losses two years[2] (in 2002, the carryback is five years) and receive a refund from the federal government and most state governments for the taxes paid in the last two years. If you wish, you also may carry forward all business losses over the next 20 years[3] and offset these losses over any income generated over the next 20 years into the future. Thus you never lose a valid business deduction.

Example: David incurs a $10,000 loss from his business. If he earns $40,000 in wages from his full-time job, his taxable income would be $30,000. He thus would pay tax on only $30,000 of income.

The IRS Works to Treat Activities as Hobbies

This all assumes that the IRS treats your activities as a business. If, however, the IRS determines that you are not engaged in the activities to make a profit, then no deduction for losses is allowed.[4] Thus your deductions from the hobby are limited to the income from the hobby. In addition, no carryover of losses or carryback of losses from the hobby is allowed.[5] (Ouch!)

Example: Carrie has a side business in travel that she operates out of her home. She spends little time operating the business, and it generates little revenue. If the IRS classifies her activities as a hobby, all losses from that business that exceed her income are disallowed.

Author's note: To classify your business as a hobby, the IRS doesn't need to attack your documentation or the legitimacy of the deduction because all deductions will be limited to the income from the hobby, with no carryback or carryover of unused deductions. Therefore, it's *vital* that you learn to run your business as a business and not like a hobby.

Presumption Based on Profit

There's a safe harbor where activities are presumed to be a business. Congress has given you a way to help solidify your business as a business so that the IRS doesn't treat it as a hobby. If your activity shows a profit for any three or more years in a period of five consecutive tax years, you are presumed to be engaged in a business.[6]

Author's note: If you're engaged in breeding, showing, training, or racing horses, this presumption test becomes a little bit better: two or more years in a period of seven consecutive tax years.[7] Even if you're not involved with horses, if you meet this presumption, you are usually home free with the IRS.

Election to Postpone Any Determination

If the IRS comes after you to disallow your losses before the full five years (or seven years for a horse-related business), you may elect to postpone any determination of being a business or a hobby until there are five consecutive tax years from the time that you first engaged in the activity (seven years for a horse-related business, as noted earlier).[8] You generally must make this election within three years of the due date of your tax return for the year in which you first started your activity.[9] You can even make this election after the IRS notifies you about this problem, as long as it's within the three-year period and you make this election within 60 days of the IRS notice. If the IRS files a suit, no election is available under any circumstances.[10]

Example: If you started your business in June 2003, you must make the election by April 15, 2007 (within three years of the due date of your 2003 return). If, however, the IRS notifies you about this problem on June 1, 2005, you have to make this election by August 30, 2005 (within 60 days of the IRS notice).

Author's note: At first glance, you may think that this election is very useful and should be used. However, there are several problems with making this election to postpone any hobby determination. First, it calls unwanted attention to yourself. Second, it extends the statute of limitations for several years for the IRS to both catch you and go after you. In short, weigh the pros and cons before making this election.

Criteria for Being a Business, Not a Hobby

So you didn't have a profit three out of five years. In fact, you may have losses for many years in the future. All is not lost. If you follow the criteria that I outline below, you'll be much more bulletproof: The IRS won't be able to treat your activities as a hobby. A large number of my students have won with the IRS after using these time-tested strategies. If you are in network marketing, have a small business, or operate a home-based business on the side, take all these strategies to heart. You will thank me forever and save yourself an enormous amount of hassle and money.

There are numerous standards that the courts use in determining whether your activity constitutes a business or a hobby. Generally, the determination is based on the facts and circumstances of each case.[11] However, some planning certainly will help your facts enormously.

One important factor is that you must show that you entered into the activity with the objective of making a profit.[12] This is true even if the chance of making a profit is small.[13]

The majority of court decisions (as well as those of the IRS) indicate that you're required to have an honest profit objective when you undertake your venture. Thus, if you have a sincere purpose of eventually reaping an overall profit, you will be deemed to have a profit motive.[14]

Author's note: It is your motives at the time that you start your endeavor that determine whether you have business intent. This can change as time goes on, but the motive at the startup becomes crucial. If you're in network marketing or franchising, you should document this intent by sending a letter to your sponsor/company to express your reasons for entering this business, emphasizing your desire to make a long-term profit and career out of this activity. If you have a small business on the side, you should document your intent with studies that show why you started this business. This point will be discussed below.

The courts have looked at the following factors in deciding if an endeavor is a business or a hobby:

1. Business plan and projections. Most court decisions have looked favorably on taxpayers who prepare business plans showing projected estimated income and expenses of their endeavor.[15] In fact, this is such an important criterion that some cases have turned just on this factor alone. Thus, in one case,[16] a sailboat chartering business was held to be a business even with years of losses because the owners had 12 years of projections of anticipated revenues and expenses and projected an overall profit. They also showed a reasonable basis for the appreciation of the sailboat.

The *key* is to project an *overall* business profit. In addition, the projected numbers should have some reasonable basis in reality. You therefore should document how you estimated each of your figures and have projections for at least 5 years, with 10 years being even better. In addition, don't have your business plan showing only estimated loss with no eventual profit.[17]

Author's note: Despite the importance of this factor, most taxpayers who have lost in court did not have a business plan with projected revenues and expenses. This is especially true for people involved in network marketing. Thus, when preparing this plan, you should seek out an expert who has been successful in your business and have him or her help you with this plan. In network marketing, seek out the experience of a very successful person in your upline or, even better, in some other line, and document this help. If you have a small business, find an expert in the field to help you prepare this plan. There are always people who are "expert consultants" in just about any field of endeavor. Also, if your business involves inventories, you certainly should have enough inventory on hand to meet your goals.

2. Your own statements. Telling your friends that you're in business to make a profit usually is deemed too self-serving to be of any use in proving a business motive. However, if you make improper statements, the court may treat your activities as a hobby and kill your deductions. For example, one person who raised dogs argued at a local zoning hearing for his home that his dog-breeding activities constituted a hobby.[18] The IRS used these words against the taxpayer, and the court held that his dog-breeding activity was indeed a hobby. Thus don't ever say, "I'm in this only to save taxes" or "I'm in this only to get a discount and save costs." This may be partly true, but don't say it.

3. Conducting the activities in a businesslike manner. This is probably the single most important factor that the IRS uses in judging a business intent. You must conduct your activity in a business-like manner and run it similarly to other businesses of the same size and type.[19] Thus you need to consult with experts about how similar businesses are run and follow their advice. It's also crucial to keep complete and accurate books and records and keep a good tax organizer or diary.[20]

It is crucial that you keep separate bank accounts and records for your business.[21] The key is not just to keep details of expenses and receipts but to have a "bookkeeping system ... that provides sufficient data for you to make informed business decisions."[22] These records must enable you to evaluate and improve your performance. What this means is that you should have the following[23]:

- A business plan showing at least 5 and preferably 10 years of projected income and expenses, showing an overall projected profit
- A marketing plan that is changed yearly to conform with what is happening
- A yearly income statement and balance sheet so that you can determine what is happening in your business and can make changes to improve profitability

If you're not making money, you should seek advice from people as to what changes you should make in your marketing and then follow through on the advice. Of course, you should document this advice. If you are in network marketing, don't just ask your upline people. Speak to different successful people to get different ideas. Don't follow the same advice from year to year if you aren't making money.[24] Businesses change the ways they market if they're not successful.

The following is a listing of activities, in addition to what was noted earlier, and the records that the courts found sufficient to enable a determination of being a business:

- *Horse breeding.* A registry of all horses bred or foaled, formal breeding, and complete breeding and medical records.[25]
- *Showing of horses.* Detailed notes on horses and horse show judges.[26]
- *Dog breeding.* Detailed records of the dogs, as required by the American Kennel Club, that allowed the taxpayer to determine the profitability of each dog.[27] This includes records of dogs bred and sold, the prices received for each dog, and the expenses incurred for each dog. Copies of advertisements showing an attempt to sell dogs and make money are also essential.

Author's note: Some cases have not mandated that you need these detailed records, but I would recommend them to be safe.

- *Charter boat operations.* An engine log, an expense log, and a revenue log indicating every financial and mechanical activity and all maintenance that the taxpayer conducted on the boat.[28] I would certainly keep a time log of business usage of the boat and a guest log.

Author's note: For network marketing,[29] in addition to keeping separate bank accounts, a tax diary, and profit and loss statements, I would keep all required receipts for travel and diary entries for appointments and meetings. I would note everyone to whom I gave marketing materials, such as tapes. If inventory is necessary, I certainly would keep some kind of inventory records and keep records that would show what was sold, given away, or used personally because personal consumption is not deductible. It is also imperative to have some form of budget, business plan, or breakeven analysis showing how much you need to sell in order to cover expenses and start showing a profit. If questioned, you should be able to explain in detail when your activity would become profitable.[30]

Author's note: Without question, network marketing has been held to be a business; however, there seems to be a higher burden with this business and with raising dogs and horses because of the popularity and social nature of these specific businesses. This may not be fair, but it's just the way it is. The key is to always try to make money and show the IRS that at least you're making a real effort, with daily activity, decent books and records, a business and marketing plan showing how much you need to sell or recruit to make money, and changes to your marketing, with the help of outside experts, if you have a loss.

4. Conducting the activities like a similar profitable business. It's essential that you show that you're carrying on your business like other profitable businesses that are similar.[31] Here is where the principle of duplication is critical. If you conduct your activity like other successful people in the same business, you have a very strong argument that you've conducted your activity like a business with the expectation of making a profit. In addition, if you follow the path of successful people, you also improve your chances of becoming successful. You actually might make a lot of money. You therefore want to adopt marketing efforts that are similar to those that are working for successful businesses.[32] Thus, you should do the following:

- Advertise your business in the Yellow Pages and the White Pages. Use the same ads in the same papers as other successful people have used. Get copies of their ads.
- Have business cards and stationery with your business name and address.
- Use a variety of marketing strategies used by successful people. Don't stick to the same thing year after year if it doesn't work.[33]

Author's note: This factor may seem similar to item 3, but there's a difference. You not only want to run your business in a business-like manner as noted in item 3, but you also want to run it the same way as people who've succeeded in similar ventures. The more you can show that you've copied the marketing and duties of successful people, the greater is your case for being deemed a business and not a hobby.

5. Prior business experiences. If you have prior business experience in this industry or with your product or service, this can make a big difference to the IRS. If you have no prior experience in this activity, your profit motive is more questionable.[34]

However, if you have no prior experience, don't be forlorn. You can overcome this deficiency with extensive study, listening to training tapes, taking seminars, and attending training meetings.

Author's note: Document in your tax organizer any training that you attended or educational tapes that you heard. You can never get enough training! If you get help or suggestions from successful people or experts related to your field, documents what was said and who helped you in your tax organizer or diary.

6. Advance research into the venture. If you were to buy a franchise or invest thousands in a business or investment, wouldn't you check it out first? Few good people start businesses without a good prior investigation of the business and any related companies. It's essential, therefore, that you investigate any business that you're considering before you get involved in it.[35]

Author's note: Many people ask me what should be done to conduct such an investigation. My suggestions depend on the type of business. If you're considering a franchise or network marketing distributorship, contact the Better Business Bureau in the area where the home company is located, and get a report in writing. Contact some franchisees/distributors and document what they tell you. Check out their products and see if you like them, see if they work, get copies of any reports on the products or any testing, etc. If you want to breed dogs, horses, or other animals, consult with experts in this area about how to run this type of business and what exactly you should be doing. The key is to consult with experts[36] consistently to keep improving your profitability and to follow what successful people are doing. The IRS doesn't care if you make money or not as long as you're trying to make a profit. Keep this in mind.

7. Devoting some time regularly to the activity. Although you certainly do not need to conduct your business full time, the more time and effort you put in, the better. Cases have shown that as little as one hour a day on average was sufficient to be deemed regular enough for a profit motive.[37]

Author's note: It seems that working one or two hours a day or more is much more important than doing nothing one week and working 20 to 30 hours the next week. Regularity seems to be important to both the IRS and tax court judges.

8. History of income/losses and measures to improve profits. Without question, your expenses certainly can exceed your income in a business. However, absent unforeseen circumstances,[38] such as theft, fire, flood, sudden market changes, etc., you should do everything reasonably possible to turn your losses into profits.[39] You should use common sense in running your business. For example, watch out for expenses that are unreasonably excessive in comparison with income. In one case, for example, a network marketing distributor's accounting fees alone exceeded his entire gross income. His travel also was 20 times his gross income. Other expenses also were very high.[40] In fact, the one taxpayer paid $2,300 in security expenses to cover $300 worth of inventory.[41] The bottom line is to use your common sense in how much you spend and on what.

Author's note: Based on numerous discussions with various IRS personnel, it seems that this concept of using excessive, unreasonable expenses as a test for a "lack of business profit motive" has been applied to a variety of endeavors. For example, one who enters the travel business and tries to deduct all his or her "familiarization trips" (otherwise known as "fam" trips), despite earning very little gross income and making little attempt to sell vacation travel, would have a tough time establishing that these trips have a profit motive. This is especially true if the cost of each trip is greater than the gross income from the entire endeavor.

In addition, some recent IRS cases have noted that although you do *not* have to make a profit, you should have some gross income during the year. Judges and the IRS just don't believe that any business can have zero gross income if someone is truly trying to make a profit. Thus, if you have zero gross income, you may well be deemed a hobby despite all the preceding discussion.

9. Income from other sources. The amount of income from other sources is used to help determine your profit motive. Although it may not seem fair, the greater your income from other sources or other businesses or jobs, the less likely it is that your loss from your activity may be deemed a business loss.[42] Although this certainly is not a determinative factor, if you have substantial income from other activities, you need to more closely dot your *is* and cross your *ts*. If you follow everything that I have discussed here, you can be a billionaire and still have your side venture be deemed a business.

10. Suspicious activities. Watch out for certain activities that the IRS considers inherently more suspect because they involve significant personal pleasure.[43] These include

- Antique collecting
- Stamp collecting
- Travel business
- Writing
- Ministerial duties
- Record recording
- Raising show horses
- Training and showing dogs
- Automobile racing

Author's note: If you're engaged in one of these activities, you must pay careful attention to the other "business versus hobby" factors mentioned.

Author's note: I've had hundreds of students who were audited because of questions about their activities being a business and have prevailed, getting their losses allowed for years! If you follow everything that I've said in this chapter, you'll have the peace of mind of being bulletproof against one of the IRS's favorite weapons.

Summary

- Losses from businesses can be used against any income, carried back two years, or carried forward 20 years to offset the next 20 years of income. No losses are allowed from hobbies, and no carryback or carryover of unused deductions is allowed. This is why classifying an activity as a hobby is the IRS's favorite weapon.
- Try to have a profit in at least three of five consecutive years. This is not mandatory, but it's nice to have because it will provide evidence of your profit motive.
- An election is available to postpone a determination of the status of your activities as a business or as a hobby. Generally, don't bother making this election.
- Document business intent by sending a letter to your manager, sponsor, or franchising company to express your reasons for entering the business, emphasizing your desire to make a long-term profitable career out of this activity.
- Have a business plan showing at least 5 and preferably 10 years of projections for revenues and expenses.
- If your business involves inventory, always have enough on hand to justify your goals and the business plan.
- Don't make any improper statements such as, "I'm in this endeavor only to save taxes" or "… to cut costs" or "… to get my products at a discount."
- Keep accurate books and records, which should include a tax organizer or diary with your daily contacts and activities. Also have yearly balance sheet and income statements prepared to help you improve your performance. Finally, keep separate bank accounts and inventory records of costs, sales, and products given away as samples or personally consumed, etc.
- At least yearly, consult with experts to find out what successful people are doing to make money in businesses similar to your own. Document who the expert was and what he or she said.
- Use advertising, telephone listings, business cards, and stationery with your business name, address, and telephone number.
- If you're not making money, change the way you market your business. It's essential that you try different documented approaches.
- Before entering your business, conduct an investigation of the industry and of any companies that you're thinking of associating with. At the least, you should get a Better Business Bureau report on any company that you're considering representing. Document your steps in this investigation.
- Keep getting trained and seeking tips on operating and improving your business. This shows that you're really interested in making a profit.
- It's much more important to work your business regularly, such as one or two hours a day, than once every two weeks for 20 hours. You should note all activities and appointments in your tax organizer or diary.

- Clearly document reasons for making any business trips.
- Try to have at least some gross income. You don't need to make money, but you should have some sales or commissions during the year.
- Be especially careful if you're engaged in one of the inherently suspicious activities.

Notes

1. Section 172 of the IRC and regulations thereunder.
2. Section 172(b)(1)(A)(i) of the IRC and see the Job Creation and Worker Assistance Act of 2002.
3. Section 172 (b)(1)(A)(ii) of the IRC.
4. Section 183(a) of the IRC and IRS Publication 535.
5. Section 183 of the IRC.
6. Section 183(d) of the IRC.
7. Ibid.
8. Section 183(e)(1) of the IRC.
9. Regulation Section 12.9(c) of the ITR.
10. Regulation Section 12.9 of the ITR.
11. Section 1.183-2(a) of the ITR.
12. Section 1.183-2 of the ITR. See also *Floyd Fisher*, T.C. Memo 1980-183.
13. Ibid.
14. *Dreicer v. Commissioner*, 78 TC 642; aff'd., 702 F.2d 1205 (CA Dist. Ct. 1983).
15. Section 1.183-2(a) of the ITR and *Bryant v. Commissioner*, 928 F.2d 745 (6th Cir. 1991).
16. *Dennis Pryor*, T.C. Memo 1991-109.
17. *Harry Van Scoyoc*, T.C. Memo 1988-520.
18. *Richard Glenn*, T.C. Memo 1995-399.
19. Section 1.183-2(c) of the ITR.
20. Section 1.183-2(b)(i) of the ITR.
21. *Frank Sutter*, T.C. Memo 1990-447; *Charles Givens*, T.C. Memo 1989-529; *Ransom v. Commissioner*, T.C. Memo 1990-381 (Amway distributor); *Frank Harris*, T.C. Memo 1992-638 (Mary Kay distributor).
22. *Thomas Burger*, T.C. Memo 1985-523, *aff'd.* 809 F.2d 355 (7th Cir. 1987).
23. *Kenneth J. Nissley*, T.C. Memo 2000-178 (Amway distributor); *Tony L. Zidar v. Commissioner*, T.C. Memo 2001-200.
24. *Kenneth J. Nissley*, cited earlier.
25. *Lawrence Appley*, T.C. Memo 1979-433. Most subsequent cases were taken from the Research Institute of America's Federal Tax Coordinator (2002).
26. *George Doyle*, T.C. Memo 1982-537.
27. *Rufus Burleson*, T.C. Memo 1983-570.
28. *Patrick Edward McLarney*, T.C. Memo 1982-461.
29. *Peter Rubin*, T.C. Memo 1989-290.
30. *Theisen v. Commissioner*, T.C. Memo 1997-539 and *Kenneth J. Nissley*, cited earlier.
31. Section 1.183-2(b)(i) of the ITR.
32. *C. Frank Fisher*, 50 T.C. 164 (1968) (acquiesced by the IRS).
33. *Sheldon Barr*, T.C. Memo 1989-69; *Kenneth J, Nissley*, cited earlier.

34. Section 1.183-2(b) of the ITR and *Ransom v. Commissioner*, T.C. Memo 1990-381.

35. *Wenzel Tirheimer*, T.C. Memo 1992-137.

36. *Sherman Sampson*, T.C. Memo 1982-276.

37. Ibid.

38. Section 1.183-2(b)(6) of the ITR.

39. Sections 1.183-2(b)(6) and 2(b)(7) of the ITR.

40. *Ransom v. Commissioner*, cited earlier, and *Abdolvahab Pirnia*, T.C. Memo 1992-137.

41. Ibid.

42. Section 1.183-2(b)(8) of the ITR.

43. Section 1.183-2(b)(9) of the ITR.

Part 2

How to Incorporate
to Shelter Your Wealth

9

Finding the Best Corporate Entity for Your Business

The beginning is the most important part of the work.

—Plato, *The Republic*

What was true for Plato 2,500 years ago still holds true today. What determines how much you can use in fringe benefits and losses, not to mention how much you can limit liabilities and how easily you can raise capital, is your business entity. It's thus crucial that you read over this chapter carefully and follow along on the flowchart (Figure 9-1). Moreover, even if an entity is great for you now, you may wish to change it as time goes by. For example, you may want to start off as a sole proprietor but later raise more capital and incorporate. Thus you will need to keep track of your "proper" business entity on a continuing basis if you want to make your life less taxing.

The flowchart in Figure 9-1 should help you to decide which form of business entity would be most appropriate for your business.

Chapter Overview
- Learn why your initial choice of a business entity is so important.
- Use a great flowchart that will easily demonstrate which entity is best for you.
- Know the pros and cons of a sole proprietorship and why it's an ideal entity for network marketers.
- Learn about partnerships and why these generally should be avoided.
- Know the benefits of being an S corporation and how this one entity can eliminate up to 40 percent of your Social Security taxes.
- Learn why a limited-liability corporation is one of the most highly recommended entities for most business owners.
- Learn about when to form a regular corporation (C corporation) and, more important, when not to.
- Learn which entity is best if you have co-owners or partners and about the one document that's crucial to your long-term success.

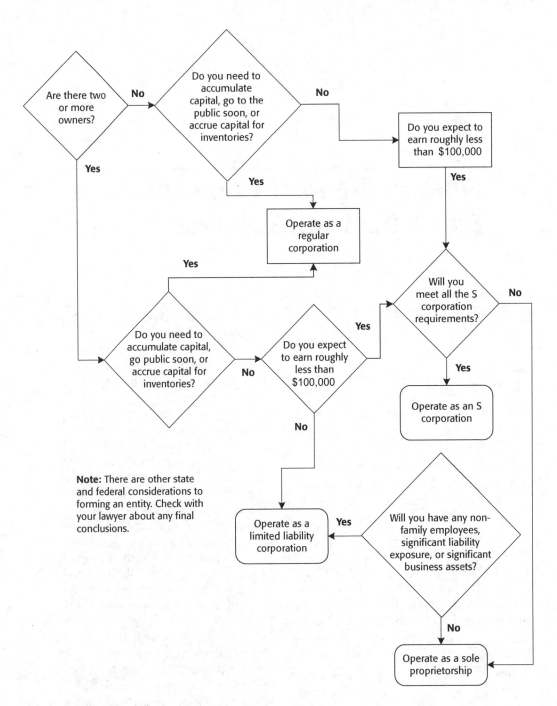

Figure 9-1. Entity selection flowchart

Let's begin by discussing the advantages and disadvantages of your entity options, with a recommendation on which types of business would be most or least appropriate for each option.

Sole Proprietorship

Sole proprietorships are great if you have no liability problems and no employees. Without question, the easiest, lowest-costing entity to run and manage is a sole proprietorship.

Advantages of a Sole Proprietorship

1. Simplicity. This is by far the least complicated form of business entity around. In fact, a sole proprietorship is defined by its lack of organization. There's only one owner. If you have no employees, there are no Internal Revenue Service (IRS) forms to file other than Schedule C with your federal Form 1040 tax return. You simply hang out a sign saying your business name, such as "Harriet Stowe, writer." Although it's highly recommended that you have separate bank accounts, you don't need to do so. You can have one account for you and your business. It doesn't get any easier than this!

2. Low startup costs. The startup costs are negligible. If you have no employees, there are no filings with the federal government, no organization documents, as with a corporation or a partnership, and no state filings unless you want to reserve a name or operate as an alias.

3. Simple control. You're in direct control all the time. There's no hassle with other owners or partners and only one layer of management—you.

4. Freely sellable. Sole proprietorships are easy to sell. There aren't a lot of hidden traps, as with corporations.

5. Great small-business tax benefits. As I've noted in prior chapters, you get lots of tax benefits being in business. However, there are limitations that apply to partnerships and S corporations that don't apply to sole proprietorships. For example, you can hire your spouse and deduct all your medical expenses with a self-insured medical reimbursement plan. (Do you remember this from Chapter 4?)

In short, this entity is cheap and simple.

Disadvantages of a Sole Proprietorship

1. Unlimited liability. Did you know that there are roughly 90 million lawsuits yearly?[1] This is certainly the $64,000 question to being a sole proprietorship. You have unlimited liability. Thus, if you are sued for any business problem or incur any debts, you're personally liable. To be sure, you can get insurance to help offset most of the potential problems, but there are a number of bankrupt people whose economic lives lie in ruin because of unlimited liabi-lity or because they didn't cover every eventuality.

If there's any chance that someone will sue your business, if you have any employees who are not immediate family, or if you have substantial assets (property) that you need to protect, you absolutely should not operate as a sole proprietorship. Pick either one of the corporate forms or become a limited-liability corporation (to be discussed below).

Author's note: If you have employees, you shouldn't be a sole proprietor. Employees who aren't your immediate family are walking lawsuits. The reason is that employers are liable for the acts of their employees. In addition, there are numerous lawsuits filed by employees over allegations of discrimination, violations of the Americans with Disabilities Act, the Occupational Safety and Health Act (OSHA), and so forth. Thus the bottom line is that if you have nonfamily employees, don't be a sole proprietor. Use another business entity.

Author's note: Whether you operate as a sole proprietorship or as a limited-liability coporation (LLC), get a liability umbrella policy for at least $2 million in addition to your regular business insurance. The cost is negligible, around $400 per year.

2. No checks and balances. Because a sole proprietorship has only one owner by definition, there is no board of directors or other partners who can oversee what the owner is doing. There's no one to say, "This is inappropriate or shouldn't be done."

3. Trouble raising capital. It's much tougher to raise capital as a sole proprietor. Basically, the assets of the owner are the primary collateral.

4. No continuity of life. If the owner dies, becomes disabled, or retires, there's usually no one who can take over the business. The business thus either dies or is sold for a very low price.

Author's note: Because of this problem, I strongly urge all sole proprietorships to have very good disability insurance and good life insurance. Thus, if the owner dies or becomes disabled, there's a continued cash flow.

Who Should Operate as a Sole Proprietorship?

Despite the wonderful simplicity of this entity, the unlimited liabilities involved should negate most reasons for operating as a sole proprietor. The only people who should consider operating under a sole proprietorship are those who have almost no chance of liability problems, *no* nonfamily employees, and little in the way of investments that need protection. Many home-based business people, especially network marketing home-based businesses, should consider this form of operation. If you're a freelance writer with no employees, this form of business also could be for you. However, if you feel or your lawyer feels that there is any significant liability exposure, take my advice: *Don't be a sole proprietor.*

Author's Note: Real Estate has large amounts of liability exposure. Thus, do NOT own investment real estate in your own name; use an LLC.

General Partnership

A partnership is essentially like a sole proprietorship but with two or more partners/owners. However, there are some more advantages and disadvantages to the partnership that a sole proprietorship doesn't offer. There are two kinds of partnerships: *general* and *limited*. Let's discuss the general partnership first.

Advantages of a General Partnership

1. Broader expertise. A sole proprietor is a one-man or one-woman shop. He or she must become a "jack of many trades"—good at management, marketing, accounting, liability protection, taxes, and much more—to become successful. With a partnership, several people can divide the work and share and develop expertise. Thus one partner can do the marketing, while another can manage the inside operation. This can result in more efficiency and can attract greater knowledge to the operation.

2. Easier to raise capital. With a partnership, you can bring in as many investor/owner partners as you want: There's no legal limit. If you need to get a loan, you have more collateral at risk for a loan because more parties are involved. Thus a partnership can attract a lot more capital than a proprietorship.

3. Easy to form. Most partnerships are very easy to form. You just need to draft up a partnership agreement showing the rights and obligations of the partners. There are very few filings with either the IRS or the states unless you have employees, although it's more complicated than for a sole proprietorship—but then, every entity is more complicated than a sole proprietorship.

4. Low startup costs. As with proprietorships, the costs are low. Since there are few required filings with either the states or the federal government, formation costs are low. You will, however, need a partnership agreement, as noted earlier, which adds to your costs. In addition, a partnership needs to file a separate IRS form (Form 1065, U.S. Return of Partnership Income). Thus the cost of filing a return is greater than for a sole proprietorship.

5. No double taxation. All profits and losses flow through to the partners. There's no double tax, as there is with regular corporations. Any losses are limited to your partnership basis. However, that basis includes what you paid for your partnership interest, the basis of any other property contributed, plus your share of the liabilities.[2] Thus you should have sufficient basis for the losses.

Example: Sam contributes $10,000 in cash, plus stock worth $20,000 for which he paid $15,000, to get a 50 percent partnership interest. In addition, the partnership gets a bank loan for $40,000. Sam's basis in the partnership is $45,000:

Cash:	$10,000
Stock (basis):	$15,000
Prorated share of debt (50 percent):	$20,000
Total basis:	$45,000

Author's note: With partnerships, you always have to worry about your basis because losses are limited to the basis. With sole proprietorships, you don't have this problem.

With these increased benefits, you would think that everyone should run out, find some good partners, and form a partnership instead of being a sole proprietorship. However, there are some major drawbacks to partnerships.

Disadvantages of a General Partnership

1. Lack of continuity. Generally, partnerships terminate on the death, retirement, withdrawal, or resignation of a partner. The IRS notes[3] that if a 50 percent partner dies, retires, resigns, or withdraws; a partnership terminates for tax purposes regardless of what happens under state law.

Author's note: This one problem can be overcome easily with a well-drafted partnership agreement that notes, "The death, disability, resignation, or withdrawal of a partner will not terminate the partnership."

2. More management. With more owners comes more management, more layers of management. Partnerships thus can't respond as quickly to changes as a sole proprietorship.

3. Complaints about money and draws. There are usually major fights among partners about how much money should be distributed to each partner based on the production or efforts involved. More partnerships have terminated because of this one factor, in my opinion, than for any other reason. With a proprietorship, you don't have this problem—unless you like to fight with yourself.

4. Unlimited liability. This is probably the greatest drawback of all. Like sole proprietors, you're unlimitedly liable for all partnership debts unless they are specifically *nonrecourse debts* (which means that you have not guaranteed the debt personally). If this isn't bad enough, you're also unlimitedly liable for the actions of your partners. They can, in effect, bind you and make you liable for a host of obligations. Yuck!

5. Good luck finding the right partners. Having a separation of duties and finding people who specialize in different aspects of the business sounds wonderful in theory. In practice, however, it's very hard to do. Many partnerships break up because one partner isn't pulling his or her weight or is failing at some important designated task.

6. Fewer fringe benefits available. Partnerships have fewer fringe benefits than regular corporations. Moreover, the benefits derived from a self-insured medical plan are more limited for both partners and for owners of more than 2 percent of the stock of an S corporation. Partners and more than 2 percent stockholders of S corporations can set up a self-insured medical plan solely for routine physicals and laboratory testing.

Who Should Operate as a General Partnership?

Take my advice: Before you decide on being a partnership, take three aspirins and lie down until the desire passes. You should *never, ever* form a general partnership.

Why not?

From practical experience, I've seen too many partnerships break up because of fights among the partners about money, power, ego, who is failing to contribute, etc. It's just horrible. If you think that divorces aren't fun, you should see what happens in court with partnership splits. It's very nasty. In addition, being unlimitedly liable for the acts of your partners and for their malpractice could be a disaster, as will be shown with the Arthur Andersen Company. Take my advice: *Don't form a general partnership.*

Author's note: In the event that you don't listen to me, at least have a buy/sell agreement with any partners. This agreement provides that if there is a death, disability, or unsolvable disagreement among the partners, you have a way to buy out a partner using a fixed formula.

Partnership Startup Checklist

In addition to all the items just noted, if you have a partnership, you should have a good partnership agreement that notes the following:

- The term of the partnership
- How new partners may or may not be added
- Provisions in the event of the total disability, death, withdrawal, or retirement of a partner

- Provisions on the timing of any profit-sharing distributions and how they are to be determined
- Listing of the initial contributions of the partners and how any excess contribution is to be allocated
- List of all duties, work hours, and profit sharing
- Provisions for management and for handling disputes
- Provisions that no person can be a partner unless approved by a percentage of the remaining partners (to prevent creditors from being partners)

Limited Partnership

Because of all the partnership drawbacks, many people set up limited partnerships, which usually are formed for investments. These are formed with one or two limited partners and one general partner who is liable for all debts. This is not normally a problem because the general partner usually is a corporation with limited liability.

Advantages of a Limited Partnership

1. Limited liability. Unlike a general partnership, the limited partners are only responsible for their initial contributions, unless they personally guarantee any debts. They are thus insulated from all partnership liabilities, like a corporation. The general partner is unlimitedly liable, but since general partners usually are corporations, their liability is limited, too.

Author's note: The limited partners enjoy limited liability, but only if they do not in any way participate in management. If they're active in management, courts have held that they are the alter ego of the partnership, which causes the limited partners to be unlimitedly liable as a general partner. Thus, if you are a limited partner, you should only contribute capital and not in any way help out the partnership or make any management decisions other than voting for another general partner.

2. Great way to raise capital. Since there can be no limit to the number of limited partners, this form of entity can raise a lot of capital. This is one of the big reasons for using limited partnerships for investment.

3. Centralized management. By definition, limited partners only contribute capital and do not participate in management. There usually is a centralized management structure that handles all the business of the partnership.

4. Transferability. Although most partnership agreements require some sort of partnership consent before transferring any partnership interest, it's usually not a problem getting consent in the sale or transfer of a limited partnership interest.

5. Continuous life. Unlike general partnerships, most limited partnerships don't terminate on the death or disability of a limited partner. If the general partner becomes bankrupt, this could be a problem unless the partnership agreement allows the limited partners to get a new general partner.

6. Estate planning discounts. Because limited partnerships are not readily sellable and have very little voting power, their value is usually discounted for estate tax purposes.[4] This is the reason why many estate planners are recommending the use of family limited partnerships for estate planning purposes.

7. Flowthrough of income. Partnerships do not pay tax. All income and losses flow through to the partners, usually in accordance with their contributions. Family limited partnerships are great ways to shift income to family members.

Disadvantages of a Limited Partnership

1. Limited transferability. There usually isn't a market for a partnership interest, so it's hard to sell. Moreover, the consent of the general partners usually is required for any sale.

2. Heavy costs. It's usually costly to set up a limited partnership because of the complexity of the partnership agreement needed and the requirement to file a Form 1065 plus K-1s for each partner at year end noting their share of partnership income and losses. In addition, since management is centralized, it must be paid, which raises the yearly costs considerably.

3. No control over the general partners. The general partner controls the day-to-day activities of the partnership. So who's overseeing the general partner? Who's on the alert for any embezzlement? Sadly, the answer is that you have an outside accountant doing the books (hopefully); however, there has been a lot of improper behavior by general partners who have taken more money than normally would have been allowed.

4. The limited partners may not participate in management. This has its good and bad points, but the limited partners must not participate in management or they'll lose their protected status as limited partners. If the general partner is running the business improperly (but not doing anything illegal), the limited partners will have very little say.

5. Passive loss problems. All limited partnerships are treated as passive activities.[5] This means that if there are losses, you can use them only to the extent that you have passive income. Passive income includes income that's not earned, such as rents, royalties, or other partnership income. Thus, if you want to use the losses, you must have some passive income for the losses to offset. If you don't have passive income, the losses get carried over to future years. Thus, as an investor, you should have some positive passive income.

Who Should Operate as a Limited Partnership?

As you can see, limited partnerships are very useful. They should be used mainly where there are investors who will not be active in the business. Real estate limited partnerships are an ideal example because all the depreciation and losses from the real estate pass through to the partners. In addition, family limited partnerships can be set up to shift income and to allow a big estate tax discount for the partnership interest. Consult a good estate planning attorney about this.

Corporations

The word *incorporate* means "to create a separate body." This is exactly what defines a corporation. It's a separate entity that, on its own behalf, can sue, borrow money, be responsible for its own debts, and run a business on its own behalf. Many entrepreneurs who are the sole owners of their corporations do not understand that they are not the business; the business is the corporation.

Advantages of a Regular Corporation (C Corporation)

1. Limited liability. Perhaps the greatest reason to set up a corporation is not taxes but liabilities. If a corporation is set up properly, and if the owners adhere to the corporate formalities, it can limit most liabilities to the assets of the corporation. The only exceptions are fraud, malpractice, and failure to adhere to the corporate formalities.

Author's note: Malpractice is a real problem for some small businesses today. The advantage of corporate status is that unlike in a general partnership, if a co-owner of a corporation commits malpractice, you would not be liable personally for it. Only the co-owner who committed the malpractice normally would become unlimitedly liable, and only the assets of the corporation are exposed.

Example: Doctors Alice, Bob, and Charley form a professional corporation. Alice commits malpractice. Alice is unlimitedly liable to the injured person, as is the corporation. However, Bob and Charley are not personally liable; the corporation has insulated them from liability.

2. Specialized management. Corporations can have as many officers as they can afford. Thus, unlike a sole proprietor, they can and usually do have different people handling different aspects of the business. In a sense, they get the same advantages in this way as a general partnership.

3. Great tax advantages. Regular corporations (C corporations) and employees of S corporations who own less than 2 percent of the stock get the most fringe benefits among all the entities. Chapter 11 will cover this, but for now here are some examples:

- 100 percent deduction for health insurance premiums for the officers and their families—a benefit that is also available to sole proprietors and partners after the year 2002
- 100 percent deduction for disability insurance premiums
- 100 percent deduction for medical expenses that are not covered by insurance, using a self-insured medical reimbursement plan
- Qualified stock options that can give capital gains
- Tax-free life insurance—up to $50,000 of group term life
- A cafeteria plan that can cover day care, unreimbursed medical expenses (with some limits), adoption assistance, and group legal service
- A fully deductible athletic facility and athletic equipment, if on the premises of the business

Author's note: Cafeteria plans, which are special legal plans that let you choose your benefits, generally are not beneficial for small and home-based businesses because not more than 25 percent of the benefits can accrue to owner/employees,[6] and there are stiff, complicated nondiscrimination rules. Moreover, the plans apply only to employees. Self-employed people and partners are not deemed employees.[7] Thus we will not be discussing this benefit in this book.

- Tax-free supper money allowance
- Qualified pensions and profit sharing that allow borrowing

4. Accumulation of capital. Unlike other types of entities, corporations are subject to their own set of tax rates. For good reasons, corporations can accrue $50,000 of net earnings each year and get taxed only in the 15 percent tax bracket. Thus, if you need to accumulate capital for marketing, business expansion, or inventories, this can be a major benefit.

5. Transferability of ownership. Unlike with a partnership or even a limited partnership, you usually can transfer your stock holding without consent from the corporation or other stockholders if you have a buyer.

6. Great for a public offering. If you want to go public and raise capital, no entity is better than a regular corporation. We have exchanges that handle the raising of capital and the transferability of shares. There's rarely a problem with disposing of publicly traded stock.

7. Ordinary losses on sale of stock. Normally, when you sell a stock at a loss, your loss is limited to any capital gains; if it exceeds any gains, you may deduct up to $3,000 of the loss against other income. Losses in excess of this amount can be carried forward and used to reduce future capital gains, up to $3,000 per year.

Example: Wendy has a stock loss of $20,000. If she made $5,000 with some stock gains, she may use $5,000 of the loss against the gains and may use another $3,000 of the loss against her salary or other income. She carries over the remaining loss to future years to use in the same way.

If you plan correctly when the corporation is formed, when you sell corporate stock at a loss, it's an ordinary loss. This means that you would not be limited to offsetting any capital gains, and there wouldn't be a limit of $3,000 per year. In fact, the maximum amount of ordinary loss that you can take would be $50,000 if you are single[8] and up to a whopping $100,000 if you are married and file a joint return![9] *Yeah!* However, you must organize your corporation so that the stock you receive is deemed "Section 1244 stock."

8. Eliminate up to 60 percent of your gain when you sell your stock. Yes, you read it correctly. If you set up a corporation, you'll probably qualify for a little-known but very available exemption, the *small-business stock exemption*. This allows you normally to deduct 50 percent of any gain on the stock from being taxed! Even better, in certain areas of the country that the president or Congress wants to help out, this exclusion is increased to 60 percent.

Disadvantages of a Regular Corporation

Despite all the wonderful benefits that are available to regular corporations, there are some major drawbacks.

Author's note: Don't you wish that there could be just one entity that has all positives and no negatives? Unfortunately, this doesn't exist. If you're considering forming a Nevada corporation, I recommend getting advice from Nevada Corporate Planners at www.nvinc.com.

1. Double taxation. Since regular corporations are treated as separate entities and have their own tax rates, you can have the possibility of double taxation: tax at the corporate level and tax for you at your rates if there's a dividend. As bad as this sounds—and it can be bad—most people who operate as regular corporations plan before year's end to pay enough in bonuses and salaries to eliminate most of the double-tax problem. However, it takes planning, and of course, this increases the cost involved.

Author's note: Before I became an S corporation, I would meet with my accountant before year's end and make projections of my yearly income and pay bonuses according to my projections.

2. Increased paperwork. Without question, operating a regular corporation is a "three-Tylenol" hassle. You *must* have yearly stockholder meetings to elect a board of directors, even if you're the only stockholder, and yearly board meetings to elect officers and approve major issues within the corporation. Also, you must keep corporate minutes. You need separate bank accounts and very good books and records. If you do not do this, your corporation will be deemed your "alter ego," and you may become liable for all corporate debts and obligations.

3. Added paperwork costs. Clearly, corporations are more expensive to operate than any other entity. You have to file a separate corporate tax return with schedules (Form 1120). In addition, you will be the employee of the corporation, so you must file with both the federal government and the state government for an Employer Identification Number (SS-4 and SS-5. Form SS-5 is Application for a Social Security Card), as well as for unemployment. Some states, such as California, have special corporate taxes that don't apply to proprietorships, which significantly increase the costs.

4. Losses don't flow through to you as stockholder. Unlike with partnerships and proprietorships, all losses in the corporation stay with the corporation. They don't flow through to you on your corporate tax return because corporations are separate entities. This disadvantage can be somewhat overcome, however, by electing S corporation status, which will be discussed below.

Author's note: I should note that the losses in a regular corporation get carried over to future years in the corporation and offset future corporate profits.

5. Lots of tax traps. Corporations have traps set up by the government to overcome perceived abuses, such as operating a corporation with a lot of unearned income (personal holding company) and accumulating too much in earnings (accumulated earnings tax).

6. Paying the highest corporate rates if you provide certain services. If all the preceding isn't enough, Congress requires corporations whose owners render almost all the services (personal service corporations) to pay a flat 35 percent rate on all income![10] This applies to most service businesses, such as doctors, lawyers, accountants, actuaries, engineers, architects, and *consultants*. However, if your main business is selling products, this isn't a problem—another example of congressional "tax simplification."

7. Stockholder fights. Corporations are run and managed somewhat like a democracy. The ones who get the most votes (based on shares) elect the board of directors, which, in turn, elects the management. Sadly, many corporate owners end up fighting over management, trying to fire each other, trying to benefit one owner over the others, etc. It becomes just as bad as fights among partners. This is especially fierce if each owner owns 50 percent of the stock. It's vital to have in place some sort of buy/sell agreement that provides both a formula and a mechanism for buying out stockholders. A good lawyer can draft one, and, I promise, it will be one of the best things that you'll ever do. Don't pass up this precaution, as many have done, to their regret.

Author's note: Many years ago, I had a corporation with a 50 percent partner but didn't have a buy/sell agreement. It took hundreds of thousands of dollars in legal fees, not to mention a huge amount of hard feelings, to settle this situation.

Who Should Operate as a Regular Corporation and Who Shouldn't

Certainly because of the personal service corporation rules, people who render mostly services and who also perform the services should *not* be a regular corporation because they will pay the highest corporate rates on all earnings. Yuck! The people who should consider being a regular corporation are those who have some liability exposure that they want to protect themselves from *and* who are in any of the following situations:

- They have substantial inventories and need to accumulate capital for this purpose.
- They need to accumulate capital in the future for marketing and other projects.
- They expect to go public in the near future.
- They need all the fringe benefits such as health insurance.

Author's note: As I said before and want to restate because it's important, the main purpose of operating as any form of corporation is to limit liability exposure or perhaps to go public. If you don't have any significant liability exposure and don't plan on having a public offering in the near future, being a corporation—especially a regular corporation—is probably not advantageous.

Author's note: From my experience, I have found that most people, despite having the best of intentions, do not keep up with the corporate formalities, annual board meetings, minutes, etc. It just doesn't happen. If you're the kind of person who won't strictly adhere to these formalities every year, do not form a corporation. Did I say that clearly enough? Form one of the other entities, such as a limited-liability corporation, which will be discussed later on.

S Corporation

There are a lot of problems inherent to regular corporations. Congress allows taxpayers to avoid most of these without many negative side effects. You do this by electing S corporation status.

An S corporation *is* a corporation. To the surprise of many people, it has the exact same formalities as a regular corporation—stockholder meetings and board of directors meetings, etc. In addition, you must make an election by filing Form 2553 with the IRS within the first 75 days of the tax year if you want to operate as an S corporation for the year. An election is just that: It's a formal choice to become an S corporation. If you don't make this formal choice, you are treated as a regular corporation.

However, there are a number of advantages that an S corporation has over a regular corporation.

Advantages of an S Corporation

1. No double taxation.[11] With regular corporations, you would take the gross income of the corporation, subtract any business expenses, and pay tax at the corporate level on the net income.

With an S corporation, this is not the case. Unless you were a regular corporation and then elected to become an S corporation,[12] there's generally no double taxation because all the income and losses flow through to you as the stockholder. S corporations thus are treated like partnerships in this way. You actually would receive a form (K-1) noting your share of the net income. Thus you don't have to go through all the complicated year-end tax planning to eliminate the double-tax problem as with regular corporations.

2. Elimination of up to 50 percent of your Social Security and Medicare taxes. As I mentioned, the main reason for setting up a corporation is to limit your liability exposure. However, there's one major tax benefit to S corporations that can be so great that many accountants have recommended setting up an S corporation solely for this benefit: the substantial saving in Social Security and Medicare taxes with the use of S corporation dividends.[13] This is especially true if you make under the Social Security maximum ($97,500 in 2007). This benefit can be so substantial that I devote Chapter 11 to discussing it.

3. Income splitting. As I pointed out in Chapter 4 on income shifting and income splitting, you're better off having various family members being taxed on shares of your income than one person—you—being taxed on the whole thing. This is so because our tax system is a graduated rate system: The rates rise as income rises. By splitting income among family members who don't have a lot of other income, the lower rates allow you to save a bundle. The rich have known this for years and have planned accordingly. An S corporation can allow you the same benefit. You can give some stock to your children or grandchildren or to anyone in a lower tax bracket than you whom you want to support. When the company earns money, they are taxed on their share of the net income based on their stock ownership. Let me give you a true example that happened to one of my friends.

Example: John and Martha have three children. They have a sole proprietorship business that had net earnings of $112,850; they paid in federal income tax alone (not counting Social Security) $24,265. I suggested that they form an S corporation and give 15 percent of the stock to each of their three children, who were attending college. Each child then was taxed on 15 percent of the gain, and the parents paid tax on 55 percent of the gain. Each child paid $2,239 in taxes, and the parents paid $10,554. The savings was $6,994 with this technique, computed as follows:

Tax payable by parents as sole proprietorship:	$24,265
Tax payable by all three children:	$ 6,717
Tax payable by parents using split technique:	$10,554
Total taxes paid by family:	$17,271
Net savings to the family using split technique:	$ 6,994

Author's note: No wonder the rich have used income splitting for years. Now that you know about it, you can do the same thing. The rich, however, have paid a lot of money in fees to find out about this; you have only paid for this book. What a deal!

4. Specialized management. Just like regular corporations, C corporations have centralized management. You have a board of directors to help oversee what you're doing and provide, in theory, some checks and balances.

5. Limited liability. S corporations limit liability to the same extent as regular corporations, no better and no worse.

6. Ordinary loss on the sale of stock. Just like a regular corporation, you can have an ordinary loss on the sale of your stock, up to $50,000 if you're single and up to $100,000 if you're married. (See the earlier discussion dealing with regular corporations.[14])

7. Elimination of up to 60 percent of gain on the sale of stock. As with regular corporations, you can sell your small business stock at a gain and avoid up to 50 percent of the gain or up to 60 percent if your business is located in certain preferred "enterprise zones." As you can see, an S corporation is a big improvement in some ways over a regular corporation.

8. Use of corporate losses. As I mentioned, an S corporation flows all income and losses to the owners. Thus, if you have a loss, the loss passes through to your individual tax return, just as with a sole proprietorship. However, there's an IRS "gotcha." The loss is limited to the basis in your stock.[15] That basis is what you paid for your stock in money plus the basis of any property contributed to the S corporation for the stock. It also includes any income that you were taxed on but didn't receive. You subtract what you received as a dividend. Thus the formula for basis is

Cash paid for stock
plus
Basis (which is usually the cost) of property contributed for stock
plus
Income that was taxed to you in the past that you didn't receive
minus
Any dividends received or losses that were passed through to you.

Author's note: Limiting your losses to your stock basis is very different from the treatment of losses in sole proprietorships, in which you can take any losses on your individual tax return. This means that you must do some planning if you expect a loss in your S corporation to ensure that you have sufficient basis for the loss.

9. Limited benefits from self-insured medical plan. As I noted earlier, owners of more than 2 percent of the corporate stock and partners generally can't benefit from a self-insured medical plan except to cover routine physicals and laboratory testing.

With all these wonderful benefits, you would think that an S corporation might be the way to go for most people. In fact, it's probably the preferred vehicle for most small businesses; however, there are some drawbacks to being an S corporation.

Disadvantages of an S Corporation

1. Severe limits on qualifying for S corporation status. There are several tests that you must meet to operate as a qualified S corporation:

- *You must have fewer than 100 stockholders.*[16] This is a strict limitation. If you exceed this number, you're disqualified. However, a husband and a wife count as one stockholder.[17] The limitation isn't too bad unless you have a large number of owners or investors. This one limitation is the reason why no public corporation is an S corporation.
- *The corporation must be a domestic corporation formed in the United States.*[18] It can't be a foreign corporation.
- *It can't be an ineligible corporation, such as a bank.*[19] For most small businesses, this is not a problem.

- *Only individuals, estates, and a certain type of limited trust can be stockholders.*[20] Another corporation, partnership, and most trusts can't own any stock in an S corporation. (Yuck!)
- *All stock must be owned by a U.S. citizen or a U.S. resident.*[21] Thus, if you have foreign investors, you can't be an S corporation. In addition, corporations, partnerships, and LLCs that are treated as partnerships can't own S corporation stock. This definitely does limit your options.
- *You can only have one class of stock.*[22] This has a number of drawbacks. First, this limits the estate planning benefits that you can do with multiple classes of stock because you can't have more than one class with an S corporation. Second, if you want to give out preferred stock that doesn't vote but is preferred in some way, you are prohibited from doing this.

Author's note: This limitation on shareholders and on not having different classes of stock provides less protection for the stock from creditors. Creditors can become stockholders with voting rights. LLCs have a real advantage here in that you can limit who becomes a member.

Author's note: You might be thinking that you would qualify for S corporation status and then, after you get qualified, violate the rules. This doesn't work. If you violate any of these six requirements, your S corporation status terminates on the first day of the violation.

2. Complete flowthrough of earnings. You can't accumulate capital at lower corporate rates as you can with a regular corporation because all income is taxed to you whether or not you receive it and taxed at your normal tax rates.

3. Limited ability to raise capital. Generally, because of the limits, the financing is done by the shareholders and is based on whatever assets they contribute.

4. Corporate debts don't increase your stock basis. With most partnerships, the partnership debt increases your basis. This is not true of an S corporation. If the corporation takes on any debt, this does not increase the basis of the stock for the stockholders. This one point makes S corporations very different from partnerships.

5. More limited fringe benefits than in regular corporations. S corporations allow fewer fringe benefits. For example, the owners don't get any major benefit from setting up a medical reimbursement plan such as a regular corporation can do and even a sole proprietorship can do by hiring a spouse. They get some fringe benefits, which will be discussed in Chapters 13 and 14, but less than with regular corporations.

Author's note: Starting in 2003, S corporations get the same benefit as regular corporations in deducting all health insurance premiums and most home health care premiums for officers and their families. In 2007, the deduction is 100 percent of the premium for medical insurance that is not subsidized by an employer.

6. Same bookkeeping hassles of regular corporations. As I said, S corporations are corporations. The S status is only to elect to have all income and losses pass through to you as the owners/stockholders. Thus you must have yearly board of directors meetings, stockholder meetings, corporate minutes, and a separate corporate bank account.

Who Should Operate as an S Corporation?

An S corporation is ideal in the following situations:

- Officers/stockholders are earning less than $84,900 in 2002.
- There's no need for any capital accumulated for inventories or marketing.
- All financing will be shareholder financing.
- You meet all the rules.

Limited-Liability Corporation (LLC)

For many years, Europe and South America have allowed a type of hybrid entity, a limited-liability corporation (LLC). For you history buffs, the LLC started in this country in 1977 in Wyoming but has been accepted gradually by all the other states.

Essentially, an LLC is a cross between a limited partnership and a corporation. If there's only one owner, it's deemed a sole proprietorship for tax purposes, and you file the normal IRS Schedule C with your federal tax return. If there's more than one owner, you file for tax purposes as a partnership and file Form 1065, which is a bit more costly.

Regardless of how you file, LLC status protects you from liabilities in the same way as corporation status.

Advantages of an LLC

1. Limited liability. As with a corporation or a limited partnership, the LLC limits liability for debts and obligations. The only time you would be personally liable is if you personally guarantee the debt, the LLC commits fraud, or you commit malpractice. Also, as with a corporation, you're responsible for your own negligence and for the negligence of those whom you supervise directly, but not for the negligence of other LLC members.

Author's note: The bottom line is that the LLC is an easier way to get the same protection offered by a corporation without a lot of the legal formalities and administrative details of a corporation. Since your liability is limited to the amount of money or other capital you contribute to the LLC, you have the same protection against obligations and lawsuits as with regular corporations and S corporations.

2. None of the restrictions of an S corporation. You can have any number of members; they can be stockholders, whether corporate or otherwise; and you can have foreign investors. Thus the LLC gives tremendous flexibility while maintaining limited liability.

3. All losses and income pass through to stockholders. Since one-owner LLCs are treated as sole proprietorships and LLCs with two or more owners are treated as partnerships, all income and losses flow through to the members. There is no double tax. LLCs thus are beneficial for operating a business as well as for holding real estate.

4. LLCs get higher basis with LLC debts. As with a partnership, if the LLC incurs any debt, the debt increases the basis of the members' portion of the LLC. Thus LLCs get the best of being a partnership without any of the drawbacks.

5. Much cheaper to operate and form than corporations. LLCs are inexpensive to form. You simply register your LLC articles with the state, and you're off and running. Moreover, unlike corporations, you don't have to have any formal meetings, minutes, or member meetings.

6. Asset protection. An LLC may protect assets better than all the entities. Yes, you read that correctly. An LLC may be better at asset protection than any other entity, even a corporation. If a partner or corporate stockholder gets sued for any reason, the creditor gets the stock or can become an unwanted partner. Partnerships and LLCs can prevent this possibility by providing in the orginal formation documents for the LLC that no new members of LLCs are allowed without the consent of the other members. This will keep creditors from becoming members.

A creditor can proceed against a member's interest in the LLC only by means of a *charging order*, which provides that any distribution made to the member who is a debtor would instead go to the creditor. This has a detrimental side effect for the creditor. If the LLC has undistributed income, the creditor would be taxed on the member's share of the undistributed income, just as the debtor-member, even though the creditor didn't receive the distribution! This makes most creditors leery about placing a charging order on the LLC member's interest.

Author's note: Think about this for a minute: What creditor would want to put a lien or charging order on a member's interest if he or she could be taxed on money that he or she never receives? This is why an LLC that's taxed as a partnership is very beneficial for asset protection. Single-owner LLCs are not as protected because a creditor may be able to take control of the LLC if there's only one owner.

As you can see, an LLC is a really great entity and, in my opinion, the entity of choice for most people. However, despite the attempts of most states to overcome most of the disadvantages of corporations and partnerships with an LLC, there still exist some disadvantages.

Disadvantages of an LLC

1. No saving on Social Security. With an S corporation, you can save Social Security and Medicare taxes by distributing dividends along with salaries. LLCs do not seem to have this advantage. All earnings are taxed like those of a sole proprietorship or a partnership and subject to Social Security.

Author's note: I should note that this isn't entirely clear. There's some argument that if you are an LLC member but have no management authority and do not actively participate in the day-to-day operations, you should be treated as a limited partner and not be subject to Social Security on your share of the earnings.[23]

2. More complicated paperwork. You have to files articles of organization for the LLC with the state in which it is formed. This certainly raises the costs. In addition, some states have a special tax on LLC income. You definitely should check with a good accountant about the state-law implications, which can result in some severe disadvantages for LLCs.

3. Lifetime limits. Some states mandate that LLCs terminate within 30 years or less. This is not true of Nevada, which is a good reason to form an LLC there (see Chapter 10). In addition, some states require dissolution of an LLC on the death or resignation of a member. This can be overcome by stating in the formation article that a termination won't occur on the death, disability, or resignation of a member.

4. May require two or more members. Some states require that an LLC have two members or more. In most states, however, this requirement is being changed to accommodate one-member LLCs. A problem arises if you form your LLC in a state that allows one-member LLCs but operate in states that don't. Your LLC in this situation may not protect you from liabilities! However, the LLC statutes in almost all states contain "nondiscriminatory provisions" that the laws of the state in which an

LLC was formed govern its organization, its internal affairs, and the liability of its members.

Who Should Operate as an LLC?

An LLC is an appropriate entity for the following:

- Individuals who expect to earn more than the Social Security maximum ($97,500 in 2007)
- Individuals who need liability protection but can't qualify as an S corporation
- Businesses that don't need to accumulate capital for inventories or for marketing
- Real estate businesses

Summary

- In choosing the best corporate entity to start your business, it's crucial to determine what fringe benefits you can obtain and whether business losses can pass through to you.
- You can always change entities as time and circumstances demand.
- A sole proprietorship is simple, simple, simple, but liability is unlimited.
- Don't operate as a sole proprietorship unless you are sure that you have the following:
  - No liability exposure
  - No significant business assets
  - No nonfamily employees
- If you even desire to form a general partnership, take three aspirin and lie down until the desire passes. In the event that your business is already a general partnership, get a buy/sell agreement immediately. "Don't pass go" until you do.
- Limited partnerships are great vehicles for obtaining investors without being subject to liability risks. They're great for investments such as real estate.
- Operate as a regular corporation only if
  - You intend to register on a national exchange soon (go public).
  - You need to accumulate capital for inventories or for mass marketing and can use the lower corporate tax rates to do so.
  - You will solemnly swear to adhere to all corporate formalities of corporate minutes, directors meetings, and stockholder meetings.
- If there are only a few corporate owners, get a buy/sell agreement as soon as possible. You'll thank me in the morning.
- Form an S corporation if
  - You make under $100,000.
  - You have some liability exposure or nonfamily employees.
  - You meet all the S corporation rules.

- To be a qualified S corporation:
  - You must have fewer than 100 stockholders.
  - It must be a domestic corporation only.
  - There must be only one class of stock.
  - There must be only individual owners and some limited trusts and estates.
  - All investors must be citizens or residents of the United States. No foreign investors allowed. Sorry!
- S corporations are corporations. You have the same formalities as a regular corporation. If you won't strictly adhere to them, don't operate as any form of corporation.
- When forming any corporation, make sure that you qualify for Section 1244, which enables you to take your stock losses as ordinary losses and not as capital losses on your tax return.
- When forming any corporation, don't forget that you may be able to avoid between 50 and 60 percent of the gain on the sale of your corporate stock if it's qualified small-business stock.
- Limited-liability corporations don't have formalities, and they protect against liabilities as well as corporations. Form a LLC when
  - You will have some liability exposure or have substantial assets in the business.
  - You make or expect to make substantially more than $97,500 per year.
  - You can't qualify as an S corporation.
  - You don't need to accumulate capital for inventories.
- If you have a few owners in a corporation, partnership, or LLC, definitely have your lawyer draft a buy/sell agreement that outlines the formula and mechanism and establishes a price to buy out a partner/co-owner. This is crucial—and you will thank your lucky stars that this book prompted you to do so.

Notes

1. Information obtained from Nevada Corporate Planners and Nevada Corporate Headquarters.
2. Sections 722 and 742 of the IRC.
3. Section 708(b)(1)(B) of the IRC.
4. *Estate of Bischoff*, 69 TC 32 (1977); *Estate of James Barudin*, T.C. Memo 1996-395 et al.
5. Section 469 of the IRC.
6. Section 125 of the IRC.
7. Proposed Regulation 1.125-1 of the ITR.
8. Section 1244(b)(1) of the IRC.
9. Section 1244(b)(2) of the IRC.
10. Sections 448 and 11(b)(2) of the IRC.
11. Sections 1361-1363 of the IRC.

12. Sections 1374 and 1375 of the IRC provide that there could be some tax at the 35 percent rate if you were previously a regular corporation with some prior accumulated earnings and profits. Check with your accountant if you are a regular corporation and want to convert to an S corporation.
13. Sections 61, 3121(a), 3306(b), Revenue Ruling 73-361, 1973-2 CB 331.
14. Section 1244 of the IRC.
15. Section 1366(d)(1)(A) of the IRC.
16. Section 1361(b)(1)(A) of the IRC.
17. Section 1361(c)(1) of the IRC.
18. Section 1361(b)(1) of the IRC.
19. Section 1361(b)(2) of the IRC.
20. Section 1361(b)(1)(B) of the IRC.
21. Section 1361(b)(1)(C) of the IRC.
22. Section 1361(b)(1)(D) of the IRC.
23. Taxpayer Relief Act of 1997 (P.L. 105-34), Section 935 (8/5/97).

10

Forming a Nevada Corporation or a Limited-Liability Corporation in Nevada

The trick is to stop thinking of it as your money.

—**IRS auditor**

Chapter Overview
Where do many movie stars form corporations? Where do most con artists form corporations? You may be surprised that these two questions have the same answer—Nevada. In fact, some of the infamous Enron partnerships were located in Nevada or in foreign jurisdictions. What these diverse groups know that you don't will be the subject of this chapter. We also will examine some of the benefits of incorporating in Nevada rather than in Delaware.

This chapter won't be long or complicated, but you'll find the information contained here to be very interesting and possibly vital to you. Perhaps this chapter really should be titled, "What the Rich Know That You Should Know." There are two major myths about incorporating in Nevada that I encounter all the time:

Myth 1: *Incorporating in Nevada will result in lower costs.* Nothing could be further from the truth. In fact, it's usually cheaper to incorporate in your home state. The reason is that Nevada has a number of fees that many states don't have, and although Nevada has no corporate income tax, you usually have to file a corporate tax return in the states where you're doing business as a nonresident. Thus you won't save money.

Myth 2: *Incorporating in Nevada will result in lower taxes.* This may be the most widespread myth of all. The truth is that incorporating in Nevada will *not* save any taxes whatsoever. You'll still have to file in many states as a nonresident. The reason that this myth is so pervasive is that some of the more unscrupulous incorporating companies emphasize the extreme privacy that Nevada provides (which will be discussed below) and, in effect, imply that no one will find out. This is not necessarily the case and is not legally correct either. Say it three times: "Incorporating in Nevada will *not* save you taxes!"

Thus, if it doesn't save taxes or costs, why do it? This is a good question. There are several good reasons to incorporate in Nevada instead of Delaware, which also has some good laws for business.

Why the Rich, the Famous, and the Crooked Incorporate in Nevada[1]

1. Greatest protection from liability. This is easily the number one reason for incorporating in Nevada.

There is a well-known legal concept called *piercing the corporate veil.* This is the process by which a court removes the protection provided to individual members of a corporation and holds these members responsible. Simply put, you'll become liable for corporate debts and obligations if the veil of your corporation can be pierced. Each state applies different tests for determining whether the court can pierce the corporate veil and hold the shareholders liable.

In many states, it's easier for this to happen than many people realize. In fact—and this may surprise you—here are the top states that allow this, in the order of occurrence[2]: California, Florida, Georgia, Louisiana, Texas, New York, and Pennsylvania. For example, many states require a lot of capitalization (or net assets) for a corporation to be respected and not pierced. In most states, the minimum capitalization is $1,000. In Nevada, it's $100. In addition, many states will hold you, as owner/officer, liable for corporate debts and obligations if you didn't adhere to the yearly formalities that I discussed in Chapter 9 concerning stockholder meetings, corporate minutes, and board of directors meetings. Nevada is much more liberal about this and usually won't pierce the veil and make the owners/officers liable for corporate debts if they haven't adhered to all the formalities.

In a famous Nevada case, *Rowland v. Lepire,*[3] the corporation committed many acts that in most states would have made the stockholders/officers liable for the corporate debts. There was minimal capitalization. There were no formal board of directors or stockholder meetings. No dividends were paid. Officers didn't receive salaries. No corporate minutes were kept or any evidence that they were ever kept. However, the corporation had a checking account in the corporate name and licenses in the corporate name. The Nevada court held that the corporate veil could not be pierced unless fraud was shown.

Author's note: Despite this great case, I would follow the formalities that I mentioned in Chapter 9. However, the case shows how far Nevada will go to protect officers and stockholders of businesses incorporated there. The catch is that the courts won't allow this protection if it can be shown that the officers committed fraud or certain other special acts, such as malpractice.

Author's observation: Based on the information researched by one of the Nevada incorporating companies,[4] Nevada has allowed a piercing of the corporate veil, thus making the stockholders liable for corporate debts, only once in 23 years! If you think about it, this is amazing.

2. Higher degree of privacy. The shareholders names are not part of the public record.[5] Many companies actually use nominees as directors so that it's difficult to find even the names of the directors. In addition, Nevada is less willing than many other states to share information about its corporations with other states and with the federal government. This also ensures a little more privacy. However, if you register in another state to do business, you may have to list the shareholders.

Author's note: Recently, I discussed this issue with various Nevada incorporators.[6] Their view is that Nevada may share information a little more freely than before owing to the terrorist activities occurring in this country. This would be especially true with the federal government. However, there's more privacy in Nevada than in other states.

3. No joint and several liability. In many states, if you are found jointly liable for a debt, you could be responsible for the entire debt if it can't be collected in whole or part from the other debtors. In Nevada, the courts must assign a percentage of responsibility. Every owner found liable is required to pay a share of the judgment no greater than his or her responsibility. Thus, if you and nine others owe $1 million, the courts would have to determine what percentage of the $1 million is your responsibility. You would not be held responsible for the others' shares if they weren't collectible.

Differences Between Nevada and Delaware for Small Corporations

You might have heard that Delaware is also a great state for incorporating. Delaware protects stockholders, especially in public corporations, by giving them lots of rights and remedies. For example, Delaware corporate takeover laws are some of the most stringent in the country.

However, for small corporations, Nevada has some advantages over Delaware:

- Nevada protects officers from liability even if they didn't necessarily act "in good faith." Delaware has no such provision.
- Nevada provides greater protection for officers against monetary damages and other types of damages than Delaware.
- Nevada protects a director even if there was a breach of his or her duty of loyalty to the corporation. No such protection exists in Delaware.
- Nevada does not require disclosure of the corporation's principal business. Delaware has no such privacy provision.
- Nevada does not require that a corporation disclose any locations or main offices located outside the state. This is not necessarily true in Delaware.
- Nevada has no corporate income tax. Delaware has an 8.7 percent corporate income tax.

The bottom line is that Nevada offers a slightly greater degree of privacy and confidentiality than provided by other states and, more important, offers some of the strongest protection possible from liabilities for stockholders, officers, and directors.

Avoidance of Sales Tax Problems and Other Liabilities

 Some of the thorniest problems for small businesses are the filing of sales tax and income tax returns in many states. The problem is that many states require companies to file a sales tax return and, in many cases, an income tax return if they do any business in that state.

Most states have an allocation formula for determining how much income is taxed in the state. You're allowed to allocate your income to other states based on your assets in each state, the employees in each state, and the income earned in each state. For example, your corporation might earn $100,000 but do very little business in California and have no employees, no office, and no assets in California. Thus the actual tax owed might be only $100, or you might even have a corporate loss. Yet California, like a few other states, assesses a flat tax of $800 for companies that have a lower tax liability.

Even worse, if you had to file state sales tax returns in each state, you could be paying more in accounting fees than you would owe in taxes, fees that could add up to tens of thousands of dollars. For a small business with little capital, this cost could be catastrophic. Thus, owing to the cost involved, many small businesses "ignore" filing returns.

However, if these states find out that you failed to file the appropriate returns, you could be hit with huge penalties, plus interest, plus the taxes owed. Even worse, your home state usually enforces these obligations and may even prevent you from doing business until these obligations are paid. Thus what can small businesses do?

The answer that many of the top accounting firms are recommending is to set up a corporation or limited-liability corporation (LLC) just for the business conducted in the aggressive states, such as California. Then, if a state attacks this entity for not filing or for past-due taxes, all other entities are protected.

Author's note: If you are doing business in various states, I would strongly advise you to contact a major accounting firm that specializes in state tax issues. States have made deals to allow one filing to take care of many problems. Hopefully, the federal government eventually will step in and help to solve this problem for small businesses.

Author's note: You may have read about the many partnerships that Enron set up that led to its collapse. One of the reasons Enron did this was to insulate the liabilities for each entity so that if one entity had problems, they wouldn't affect the others. In addition, it ensures greater privacy: One entity may be uncovered, but not necessarily the other entities. This is one big reason why most Enron partnerships were formed outside the United States. Essentially, this technique is used for a wide variety of potential problems.

Summary

- Incorporating in Nevada will not be less costly or save you taxes.
- Incorporating in Nevada will provide some of the strongest liability protection of officers and directors of any of the states.
- Incorporating in Nevada will give you greater privacy than in most other states, unless you register in other states.
- In many cases, incorporating or forming an LLC in Nevada will avoid a lot of possible joint and several liability problems.
- As shown with Enron, forming separate entities such as corporations, limited partnerships, and limited-liability corporations will limit the liability problems to that entity and not taint other assets.[7]

Notes

1. Much of the information presented was provided by Scott Letourneau of Nevada Corporate Planners. If you need to consult with him about forming a Nevada corporation, you can reach the company at 888-627-7007 or www.nvinc.com.

2. *Cornell Law Review*, Vol. 76 (1991), p. 1050.

3. *Rowland v. Lepire*, 662 P.2d 1332 (1983).

4. Nevada Corporate Planners.

5. Nevada Secretary of State Web site at sos.state.nv.us/comm_rec/whyinc.htm.

6. Nevada Corporate Planners, Nevada Department of Revenue.

7. Nevada Corporate Planners.

11

How to Eliminate up to 40 percent of Your Social Security and Medicare Tax with an S Corporation

It's a game. We [tax lawyers] teach the rich how to play it so they can stay rich—and the IRS keeps changing the rules so we can keep getting rich teaching them.
—John Grisham, lawyer and author, *The Firm*

I should note that this chapter won't be long or complicated. In fact, it will probably be one of the shortest in the book. However, don't let the short length fool you. The tax benefits here alone could make you a millionaire, if you invest the tax savings yearly.

> **Chapter Overview**
> Have you ever heard that tax planning is beneficial only to the rich and not to Middle America? Well, this is a myth, as you now know from the previous chapters, which offered information applicable to everyone.
>
> However, this chapter is different. It primarily applies to Middle America and not the rich, since it works best for taxpayers who have a net income, after business deductions, of $97,500 or less per person. It is a proven loophole that accountants have been using for decades—using an S corporation to eliminate self-employment tax.

Overview of Taxation for S Corporations

Unless you converted from a regular corporation to an S corporation[1], an S corporation is not subject to any tax.[2]

You would compute the corporation's gross income and subtract any business deductions to arrive at the net taxable income. You would

165

then file an individual return on your pro-rata share of the corporation's net income or loss.[3] The S corporation would not pay any tax on the income.

Example: Mary is a 50 percent shareholder in an S corporation. The corporation had gross sales of $500,000 and deductions of $400,000, for a net income of $100,000. Since Mary owns 50 percent of the stock, she would pay tax on onehalf of the $100,000, which is $50,000.

Author's note: You pay tax on the net income of the corporation whether or not it's distributed to you. Thus, if all the income were left in the corporation for growth, Mary would still pay tax on $50,000. This undistributed amount would raise her stock basis, however, as if she had paid $50,000 more for stock. If she receives any dividends, this would reduce the basis.

Some income items and deductions get separately stated on your individual return as if you'd earned them.[4] Thus, such income items as tax-exempt income and capital gains and some deductions, such as charitable contributions, would be separately stated on your Form 1040 as if you'd earned these items.

The key to saving Social Security taxes is that with an S corporation you pay self-employment tax on wages, salaries, and bonuses but not on dividends.[5] Your share of undistributed earnings is deemed dividends and not wages and is treated as any actual dividend distribution. Let me repeat this again because it is worth repeating: *dividends and undistributed earnings are not subject to self-employment tax.*

Thus, the key is to pay yourself as little in salary as possible and as much in dividends as possible and wipe out most of your Social Security tax.

Example: John has a net income of $80,000 from his S corporation. If he receives this amount in the form of salary, all of it would be subject to self-employment tax at the 15.3 percent rate, so he would pay $12,240. If, however, John pays himself a reasonable salary of $40,000 and takes the other $40,000 as a dividend, he would save 15.3 percent on the dividend, a savings of $6,120 each year that he does this! Not bad, huh?

You may be thinking that this sounds fabulous. Why not pay zero salary and take all the earnings as dividends and completely eliminate all selfemployment tax? Unfortunately, the IRS has thought of this.[6] The IRS requires you to pay yourself a "reasonable" salary. If you don't, the entire dividend and undistributed portion of the net income from the S corporation will be reclassified as wages, which are fully subject to self-employment tax. Yuck! In fact, all taxpayers who didn't understand this rule have ended up losing in court.

My favorite case involved an attorney named Joseph Radtke.[7] Radtke thought the same way. He formed an S corporation and paid himself no salary. He treated the entire net income as a dividend. The tax court rightly reclassified the dividend as wages, and poor Radtke had to pay self-employment tax on the entire amount. Thus, you must pay yourself some reasonable salary.

What Is a "Reasonable" Salary?

Good question! The IRS defines "reasonable compensation" as what would ordinarily be paid for like services, by like enterprises (similar in size and business to your own), under like circumstances.[8] This is generally inter-preted to mean "what you would pay an outside agency or person to do the same duties."

There are a lot of factors that determine what is reasonable, such as:

- Actual services performed
- Responsibilities involved
- Time spent
- Size and complexity of the business
- Prevailing economic conditions
- Compensation paid by comparable firms for comparable services
- Salary paid to company officers in prior years

Sadly, as you can see, the factors are not very clear. I would highly recom-mend that you check with a good accountant or tax attorney when setting any salaries and bonuses for you. Get comparable salaries from government publications.

Author's note: Most people want a nice flat number or a flat percentage of income as the litmus test for reasonable compensation. Sadly, I can't give a number, because it varies from business to business and according to a number of factors. However, from the many cases that I have read, I have found that in most cases where salary paid was approximately between 40 percent and 60 percent of net income, this amount has been deemed reasonable.[9] Also, if there are unrelated minority stockholders, if they approve some compensation for the officers who are also majority stock-holders, courts tend to give weight to this approval from the Board of Directors or stockholders, since the minority stockholders would then be receiving less in dividends.[10] The bottom line: check with a good account-ant and tax lawyer about setting any salaries and bonuses in order to min-imize your salary and minimize your self-employment tax. Here, an ounce of prevention is worth a bundle in wealth!

Summary

- This strategy is especially great for Middle America.
- S corporation salaries and bonuses are subject to self-employment tax.
- Dividends and undistributed earnings (which are treated as dividends) are not subject to self-employment.
- If you're an S corporation, pay yourself as little as possible in salary, as long as it's reasonable, and as much as possible in dividends.
- Use a good accountant and/or tax attorney to help you establish what a minimum reasonable salary should be. Failure to do this would be a hazard to your wealth.

Notes

1. Section 1374(a) of the IRC. This deals with built-in gains where you have accumulated earnings and profits for a regular corporation. If you started as an S corporation and never operated this entity as a regular corporation, this is not an issue.
2. Section 1363(a) of the IRC.
3. Section 1366 of the IRC.
4. Section 1366 of the IRC.
5. Section 1402(a) of the IRC.
6. Revenue Ruling 74-44, 1974-1 CB 287.
7. *Joseph Radtke v. United States*, 895 F.2d 1196 (7th Cir. 1990).
8. Section 1.162-7(b) of the ITR.
9. *Hamilton and Co.*, T.C. Memo 1959-153.
10. *Gilles Frozen Custard, Inc.*, T.C. Memo 1970-73; *William J. Hertz*, T.C. Memo 1998-210.

12

How to Get Assets and Money into a Corporation Tax-Free

Forming a corporation is similar to getting married. It is easy to get into but much harder to get out of.

—Sandy Botkin

Many times people want to start their corporate business by transferring personal assets to their corporation. Let's face it—it's certainly a lot cheaper and easier to use assets that you already own than to purchase new assets.

You can transfer property to a corporation easily and tax-free if you

Chapter Overview
- You'll learn about the requirements for transferring property tax-free to a corporation.
- You'll be aware of the congressional "gotchas" and how to avoid them.
- You'll understand why you should rarely own real estate in a corporate name, especially in regular corporation.
- You'll understand the IRS filing requirements that will keep your transfers tax-free.

know what you're doing. Generally, no gain or loss is recognized on the transfer of property to a corporation solely in exchange for stock in that corporation.[1]

Author's note: As noted, you can't take any loss on the transfer. Thus you generally should *not* transfer property that would result in a tax loss to you if you sold it. You're better off selling the property and taking the loss. You then can transfer the net cash received to the corporation.

To have no gain or loss apply, you must meet certain easy conditions:

1. You must transfer assets. It can be almost any property, such as other stock, real estate, cash, patents, copyrights, etc.[2] In fact, there's a lot of flexibility. However, and this is a *big however,* you cannot transfer services for

169

stock tax-free. It doesn't matter if the services have been rendered in the past or will be rendered in the future.[3] If you do, you will be taxed as ordinary income on the fair market value of what you receive.[4] If you both transfer property and render services for the stock, you will be taxed as compensation (ordinary income) on the portion of the stock received that applies only to the services.

Example: Ted and Carol form a corporation, and each receives 50 percent of the stock. Ted transfers $100,000 cash and Carol performs some legal services and incorporation services and transfers $50,000 cash. Since some of the stock that Carol received was for services, she would be taxed on the portion that relates to the services.

2. You must receive stock for your property.[5] This sounds very clear-cut, but there are a few issues that you should know about. First, *stock* means stock and not warrants, calls, puts, or any other options.[6] Second, it doesn't have to be solely for voting stock. It can even be preferred stock if you want some investors to get preferences as to dividends.

For those who don't know what preferred stock is, here's a great definition: *Preferred stock* is "stock that is limited and preferred as to dividends and does *not* participate in corporate growth to any significant extent."[7] Thus preferred stockholders would get a flat, fixed dividend, similar to a bond. They don't get to vote and don't benefit significantly from the growth or equity of the company. In addition, if the company makes a lot of money, the preferred stockholders don't get larger dividends. The use of preferred stock is normally to fix the value for estate planning and to bring in investors who want greater security in their dividends.

3. After the transfer, you must control at least 80 percent of the voting stock and at least 80 percent of all other shares of any other class of stock.[8] This simply means that you can have some stockholders getting voting stock and some getting other types of stock, such as nonvoting or preferred stock, as long as everyone together owns at least 80 percent of the voting stock and 80 percent of all the shares of the other stock.[9]

Author's note: If you and some others are organizing a newly formed corporation, you will, in all probability, receive over 80 percent control of all stock. Thus this third requirement is not normally a problem for new corporations. Also, and this is important, if you want to give away your stock (such as to your children or grandchildren) after the transfer, you may do so as long as you're not obligated to retransfer the stock. All stock should be issued to you first; then you can do with it as you please, as far as the Internal Revenue Service (IRS) is concerned.[10]

Traps in Transferring Property to a New Corporation

The bad news is that Congress created several traps that would result in tax to you on incorporating. The good news is that I'll show you how to avoid them easily.

Trap 1: Don't Place a Debt on Transferred Property Right before Forming the Corporation

As I said earlier, when you transfer property for stock in a corporation, you avoid all gains and losses. The corporation can even assume your indebtedness on the transferred property without any gain recognized by you or any other person who transfers property.[11] However, if it appears that the principal purpose of the assumption of debt was to avoid federal income tax on the exchange, then the debt will be treated as money received and taxed to you.[12] Yuck!

Author's note: Generally, if a debt has been on the property for a while, at least one year, you won't have a problem. If you place the debt on the property just within the last four to six months,[13] you'd better have a great reason for doing this. An example of a good reason actually given by the IRS would be to replace an existing debt on property.[14] Another good reason, in my opinion, would be to refinance an existing debt at a lower interest rate.

Example: Sue transfers for stock property worth $200,000, but with a debt of $50,000; the corporation assumes Sue's debt on the property. This would be a tax-free transfer.

Example: Assuming that Sue placed the debt on the property two months before transferring the property to the corporation, she probably would be taxed on the liability assumed by the corporation because the transfer was to avoid taxes.

Trap 2: Don't Receive Cash or Other Property Back from the Corporation

You must transfer property for stock. If you receive anything else besides stock, such as cash or other property, you will be taxed on the receipt of the cash or property received.[15]

Example: Mike and Gloria transfer property to form their corporation. Mike transfers $100,000 in cash, and Gloria transfers real estate worth $120,000 but gets the same amount of stock as Mike. If Gloria receives back $20,000 in order to equalize the transfer, she will be taxed on the $20,000 that she receives.

Trap 3: Don't Transfer Any Property That Has Debt Greater than Your Basis[16]

What does this mean? This is where you transfer property whose adjusted basis to you (cost plus improvements less depreciation taken) is less than the debt on the property. This can happen in a number of ways.

Example: You pay only $100,000 for some real estate that skyrockets to $600,000 in value. You then go to a bank and refinance the property and get a loan for 80 percent of the value, or $480,000. Your basis was $100,000, which is what you paid,[17] but your loan on the property is now $480,000, which is $380,000 more than your basis. If you transfer this property with this debt, you will pay tax on the $380,000! How's that for a congressional "gotcha"?

This also can happen if you take a lot of depreciation but your debt gets paid off over a longer period than the depreciation. Your property could be completely written off, but you still have some debt.

Author's note: There's a great way around this problem. In fact, if you ever have this problem, this book will pay for itself many times over.

Here's the IRS rule: You pay tax on the excess of your liabilities over your basis of the property transferred, but it's the sum of *all* the liabilities for each transferor over the sum of *all* the adjusted bases of the properties transferred by each transferor.[18] What this means to you is this: Transfer more property to the corporation so that the *total* basis of what you transfer exceeds the *total* debt on the transferred property.

Example: Calvin transfers some real estate to a corporation for stock. His real estate has a basis of $50,000, but there's a mortgage of $100,000 on the property. If Calvin transfers this property alone for stock, he would pay tax on $50,000. Thus he should either not transfer this property or add some other property so that the total basis equals or exceeds the total debt. Thus, if he also adds $50,000 in cash as part of the transfer, his total basis in the real estate and cash is $100,000, which equals the debt. Thus no tax! Pretty slick, isn't it?

If Possible, Don't Transfer Real Estate to a Regular Corporation

As my opening quote notes, it's hard to get property out of a corporation, especially a regular corporation. If you have real estate in the corporation that appreciates in value, which real estate tends to do, you may have to pay tax at the corporate level on the appreciation whenever you sell the property or liquidate the corporation[19] and probably pay tax at your individual level, too. That's double taxation! There are ways around it with reorganizations, etc., but it takes some knowledgeable tax planning.

The rich have known this for years. Thus what many top tax experts are recommending is to form an LLC or a limited partnership that would own the real estate and then lease it to the corporation. In this way, you don't have to worry about the real estate appreciation being "trapped" in the corporation, and you or your family members can receive the lease payments. Thus you can shift income to your family at lower tax brackets. Even better, you don't need to worry about the liability being over the basis because the property wasn't transferred to the corporation. Finally, you can take a deduction for the depreciation of the real estate on your individual tax return or the tax return of your family members if they're part owners. The real estate losses and depreciation won't be locked into the corporation because a flowthrough entity owns the real estate, so all losses flow through to you and your family or the owners of the flowthrough entity. What a great country this is!

Don't Forget to Attach the Required Schedules to Your Tax Return

There's a price for all these nice tax-free goodies: You get to somewhat enrich your accountant. The IRS requires a statement to your tax return noting a complete description of the property transferred, a complete description of what you received in exchange (including other property received), a complete description of the stock received, and a description of any liabilities that were assumed.[20] In addition, if this isn't bad enough, you need to attach a similar description to the corporate tax return.[21]

Summary

- To transfer property to a corporation tax-free, transfer it for the stock in the corporation.
- Do not receive warrants or options. This isn't deemed stock.
- The stock can be preferred stock as long as there's no mandatory buyback.
- Don't transfer property that would result in a loss if sold. You will lose the loss. It's better to sell the property and transfer the cash instead.
- Don't transfer services for stock, or you'll be taxed on the fair market value of the stock attributable for those services.
- All the transferors in total should own at least 80 percent of the voting stock and 80 percent of all shares of other stock issued.
- You can have the corporation assume any liabilities on the transferred property. Just don't place any liabilities on the property within one year

(to be safe) before the transfer, unless you have one heck of a good corporate reason.

- Don't transfer property whose liabilities exceed your basis. If this is a problem, transfer other property so that the total basis of the properties transferred equals or exceeds the total of the liabilities assumed.
- Don't forget that if you receive anything other than stock from the transfer, you may pay tax on what you receive.
- Don't have a regular corporation own real estate. Do what the rich do: Form either an LLC or a limited partnership to own the real estate, and lease it to the corporation.

Notes

1. Section 351(a) of the IRC.
2. *George Holstein*, 23 T.C. 923 (1955); *DuPont de Nemours and Co. v. United States*, 471 F.2d 1211 (Ct. Cl.1973).
3. Section 1.351-1(a)(1)(i) of the ITR.
4. Section 351(d)(1) of the IRC and Section 1.351-1(a)(1) of the ITR.
5. Section 351(a) of the IRC.
6. Section 1.351-1(a)(1) of the ITR.
7. Section 351(g)(3)(A) of the IRC. I should note that when the preferred stock is sold, it could result in ordinary income and not capital gain under Section 306 of the IRC.
8. Sections 351 and 368(c) of the IRC.
9. *Marsan Realty Corp.*, T.C. Memo 1963-297; see also IRS Letter Ruling 8230028.
10. *Wilgard Realty Co., Inc. v. Commissioner*, 127 F.2d 514 (2nd Cir. 1942).
11. Section 357(a) of the IRC.
12. Section 357(b)(1)(A).
13. *W. H. B. Simpson v. Commissioner*, 43 T.C. 900 (1965); *W. H. Weaver v. Commissioner*, 32 T.C. 411 (1959); *Drybrough v. Commissioner*, 376 F.2d 350 (6th Cir. 1967).
14. Revenue Ruling 79-258 1979-2 CB 143.
15. Section 351(b)(1) of the IRC.
16. Section 357(c)(1) of the IRC.
17. For purposes of simplicity, I've ignored any depreciation that you may have taken. This would reduce your basis.
18. Revenue Ruling 66-142, 1966-1 CB 66.
19. Section 336(a) of the IRC.
20. Section 1.351-3(a) of the ITR.
21. Section 1.351-3(b) of the ITR.

Part 3

Every Fringe Benefit Available to Small and Home-Based Businesses

The following table summarizes the many deductions discussed in Chapters 13 and 14. (Legend: C = Corporations; P = Partnerships; SP = Sole Proprietorships)

Benefit	Available to	Discrimination Allowable?	Limitation on benefits to owners or highly compensated employees?	Other special rules and limitations
Working condition fringe benefit (tax-free use of equpment and services)	All entities, although proprietors deduct those as expenses	Yes	No limits	
No-additional-cost benefit	All	No	No limits	
Tax-free day care	All	No	Yes: no more than 25% of the benefits can go to 5% or more stockholders or owners	Limit: $5,000 per year and $2,500 for married filing separately
Adoption assistance	All with some limitations	No	No, but benefits phase out based on income	Limit: $10,960 per child Benefit starts phasing out as AGI goes over $164,450 and completely out at $204,450

Benefit	Available to	Discrimination Allowable?	Limitation on benefits to owners or highly compensated employees?	Other special rules and limitations
Health insurance	Fully deductible for all entities.	No	No limits	
Self-insured medical reimbursement plan	C, SP (with hiring spouse)	No, but exceptions exist (under age 25, less than three years of service, works less than 25 hours per week)	No limits, other than that overall wages must be reasonable	
Disability insurance	All except owners of SP	Yes, apparently	No limits	
De minimis fringe benefits and occasional supper money	All except owners of SP	Yes	No limits	
Qualified employee discounts	Yes	Yes, but some limited exclusions allowed	No limits	Maximum discount allowed: for services, 20% of normal charge; for property, sale price less profit margin
Gym and athletic facilities	All	No	No limits	
Retirement advice	All	No	No limits	
No-interest or low-interest loans	All except owners of SPs	Yes for loans under $10,000 No for mortgage loans	No limits	Exceptions: 1. Loans under $10,000 2. Relocation mortgage loans 3. Bridge loans

Benefit	Available to	Discrimination Allowable?	Limitation on benefits to owners or highly compensated employees?	Other special rules and limitations
Educational assistance plans	All	No	Yes: no more than 5% of benefits to 5% or more stockholders or owners	Limit: $5,250 per employee per year
Reimbursed dues for country and health clubs	All	Yes	No limits	Either company gets deduction or employee gets business use tax-free—but not both!
Company-provided trips for employees and spouses	All	Yes	No limits	For tax-free reimbursement for spouse, spouse must be licensed in business, work for company, or provide convention duties
Company purchase of homes	All except the owner of a SP	Yes	No limits	Used only when house depreciates in value from cost
Reimburse-ments for moving and relocation expenses	All	Yes	No limits	
Tax-free transportation, limos, and chauffeurs	All except owners of SPs and those not paid overtime for overtime work, which is usually salaried people	Yes, but not available to people who are exempt from Fair Labor Standards Act	No limits	Nice, but limited benefit: can't be provided tax-free to the ones to whom most businesses want to provide it— the major officers— unless they get paid time-and-a-half for overtime work

Benefit	Available to	Discrimination Allowable?	Limitation on benefits to owners or highly compensated employees?	Other special rules and limitations
Vanpools, transit passes, and free parking	All except owners of SPs and 2% or more stockholders of S corporations	Yes	Yes: not available to owners of SPs and 2% or more stockholders in S corporations	Monthly limit on qualified parking: $205 per employee Monthly limit on transit passes and vanpools: $105 per employee
Company-provided vehicles	All	Yes	No limits	The catch is how vehicles are taxed. Use cents per mile for vehicles that cost under $15,000, or use commuting method if available. If using annual lease value, company should pay for all insurance, repairs, and gas.
Cafeteria plan	All	No	Yes, strict (next column)	Limits on owners and officers. No more than 25% of benefits can go to any officer who earns over $130K or any 5% or more stockholder. No more than 25% of benefits can go to any 1% or more stockholder who earns over $150K.
Restricted stock	C	Yes	No limits	Taxation occurs at earlier of two dates: when stock is sold or when restrictions lapse. Company gets deduction when employee gets taxed.

Benefit	Available to	Discrimination Allowable?	Limitation on benefits to owners or highly compensated employees?	Other special rules and limitations
Phantom stock	C	Yes	No limits	
Qualified stock options	C	Yes	Yes: not available for 10% or more stockholders unless strike price is 110% of market value at time of grant and option is exercised within five years of grant	Limit: generally $100,000 per year of stock per employee. Employee can get long-term capital gains rates on stock sale. However, there are specific rules that both the corporation and the employee must follow or it becomes ordinary income to the employee.
Tax-free lodging	All except owners of SPs	Yes	No limits	
Tax-free meals	All except owners of SPs	No, with some exceptions for restaurant employees, emergency work, and lunch conferences	No limits	Many ways: 1. Short business meal 2. Employees live on premises 3. Meals furnished for restaurant employees 4. Meals furnished if employees must be available during lunch for emergencies 5. If no nearby eating facilities 6. Meals provided to over 50% of staff 7. Staff lunch meetings and conferences

Benefit	Available to	Discrimination Allowable?	Limitation on benefits to owners or highly compensated employees?	Other special rules and limitations
Qualified pension and profit sharing	All	No, but some exceptions, such as three-year waiting period	No limits to certain people but overall contribution limits	Recommended plans: 1. Profit sharing: best for companies with varying incomes, limit: $45,000 2. SEPs: great especially if few employees, contribution limit: $45,000 3. Simple IRAs: best for companies with many employees, limit: $10,000 plus company contribution 4. Defined benefit: great for older employees, contribution limit: $175,000

13

Fringe Benefits You Will Love, Part 1

The proper avoidance of taxes is the only intellectual pursuit that still carries any reward.

—John Maynard Keynes, economist,
***Economic Consequences of the Peace* (1920)**

One of the biggest questions that I get at my seminars is, "How do I get money tax-free out of my corporate business?" The answer is to establish a load of tax-free fringe benefits. In fact, this chapter could be subtitled, "Getting Money Out of a Corporation Tax-Free."

If starting a successful small business is the engine behind riches, then fringe benefits are the wheels and the frame around this engine.

You've probably heard about how many of the big, rich corporations are providing a host of benefits to their employees. The interesting fact is that most of these benefits can be provided

Chapter Overview
• Learn about one of the fringe benefits that all corporations should have: tax-free use of property, equipment, and services, also known as *working-condition fringe benefits.*
• Understand the little-known way to get many fringe benefits with the no-extra-cost approach.
• Learn how to get day-care assistance for you and your employees on a tax-free basis.
• Understand the new and improved rules for company-provided adoption assistance.
• Learn why you should get your medical, dental, and nursing home insurance for yourself and your employees tax-free.
• Set up a self-insured medical reimbursement plan.

by small businesses as well. It's just that most small business owners never find out about what choices are available to them.

Author's note: The myth that "my accountant takes care of my taxes" has kept people ignorant about all the amazing fringe benefits that are available.

You will find some fabulous information in this chapter that, in many cases, isn't available elsewhere. It will give you a good overview of every available fringe benefit that I can suggest for small and mid-sized businesses. Use the various benefits as a checklist for your business.

Although time and space do not permit me to discuss every detail involved in all fringe benefits, and a whole book could be devoted to this subject alone, I give a good overview of what's required to establish each benefit and to bulletproof the benefit from the Internal Revenue Service (IRS). I also discuss any drawbacks to each benefit that you should be aware of, such as discrimination problems.

I should note that I discuss only benefits that would be available to small-business owners and not necessarily only to publicly traded corporations, although all the benefits mentioned here can and have been used by even the biggest companies.

Pay particular attention to which benefits can be offered to both owners and employees, which benefits can be offered only if you don't discriminate (which would be most of the benefits), and which benefits have limitations on what can be offered to owner/stockholders. In addition, although all these

---

Chapter Overview (Cont.)

- Learn about providing tax-free disability insurance, and understand the one IRS loophole to obtaining the benefits tax-free.
- Understand the little-known de minimis fringe benefits.
- Learn when you can give property at a sizable discount to employees (qualified employee discounts).
- Learn how you can deduct your exercise equipment and set up a gym courtesy of the IRS.
- Have your company provide retirement advice tax-free.
- Learn how to get a low-interest or even no-interest loan from your company tax-free.
- Learn how you can get your company to pay for employee educational expenses and have them be tax-free to the recipient.
- Understand the rules for obtaining as much as $5,250 per year of educational assistance for employees' children for college costs tax-free.
- Learn when you can pay country club and health club dues and have the benefit be tax-free to the employee.
- Understand when company-provided trips to wonderful destinations can be tax-free.
- Learn about the benefit to your company of buying your home and getting all those closing costs tax-free.
- Learn why your company should provide tax-free moving expenses for you and your employees.
- Learn about when you can have employer-provided transportation, such as limos and chauffeurs, tax-free.

benefits assume that you're operating as a corporation, many also apply to other entities, such as limited-liability corporations (LLCs) and sole proprietorships. All in all, using the information in this chapter will result in huge tax savings that will pay for this book many times over.

Author's note: For a number of benefits, you cannot discriminate in favor of highly compensated individuals, stockholders, or owners of a 5 percent or more of stock or profit interest. Highly compensated people for purposes of this book are people who make over $100,000 per year or who own 5 percent or more of the stock or who own 5 percent or more of the business. Thus, throughout Part 3 of this book, this is what I mean when I state that you can't discriminate in favor of highly compensated people.

Tax-Free Use of Property, Equipment, and Services

You're going to like this. This is one of the broadest ways to obtain tax-free fringe benefits. This benefit is also known as *working-condition fringe benefits.* These types of benefits are defined as "any property or services given to an employee by an employer that would have been deductible or depreciable by the employee as a business expense had the employee paid for the property or services."[1] It applies, however, only to employees and not to their dependents—sorry![2] Here are some examples:

- Most business publications
- Business-oriented books
- Use of employer-provided cars to the extent used for business
- Computers used for business
- Cell phones
- Fax machines
- Memberships in business-oriented associations
- Memberships to business-oriented Web sites
- Job-placement assistance if it results in some benefit to the employer, such as raising the morale of remaining workers, and the placement is in the same or similar trade or business

Example: Sam runs his insurance business as a corporation. He wants to receive memberships in the local Chamber of Commerce and life underwriters association. He also wants to receive various publications for insurance agents and various sales publications. His corporation may provide Sam with these memberships and subscriptions as tax-free working-condition fringe benefits because Sam could have deducted the cost of these publications and memberships had he spent the money himself.

Author's note: You may be wondering why a working-condition fringe benefit is such a good deal because the employee could have deducted the cost of such an item anyway. Good question! The reason is that when an employee takes a deduction for business-related expenses, it's as an itemized, nonbusiness deduction. These types of deductions have phaseouts and must exceed a threshold amount of 2 percent of your adjusted gross income (net income from a business plus wages, dividends, pensions, rents, etc.). However, if the employer provides these benefits, they are fully deductible by the corporation and tax-free to the employee. There are no phaseouts and no threshold amounts that they must exceed. Thus you get the full benefit of the deduction.

Example: Marjorie operates her network marketing business as an S corporation. She wants to subscribe to various home-based business publications and subscribe to special services for networkers, such as The Greatest Networker Web site maintained by the well-known John Milton Fogg George Madeau. If her corporation pays for these subscriptions, she may receive these benefits tax-free.

Discrimination Is Fully Allowable

This is one benefit in which Congress allows for any type of discrimination, even if the benefit is provided only to the officers or directors or other highly compensated employees of the company. You just can't discriminate when providing any product testing. Don't ask me why![3]

Example: Sock'em Corporation provides cell phones and computers only to its executive officers. These benefits are fully deductible by Sock'em and tax-free to the employees even though they're not provided to all employees.

What Is an Employee?

The working-condition fringe benefit applies to employees. Strangely, however, Congress allows many people to be treated as employees that you would never have thought would qualify for this one benefit. For example, for purposes of this rule, *employees* would include partners and members of the board of directors (although board members can't be used in any product testing).[4] In addition, independent contractors are allowed to be given working-condition fringe benefits on a tax-free basis as long as they don't involve parking or product testing.[5] Self-employed owners are not deemed employees under this rule; however, they can deduct these items anyway as business deductions without any limitation. Thus, in effect, they get the benefits too.

Author's note: I often wonder what Congress was thinking when it carved out such limited exceptions as product testing and parking for independent contractors. This simply adds needless complexity for some narrow exceptions.

Consumer Testing of Products by Employees

Your corporation can provide employees with products to test and evaluate that are manufactured by you for sale to customers. However, to avoid taxation of the employee on the receipt or use of these products, you must meet the following conditions[6]:

- It would be a normal expense of the employer (which is usually the case).
- Valid business reasons necessitate that the products be tested off the premises of the employer.
- The products are indeed furnished for testing and evaluation.
- The products are available to the employee for a period that isn't longer than needed for testing and evaluation.
- At the end of the testing period, the item is returned to the employer.
- The employee must submit detailed reports on his or her evaluation.
- The length of the testing and evaluation period is reasonable for the product.
- The employer imposes strict limits on personal use, such as a prohibition against nonemployees using the product.[7]
- The employer does not discriminate against highly compensated people in the testing unless it can show a good reason.

No-Additional-Cost Fringe Benefits

A company may provide services to employees on a tax-free basis and IRS bulletproof this benefit if it meets these conditions:

- The services are offered to customers in the ordinary course of business.
- The company doesn't incur substantial additional cost in providing these benefits.[8]

You could provide services at no additional cost, for example, when you have excess capacity.

Example: The Shipandstore Corporation provides air transit services and hotel rooms to customers. If there are some free spaces in the plane or some unoccupied hotel rooms, the corporation may provide these tax-free to its employees.

The key to this fringe benefit is that the services offered are in the same line of business as the employer and normally are offered to nonemployee customers.

Example: The Foolproof Bank offers car washes to nonemployees in order to raise funds for charity. This is not the business of the bank, and free car washes provided to employees would not qualify as no-additional-cost fringe benefits.

Author's note: Even if the employee agrees to reimburse the employer for the increased cost, this would not qualify as a tax-free fringe benefit. The following example illustrates this point.

Example: High-Cost Computer, Inc. (HCC), repairs computers. Jane is an employee with some big computer problems. HCC fixes her computer. The normal retail cost to fix it would have been $500 for labor and materials, but the actual out-of-pocket cost would have been only $100. Even if Jane reimburses HCC for the $100 cost, she would be taxed on the $400 of extra benefit. This is not a no-additional-cost benefit because HCC paid $100 to provide $500 worth of benefits. Jane's reimbursement does not alter this fact.

Discrimination Toward Owners or Highly Compensated People *Not* Allowed

Sadly, you can't discriminate in favor of highly compensated people or owners of the business who hold 5 percent or more of the stock.[9]

The Bottom Line

For this benefit to be tax-free, the employer must not incur any extra cost, and the benefit provided must be the same services as provided to customers in the employer's normal course of business.

Tax-Free Day-Care Assistance

You can provide day care tax-free to all employees[10] up to a maximum of $5,000 per year ($2,500 if married filing separately).[11] The self-employed are considered employees under this rule. Hooray! Even partnerships can offer this benefit to partners who are treated as employees.[12] Moreover, you can either pay for the employees' day care directly or reimburse the employees for the expenses.[13] How's that for flexibility? However, you *cannot* discriminate in favor of highly compensated people or owners or stockholders who have a 5 percent or more interest in stock or profits of the company, and there are limitations on the benefits that can accrue to the owners as well. This will be discussed below.

Requirements to Bulletproof Tax-Free Day Care from the IRS

In order to receive this benefit tax-free, you must meet all the following requirements:

- The plan must provide employees with dependent care to children who are under age 13 or to any other dependents who are either physically or mentally incapable of caring for themselves.
- You must have a separate, written plan. It doesn't have to be long and fancy, but you must have a plan in writing that shows who will get the benefits and what these benefits will be. You also have to notify the other employees of the availability of this benefit. You just can't keep it secret. Nice try!
- A company cannot discriminate in favor of highly compensated employees, more than 5 percent owners, or more than 5 percent stockholders. However, even if a company is found to be discriminating, those employees who are not highly compensated or do not own 5 percent or more of the stock or more than 5 percent of the business will have their benefits tax-free.
- The employee must provide some documentation to the employer, such as the name, address, and Social Security Number or Taxpayer Identification Number of the provider. See your accountant about this.
- Even if you give this benefit to everyone, you can't have more than 25 percent of the total benefits go to any stockholder or business owner who owns more than 5 percent of the stock or the business.

Author's note: I personally find this extremely irritating, not to mention idiotic, that Congress would place a limit on the benefits available to owners even if they don't discriminate. This only complicates the tax law. Why place a limit on benefits to business owners if there's no discrimination? In addition, placing limits on benefit to owners hurts the small-business owner who may not have lots of employees, and in many cases, these people need the help the most.

I should note that you cannot have your child be the day-care provider if he or she is under age 19 by year's end or your dependent even if over age 19. Once your child hits age 19 and stops being your dependent, he or she can be a qualified provider for the other children.[14]

Author's note: The same rule would apply to any other relative, such as an employee's parents. If an employee pays one of his or her parents to take care of the employee's children, these payments would be tax-free if the parent was not a dependent of the employee. This might be a great way to get your parents some money and to take care of your child-care problems at the same time.

Company-Provided Adoption Assistance

There's a big demand from couples to adopt children. Because of this, Congress created a nice fringe benefit for adoption expenses. A company can set up a qualified plan and pay up to $11,390 of adoption expenses per child[15] on a tax-free basis.[16]

Qualifications Needed to Bulletproof This Benefit from the IRS

In order for a company to provide these benefits tax-free, the adoption assistance must meet the following criteria:

- The plan must be in writing, and all eligible employees must be notified.
- The plan must be nondiscriminatory. However, unlike the day-care assistance benefit, there's no limit on how much goes to the owners or stockholders. The plan just can't discriminate in favor of highly compensated people, 5 percent or more stockholders, or 5 percent or more owners.

Unfortunately, what Congress gives, it also takes away. The tax credit for the benefits starts phasing out as your adjusted gross income (AGI) exceeds $170,820 and completely phases out when your AGI exceeds $210,820.[17] As a reminder, your AGI generally means any net income from a business plus dividends, interest, rents, penalties, and wages, with a few further modifications. The following examples will illustrate how the phaseout works.

Example: John and Mary have an AGI of $190,820. If they receive from Mary's employer $6,000 of expenses, only one-half, or $3,000, is tax-free. The other $3,000 is taxable. The reason is that they earn $20,000 more than the allowable $170,820, halfway to the $40,000 phaseout. If their AGI were $180,820, one-fourth through the $40,000 phaseout range, one-fourth ($1,500) would be taxable and three-fourths ($4,500) would be tax-free.

Author's note: Although this is not a tax policy book, think about what Congress has done. This program essentially subsidizes poor to middle-class taxpayers to adopt children and discourages wealthy people, who can best afford children.

Tax-Free Health Insurance

One of the big disadvantages of being solely an employee (among the others mentioned in Chapter 1) is that you can deduct only medical insurance premiums and other medical expenses that exceed a very high threshold, 7.5 percent of your AGI—your net income from a business plus wages, interest, dividends, pensions, and some other modifications.[18] Thus, unless you have a huge amount of medical and dental expenses, you likely won't get any deduction for these expenses.

However, if you have a side business, your business can provide you and your employees and their families with health insurance 100 percent tax-free starting in the year 2003 and thereafter.[19] Moreover, you just need to pay for the insurance premiums. No written plan is required, and the benefit is available to all forms of business, whether incorporated, partnerships, or even self-employed.[20]

In fact, health insurance almost always should be provided owing to the tremendous flexibility of this benefit. For example, long-term care insurance is deemed to be health insurance,[21] as are Medicare supplement premiums.[22] Companies even can cover domestic partners, although for the payments to be tax-free for an employee, the domestic partner must qualify as a dependent of the employee.[23]

In addition, a company even can reimburse the employee for the insurance premiums paid under the following conditions[24]:

- The employer has a plan for health insurance coverage.
- The employer requires the employees to prove what actually was spent on health insurance.

Author's note: Being able to reimburse employees becomes essential, especially for small-business owners, whenever an employee would not be able to get coverage owing to preexisting conditions.

Finally, and this is my favorite benefit of providing health insurance premiums, the health insurance can be provided on a discriminatory basis. You just can't discriminate based on health factors,[25] and it must seem to cover employees, not just stockholders or owners.[26]

Example: Harry provides health insurance to all his full-time employees but charges a premium for those with prior health problems. This would be prohibited. However, if Harry provided health insurance to all the officers, regardless of health problems, and a lesser plan to other employees, this would be allowable.

The bottom line is that this is a great, flexible fringe benefit that most firms should provide regardless of size and regardless of entity.

Set Up a Self-Insured Medical Reimbursement Plan

This is a plan that covers all your medical expenses that are not covered by insurance, such as mileage to and from the doctor, deductibles, coinsurance, braces and other dental expenses, hearing aids, chiropractic therapy, over-the-counter medication that alleviates a medical condition, and much more. This is in addition to your health insurance. You're not dropping your health insurance coverage. See the detailed discussion in Chapter 4 on this topic.

Provide for Disability Insurance

Disability insurance covers two situations: loss of income owing to being disabled from an accident or illness and payments for the loss of a bodily function, a limb, or an organ.

Loss of a Bodily Function, a Limb, or an Organ

Payments made for the loss of a bodily function or a limb are tax-deductible for your company and tax-free for the employee.[27]

Example: Juan works in a machine shop and loses an eye. The company provides disability benefits, paying $100,000 for the loss of a bodily function or an organ. The $100,000 that Juan receives is tax-free.

Disability Owing to Accident or Illness

Today, there's a much better chance of being injured by accident or suffering a long-term illness than dying. Sadly, when a catastrophe of this nature occurs, few would have the ability to continue their income if they could not work. This is the purpose of disability insurance.

Interestingly, companies have two options regarding disability premiums paid to an insurance company. The premiums can be either tax-free to the employee or taxable to the employee.[28] There's a drawback to each option. If they're tax-free to the employee, then the benefits would be taxable to the employee if he or she gets paid on the policy. However, if the employee gets taxed on the premiums or in fact pays the premiums, then the benefits are taxable.[29]

Example: Wise Corp. provides disability insurance on all its employees tax-free. Joan, an employee, becomes seriously injured in a car accident that keeps her out of work for six months. All payments to her will be fully taxable because the premiums were tax-free.

IRS-Approved Tax-Planning Strategy

The IRS has ruled in a private ruling[30] that an employee who had paid the total premiums for disability coverage in the *policy year* in which he suffered a disability and received payments would not be liable for taxes on those payments, even though his employer had paid the premiums in previous years. In other words, all disability payments that the employee received would be allocable to his payments and would not be taxable.

Isn't this an amazing country?!

What this means to you is simple. Have your company deduct all premiums and treat them as tax-free to all the employees. However, in the year of a disability, have the company treat the premiums as taxable to the disabled employee; thus it will make the benefits tax-free.

Example: Joan is permanently injured in a car accident. If in the year of the injury she were taxed on the premiums paid by her employer, the benefits would seem to be tax-free.

As a final note, self-employed taxpayers or S-corporation shareholders who own more than 2 percent of the stock or partners are *not* employees.[31] Thus a self-employed person cannot deduct disability insurance premiums. However, the benefits then would be tax-free.

The Bottom Line

All companies should provide for disability coverage and should both deduct the premiums and treat them as a tax-free benefit to the employee. If the benefit is for loss of a bodily function, the benefit is always tax-free. If the benefit is for loss of income owing to sickness or accident, treat the last year's payment as income, and the benefits should become tax-free as well, not withstanding what was done in the prior years.

De Minimis Fringe Benefits and Occasional Supper Money

Your company can provide any employee—even if it discriminates in favor of officers or highly compensated people[32]—property or services under both the following conditions[33]:

- The value of the property or services is so small or inconsequential as to not warrant an accounting.
- The property or services are not provided too frequently.

Thus, even if a fringe benefit were small in value but provided daily, it would *not* be deemed de minimis. It must be *both* infrequent and inconsequential to be a de minimis fringe benefit.

Example: Financial Destiny is a small corporation that provides income opportunities. If it provides a one-time payment of $1,000 to an employee, this would not be deemed inconsequential and would be fully taxable.

Example: Financial Destiny also provides bus fare for some employees daily. Even though the value of this benefit is inconsequential, it's provided too frequently, so the total value of the fares would not be considered inconsequential.

Author's note: Any use of an employer-provided car, constant use of a season's ticket, or membership in a country club would not be a de minimis benefit. Such benefits may qualify as working-condition fringe benefits, however.

Examples of De Minimis Benefits

Now that you know what benefits are not de minimis, here are some de minimis benefits that can be provided:

- Occasional typing of a personal letter by a secretary
- Weekly coffee and donuts
- Holiday gifts of low value
- Holiday turkeys if cost is usually less than $25
- Occasional theater and season's tickets
- Free soft drinks
- Occasional use of the copy machine, fax machine, or other similar equipment if personal use is less than 15 percent[34]

Author's note: The IRS strangely has noted that monthly transit passes that cost no more than $21 would be deemed de minimis if paid to an employee.[35] But it doesn't treat the self-employed as employees. Sorry!

Occasional Supper Money

The IRS allows the payment of occasional supper money under all three of the following conditions[36]:

- The supper money is provided occasionally and not regularly.
- The supper money allows an extension of the normal workday.
- The supper money enables the employee to work overtime.

Author's note: This benefit applies only to employees. Thus, if you're self-employed, you can't give yourself supper money. You can, however, give it to any employee of yours. In addition, if you incorporate your business, you then become an employee of that business and are eligible to receive supper money.

The key is that supper money can be provided to anyone or everyone if there's a need for emergency overtime. It can't be based on hours worked, such as $3 of supper money for each hour of overtime. Thus, if you have a business that requires some overtime owing to a time crunch or emergency, you can provide supper money.

Example: Footer Podiatry, Inc., has a crunch of business once or twice a month. If the employees work two extra hours of overtime, the company can provide tax-free supper money. If this happens every week, this probably would be deemed too frequent and would be taxable.

Author's note: I've spoken with the IRS ruling division about this. Their policy is to allow supper money if it isn't provided too frequently, such as two or three times a month. Thus, if you have overtime required of employees that does not exceed three days a month, you should be able to provide a reasonable amount of supper money tax-free. Limit the money to what it would cost one person to eat in a medium-priced restaurant. Paying $100 per day for supper money probably would not be reasonable.

The Bottom line

I don't consider de minimis fringe benefits the top benefit in this chapter. They have a narrow application and, as the name indicates, can't be too beneficial. However, when you consider all the items that can be deemed de minimis, such as monthly transit passes under $21, these benefits can add up and not be de minimis to you or your company.

Qualified Employee Discounts

How would you like to be able to provide your employees with tax-free discounts on a wide range of products and services? Well, you can, and it's easy to implement in any company of any size.

The term *qualified employee discounts* means giving your employees property or services that you normally provide to the public in your company's ordinary course of business but you provide them at a discounted price to your employees. If you provide qualified employee discounts, the employees receive the property or services tax-free.[37]

Example: Safecracking, Inc., runs a nationwide banking consulting service. If the company provides discounts on banking fees to its employees, this would be a qualified employee discount. However, if it purchases and distributes season's tickets for the Redskins football games, this would not be a qualified employee discount because the company is not in the business of selling season's tickets.

A company can provide discounts on any product or service that it offers to the public—with the following exceptions:

- Stocks and bonds
- Commodities
- Real estate
- Money

Author's note: It's too bad that Congress passed these exceptions. I would have loved to work for a currency house or a bank and get discounts on money. Wouldn't you?

Limitations on Qualified Employee Discounts

Besides limiting discounts to qualified property, Congress has placed some limitations on the amount of the discount. As a result of some "tax simplification," the rules vary depending on whether you're providing services or property.

If you're providing a service, such as a flight or legal service, you can allow up to a 20 percent tax-free discount.[38]

Example: The law firm of Shaft and Shaft provides legal services to all its staff members at a discount. If the normal fees are $300 per hour, it can offer the legal services at a 20 percent discount, charging $240 per hour. If it offers these services for $100 per hour, the $140 "excess" discount would be taxable to the employee.[39]

If your firm provides discounts on property, the amount of the discount can't exceed the gross profit percentage.[40] You might be wondering what this means! The *gross profit percentage* is the sale price minus the cost of the property. Thus, in effect, you can offer the property at your company's cost.

Author's note: Why Congress couldn't use the term *cost* of the property instead of *gross profit percentage* is beyond me.

Example: IBM offers computers to its employees at a discount. If the normal price of a computer to customers is $2,000 but the profit that IBM makes on each computer is $500, the company can offer its computers to its employees at $1,500. Anything above this discount would be taxable to the employee.

Nondiscrimination Rules

In order to provide qualified employee discounts, you must offer them on a nondiscriminatory basis. You can't give the discounts just to the officers and other highly paid individuals. However, if you do discriminate, the discounts are still tax-free to employees who are not 5 percent owners of the stock or business or who make less than $100,000 per year.

There's a bit of sunshine here. There are some employees who can be deemed ineligible for the discounts:

- Employees who have less than one year of service with the company
- Employees who normally work less than 17.5 hours per week
- Seasonal employees who normally work less than six months per year
- Employees who are under age 21
- Employees who are subject to a collective-bargaining agreement (union contract)
- Employees who normally work less than 1,000 hours per year[41]

Author's note: As you can see from some of the fringe benefits, part-time workers need not be offered many benefits. Maybe this is the reason so many companies are hiring employees on a part-time or seasonal basis.

The Bottom Line

Qualified employee discounts can be a real benefit to companies and to their employees. They're available, however, only for products and services normally provided to the general public. Also, if they are services, the discount is limited to 20 percent. If the discounts are for property, they're generally limited to the gross profit percentage, which means that the employee can pay the cost of the property.

Deducting Exercise Equipment and a Gym

As we've read in many news articles, exercise is being touted as a partial cure for many ailments. Wouldn't it be great if you could deduct the cost of exercise equipment, tennis courts, and even a gym and provide these items tax-free to your employees and, if incorporated, to yourself? The answer is that you can!

Requirements to Bulletproof Company-Provided Athletic Facilities from the IRS

In order to make this benefit tax-free, you must meet several well-defined tests[42]:

- The equipment or gym generally must be on the company premises or leased or owned by the employer. (Thus it doesn't have to be physically in the same building as all the employees.)
- The equipment or gym must be operated by the company.
- The equipment or gym must be used substantially by employees of the company, their spouses, and their dependent children.

There are a couple of implications that can be derived from these rules. First, you can't pay for a health or country club membership because these clubs would be used by the general public and not substantially by your employees.[43] Second, the facilities must be run or operated by the company. This means that you can't deduct the use of a resort with facilities such as tennis or a swimming pool, which would be part of the association dues.

In addition, the IRS has noted that *employees* can include partners and employees who are separated from the company (either through retirement or disability).

Example: Your company provides a gym in the office for your employees. The gym is staffed by personnel paid by the company. The gym would be fully deductible and tax-free to the employees. If the company paid for health club memberships, on the other hand, this would not be tax-free to the employees. In addition, the athletic facility must not be offered only to officers or highly paid employees. Most staff members should be allowed to use the facility.

Author's note: Self-employed individuals ordinarily cannot give themselves this fringe benefit because self-employed individuals are not considered to be employees. However, if you're self-employed and you hire your spouse and/or other family members, they become your employees. If you place a gym in the location where your family employees work, you may be able to deduct the cost of the gym and the equipment. It's vital, however, that only employees or their family members use this facility. Thus don't let your friends use the gym. Keep an exercise log for everyone using the facility.

What Types of Facilities Can Be Operated under This Fringe Benefit?

Under this benefit, you can deduct and provide on a tax-free basis the following types of items:

- Gyms
- Exercise equipment
- Tennis courts
- Swimming pools
- Golf courses

Author's note: I really like the idea of being able to provide a golf course to my employees tax-free; however, the cost would be prohibitive to small businesses. However, remember what I stated earlier: "Where there's a will, there's a lawyer." Check out the next exception.

In case you don't have the hundreds of thousands or, in the case of golf courses, millions necessary to provide this benefit to your employees, there's a great exception from having your company pay all the costs.[44] A company can have an agreement with other employers to operate the gym, golf course, or swimming pool. Thus you find a company currently providing this benefit to its employees and cut a deal to pay rent or a fee so that your employees can use this facility. I should note that you must cut a deal with another company that provides this benefit solely to its employees. You can't go to a general health club or a country club and do the same thing.

Author's note: This is another idiotic rule passed by Congress. I can pay IBM to let my staff use a golf course that it owns and operates, along with employees of other companies that pay IBM for use of this course, but we can't pay a health club or a country club to do the same thing. Am I missing the point, or is this dumb?

Sandy's tax tip: Normally, self-employed individuals (otherwise known as sole proprietors) can't set up a deductible gym for themselves. However, if you were to hire your spouse and provide the gym in the location where your spouse works, such as your home, the gym should be deductible if used by you and your dependent children as well. This option, however, has not been tested yet.

The Bottom Line

This is a terrific and often overlooked benefit. Just have your company either operate the athletic facility or pay rent to another company that's operating a facility for its own employees.

Retirement Advice

Congress has been concerned recently with the lack of retirement planning of most people. In fact, according to a Harvard University study, only 2 percent of the population can retire by age 65 on the same standard of living that they had before retirement. Thus, starting in 2002, companies now can provide qualified retirement services to their employees and their spouses.[45] However, the employer must have some kind of "qualified plan" in place, such as a pension, a profit-sharing plan, a simplified employee pension (SEP), or even a simple individual retirement account (IRA) (most of these plans will be discussed later in this chapter) so that the employees can see where this benefit fits in with all the other retirement planning.

Example: Stop the Clock, Inc., wants to provide retirement planning for its employees. It hires a financial planner to meet with each employee about his or her retirement and to set up individual retirement plans for each employee and his or her spouse. If the company pays a fee for these services, it can deduct the fee, and the benefit would be tax-free to each employee if there were no discrimination.

In addition, anyone, even highly compensated employees and officers, can have this tax-free benefit as long as it doesn't discriminate.[46] Thus provide it to all full-time people.

The Bottom Line

This is both a great benefit and a needed benefit. You'll have happy and economically healthier employees by providing this benefit. Remember, however, that this benefit must be nondiscriminatory.

Company-Provided Low- or No-Interest Loans to Employees

This has got to be one of the most used and yet misunderstood fringe benefits. Unfortunately, few companies are using this benefit correctly. However, you, my faithful reader, will not have this problem because you will learn exactly what you need to do to make these loans tax-free.

The rules provided by Congress are entitled, "Treatment of Loans with Below-Market Interest Rates." These are defined as loans made to employees or even independent contractors at rates that are below the minimum rates allowed by the IRS, which are also known as the *applicable federal rates*. Thus, if you want to make the interest rates on these loans tax-free, there's a minimum rate that you must charge, or the employee is taxed on the foregone interest that he or she should have paid at the applicable federal rates.[47]

Example: Alice borrows $50,000 from her corporation for a 10-year period, interest-free. Because she didn't pay interest equal to the applicable federal rate, she would be taxed on the foregone interest using this rate each year. Yuck!

Applicable Federal Rates

The IRS publishes the applicable federal rates each month. They're available in your accountant's office, or you can call the IRS at 800-IRS-1040. (Isn't that a cute number?) There are three federal rates:

- *Short-term rates*—for loans of three years or less
- *Middle-term rates*—for loans over three years but not over nine years
- *Long-term rates*—for loans over nine years

Author's note: You would determine how long you want the loan and find out the latest applicable federal rate for the duration of the loan that you want. As long as you charge at least that rate, you can get these below-market loans tax-free. Also, as an estimate for you, the rate for long-term loans (over nine years) approximates the prime rate, whereas the rate for short-term loans is approximately one-half the prime rate. Thus the longer the duration, the more you must charge in interest.

Fabulous Exceptions to the Below-Market Loan Rules

1. $10,000 de minimis exception. The below-market loan rules do not apply to loans of $10,000 or less, which means that you can charge no or little interest.[48] However, if the amount is above $10,000, the rules apply even if you pay down the debt below $10,000.[49]

Example: You borrow $10,000 from your corporation, interest-free. This would be an exception to the rules, and you would not pay any tax on the foregone interest.

Example: You borrow $15,000 from your corporation, interest-free. This would not be an exception even if you pay the loan down below $10,000. You're taxed on each year's foregone interest.

2. Employee-relocation mortgage loans made in connection with a new place of work. One fabulous exception would be to provide mortgage loans to employees as part of a transfer to a new location.[50] Your new job location has to change, so you would qualify for the moving deduction. Generally, this means that your new job location should be on the other side of the city at least 50 miles away or, even better, in another city or another state. If you qualify, you can charge little or no interest.

The new workplace would have to be at such a distance from the employee's old residence as to require at least an additional 50 miles of commute. In other words, if the distance between the new site and the old residence is at least 50 miles greater than the distance between the old site and the old residence, the distance requirement is fulfilled.

Author's note: Hooray! Remember that I told you that we have good tax laws. You just have to know about them.

Requirements to Bulletproof Relocation Loans from the IRS

Nothing comes for free. To qualify, you must meet the following five easy tests[51]:

- The loan can't be for the purpose of avoiding taxes. This isn't usually a problem unless, for example, only the owner of the company gets it, and it isn't provided to other relocating employees.
- The benefits of this loan aren't transferable to a new buyer.
- The benefits of this loan are conditioned on continued future performance of substantial services by the employee. Thus the loan agreement could provide that "if the employee ceases working for the company, the applicable federal rate of interest will be charged the employee" or that "the loan will terminate and must be paid off within six months of termination."
- The employee must give a statement that the employee would itemize deductions on his or her tax return for each outstanding year. In other words, the employee would certify that he or she would be able to take a deduction for the interest on his or her federal tax return.
- The loan agreement provides that the mortgage money can be used only to buy a personal residence and not an investment property.[52] In short, you have to use the residence as your home and not rent it out.

Example: Karen works for the I've Been Moved Company (IBM). She is relocated from New York to California, and the company provides a no-interest mortgage for 15 years. As long as she uses the mortgage to buy a principal residence, is required to work for the company in order to keep receiving this benefit, and certifies that she will file an itemized return (Schedule A) with her federal tax return, the foregone interest would be tax-free.

Author's note: Any company of any size can offer this benefit to any employee of the company. Self-employed individuals are not employees, nor are independent contractors. This benefit is also very good for motivating and retaining an employee. What employees would want to leave a job if they were getting a tax-free mortgage that they would have to refinance at the going market interest rate if they quit?

I should note that this benefit is also available to corporate officers and to corporate owners as long as they are employees of the company.

3. Bridge loans. If you don't want to tie up your company's money in a mortgage, you can provide a no-interest or low-interest bridge loan to hold an employee until he or she is able to get a permanent mortgage on the real estate. To make this benefit tax-free, you must meet not only *all the criteria* for mortgage loans but also the following three criteria[53]:

- The loan agreement with the employee must provide that the employee must pay off the loan in full within 15 days of selling his or her principal residence.
- The total amount of all bridge loans must be less than the equity of the old house sold.
- The old house must be sold and not converted into investment property.

Author's note: As you can see, making a tax-free temporary loan (bridge loan) is more complicated than simply providing a mortgage. However, you many not want to tie up company funds in a long-term interest-free or low-interest commitment. Bridge loans are ideal in that they are short-term, temporary loans provided until the employee sells the former residence and has the funding to buy a new home. A corporation may provide bridge loans to the owners/stockholders. A sole proprietorship may provide them to employees–but not to the owner!

The Bottom Line

In order to provide tax-free below-market loans, either you must charge what the applicable federal rate would be for your loan's duration (which can be obtained from the IRS or your accountant) or you must meet one of the exceptions—loans of less than $10,000, relocation mortgage loans, or bridge loans. Make sure that you meet all the criteria noted in this book, and you will bulletproof this nice tax-free fringe benefit from the IRS. It also will provide for much more loyal employees because if they leave, this benefit can terminate.

Employer Educational Assistance and Other Tuition Plans

One big question that I get from most small-business owners is, "Can I provide my employees or my employed children with a tax-free tuition payment each year?"

There's good news and bad news here. The good news is that there are several possible ways to provide for tax-free tuition money: an educational assistance plan or tax-free use of property, equipment, or services, otherwise known as a *working-condition fringe benefit*. We'll discuss each of these in the order presented. The bad news is that for small businesses, most of these plans won't benefit the owner significantly but will benefit most of the employees of the business.

Generally, any educational expense paid for an employee or for a member of an employee's family is deductible by the company but taxable to the employee, unless you meet one of the exceptions noted below!

Educational Assistance Programs

You can set up an educational assistance program for your employees and pay up to $5,250 per year for tuition, fees, books, and supplies.[54] However, you cannot provide meals, lodging, transportation, or payments for sports, games, or hobbies unless they are part of a degree program.

Example: Jim is studying computers and takes some gym courses to keep in shape. His employer may not reimburse him for the gym courses. However, if Jim were studying exercise physiology and the gym courses were part of the curriculum, his employer could make such payments tax-free.

No discrimination is allowed in favor of business owners or highly compensated employees; however, employees of sole proprietorships can use this benefit. Now, for the bad news: No more than 5 percent of the total benefits can be paid to a stockholder who owns more than 5 percent of the stock or to an individual who owns 5 percent or more of the business even if you don't discriminate in any way. Yuck!

Author's note: If you have very few employees using this plan, you won't meet this requirement because more than 5 percent of the benefits will be benefiting the owner. Thus small-business owners get shafted because they can't avoid this 5 percent coverage, but larger businesses won't have a problem. You can, however, provide this assistance to your employees who do not have a 5 percent or more stock or business ownership interest.

Working-Condition Fringe Benefit

Although this was covered earlier, some special rules are applicable here. Even if you don't qualify for tax-free treatment as an educational assistance program, you may be able to deduct the courses and provide tax-free assistance as a working-condition fringe benefit if you meet certain criteria[55]:

- The educational expense would have been deductible by the employee if paid by the employee. This means that it doesn't qualify the employee for a new trade or business. (See Author's note below for further explanation.)
- The courses taken are related to the duties performed by the employee on the job.[56]
- The employee submits receipts and an expense report for all educational reimbursements.[57]

Author's note: There's only one unclear issue here: When can an employee deduct the educational expenses? The answer is that the course must be to maintain or improve the skills needed by the employee for his or her current duties *and* cannot be part of a program of study to qualify the employee for a new trade or business. Thus college courses that lead to a basic college undergraduate degree would qualify for a new trade or business, as would law school and medical school courses. However, courses that would not qualify for a new trade or business, such as many postgraduate courses, would qualify as a working-condition fringe benefit. Let's take some examples to illustrate all this.

Example: Chan works for Hackers, Inc., a computer repair facility. He's studying computers at the local college. If the company pays for his tuition, without it qualifying as an education assistance program, it would be fully taxable to Chan because he's seeking an undergraduate degree, which is deemed to qualify most people for a new trade or business.

Example: Let's assume that Chan already has an undergraduate degree and is seeking a master's in computers. Now, Hackers, Inc., can pay for any computer courses because these courses would be related to his job duties and would not qualify him for a new trade or business.

Example: Marcia works for an accounting firm by day and goes to law school and takes some tax courses in the evening. If her firm reimbursed her for these courses, none of reimbursement would qualify as a working-condition fringe benefit because Marcia cannot deduct law school courses that lead to a doctor of law degree. If she already had a law degree, however, and took some graduate law courses in taxation, she could receive reimbursement tax-free.

The Bottom Line

An educational assistance program is great, but you can't discriminate and can't have over 5 percent of the benefits go to the business owners or stockholders who own more than 5 percent of the stock. You also have a "fallback" position as a working-condition fringe benefit if the course is related to the employee's duties and the course doesn't qualify the employee for a new trade or business. Basic undergraduate courses, basic law courses that lead to the practice of law, and medical school courses that qualify a person to practice medicine would not qualify as a working-condition fringe benefit.

Reimbursed Country Club and Health Club Dues

Before 1987, country club dues were deductible to the extent used for business. Sadly, Congress did some "tax simplification"; thus, you know that you were shafted.

Today, there's generally no deduction for you or your company for country club or health club dues.[58] However, if an employee uses the club for business, any payments made for club dues would be deemed tax-free to the employee to the extent that the club is used for business under the working-condition fringe benefit rule, as discussed earlier.[59]

Author's note: Thus, if the club were used in part for business, some of the club dues would be tax-free to the employee using the club. The dues, however, would not be deductible by the company as a result of the "tax simplification" law.

Example: The Getwithit Corporation pays $2,000 a year to a health and golf club for use by its marketing employee. If the employee uses the club 40 percent for business, 40 percent of the $2,000, or $800, would be tax-free to the employee, who would be taxed on the remaining $1,200.[60] The employer would get no deduction for the dues.

However, if the company treated the club dues as fully taxable compensation, it could deduct the entire amount as compensation and not club dues, but the employee would be taxed on the full amount.[61]

Example: If, in the preceding example, Getwithit treated the $2,000 as additional compensation, it could deduct the entire amount as compensation, and the employee would get taxed on the full amount, even the portion that he or she used for business. So much for tax simplification!

Thus the bottom line is that either the employer gets a deduction and the employee gets taxed on all the dues, or the employer gets no deduction for the dues and the employee pays taxes on some of the dues.[62]

Sandy's tax tip: The key is to have your company reimburse employees only for the business use of the club. Thus only the business portion would be disallowed as a deduction by the corporation, but the employee gets that portion tax-free. The corporation should treat the portion that's not used for business as "additional compensation" to the employee in order to take a deduction for this portion.

Author's note: An employee would establish business use by keeping some form of tax diary or tax organizer showing what business was discussed each day that he or she used the club for business and the name of the person with whom it was discussed. One final point: The disallowance of the club dues deduction by Congress does *not* apply to other types of expenses. Thus business meals at your club would be deductible.[63] The same reasoning would apply to golf caddie fees, green fees, tips, etc.

The bottom line is that health club, golf club, and country club dues are not deductible by a company unless it treats them as additional compensation to the employees who use the club. The company can forgo the deduction so that the employee could receive some of the benefits tax-free, but only to the extent that he or she used the club for business.

Company-Provided Trips for Employees and Spouses

Many companies provide their top salespeople with conventions in very desirable places as both a morale booster and, frankly, a reward for good performance.

Author's note: Unfortunately, as a speaker, I always seem to go to Arizona in the summer and Michigan in the winter. I'm definitely doing something wrong!

We discussed in great depth in Chapter 3 the rules for employees to deduct business trips. Generally, for a trip to be tax-free, the majority of the days must be for business. Training activities must predominate each day, other than weekend days that are sandwiched between business days. In addition, each day would be a business day if the employee attended at least four hours and one second of meetings or it were either a travel day or a sandwiched weekend day. See Chapter 3 for a more detailed analysis of this.

The key question that often arises is what happens if the spouse comes along? Congress actually has thought of this and provides that you can bring your spouse and either get a tax-free reimbursement or deduct the cost if you are not reimbursed—if you meet one of two tests:

- Your spouse is licensed in your business. (If you are an insurance agent, for example, your spouse would have to be licensed in insurance.)
- Your spouse can make money for you or the company at the convention! (You've got to like this one!) But what does this mean?

Requirements to Bulletproof Tax-Free Reimbursements for Your Spouse's Travel from the IRS

The IRS provides that if your spouse is not licensed in your occupation, the company may pay his or her travel and lodging expenses under all the following conditions:

- The spouse is there for a bona fide business reason and not just to keep you company.
- There is proper substantiation for the expenses that the spouse incurs, by keeping some form of expense log, tax diary, or tax organizer.[64]
- The spouse is an employee of the taxpayer.[65]

Author's note: The last requirement is waived if the spouse performs convention duties, such as registering guests and monitoring attendance at the meetings, etc.[66]

Example: Richard takes his wife to the company convention in Orlando. Her only duties are to accompany Richard and attend some seminars for spouses. The company could either deduct none of her expenses or deduct her expenses and treat them as taxable compensation for Richard.

Example: If, in the preceding example, Richard's wife also were an employee of the company, she could attend the convention and not be taxed on the reimbursed expenses if she either attends courses related to her duties or performs functions at the convention, such as registering guests.

Author's note: Self-employed taxpayers have the same rules for deductibility of their spouses' expenses on business trips.

The Bottom Line

The predominant reason for the trip must be business or training. Each day should consist of at least four hours and one second of training. For a spouse's expenses to be deductible and tax-free to the spouse or the employee, there must be a valid reason for the spouse to be there, such as convention duties, or the spouse must work for the company and attend meetings related to his or her own job duties.

Corporate Purchase of an Employee's Home That Has Declined in Value

I'm not sure that this is as much a fringe benefit as a tax loophole. But I should tell you about it.

If an employee sells a home to his or her corporate employer, it would be considered a sale as if the employee sold it to a stranger.[67] Thus there's little benefit to selling your principal residence to your corporation if it has appreciated in value.

However, if the home has declined in value, there's a possible benefit to the employee. If any employee, even an employee who owns 100 percent of the stock, sells his or her principal residence to the corporation at a loss, none of the loss would be deductible.[68]

Author's note: I find it interesting that if you have a gain on your home, you are taxed on the gain, but if you have a loss, the government wants no part of your loss! This is another example of the "golden rule": "He who has the gold makes the rule."

Even worse, if there are sales expenses such as commissions, appraisal fees, bank fees, etc., the employee gets no benefit from these fees. It just accentuates the loss! Even worse, if your company reimburses an employee for the loss, the employee gets taxed on the reimbursement.[69] Yuck!

Sandy's tax tip: If an employee would have a loss on his or her residence, have the corporation purchase the house at the appraised fair market value, and then resell the house and pay all the selling expenses, although the employee would not be able to deduct the loss and also would not pay any tax because a loss would have resulted,[70] he or she won't incur additional nondeductible closing costs such as commissions. However, when the corporation incurs these expenses, it can deduct them as part of the resale of the house. Thus, in effect, the corporation is able to deduct the closing costs!

Example: Martha purchased a home for $300,000 several years ago. As a result of a bad real estate market, her home is now worth $250,000. If she sells it for the fair market value of $250,000, she cannot deduct the $50,000 loss (except to the extent that she may have claimed an office in the home). Even worse, if she were to incur $15,000 in real estate commissions and $5,000 in other closing costs, she couldn't deduct these either.

Example: Assume that Martha's company purchases the house from her for the fair market value of $250,000 and then resells the house for the same amount and, in addition, incurs the $20,000 of closing costs that Martha would have incurred. The corporation could deduct the $20,000 of costs as a loss. Everyone wins except the IRS.

Author's note: This will work for any corporation, whether a regular corporation or an S corporation. It also should work if you're running your business as a partnership or a multiple-owner limited-liability corporation. It will even work for a sole proprietorship, but only for the employees of the proprietorship, not the owner.

The Bottom Line

If you're incorporated or an employee in any business entity and you own a principal residence that has declined in value, let the corporation purchase the home at the fair market value and resell the home. The company then can deduct the closing costs incurred as a loss.

Reimbursement for Relocating Expenses for a Qualified Move

A company can reimburse tax-free the cost of relocating employees who would have qualified for the moving-expense deduction.[71] This means that if an employee makes a qualified move, the corporation can reimburse for the cost of the following:

- Transporting all household goods and furnishings
- Lodging for all family members incurred during the move
- The cost of the transporting the family members to the new location

Author's note: The employee must give the company an itemized record, including receipts for all expenses incurred, or he or she will be taxed on the reimbursement. If this is your corporation, you may use this fringe benefit as if you were an employee.

What Is a Qualified Move?

The IRS defines a *qualified move* this way (Publication 521): "Your move will meet the distance test if your new main job location is *at least 50 miles* farther from your former home than your old main job location was from your former home." It adds the following explanation: "The distance between a job location and your home is the shortest of the more commonly traveled routes between them. The distance test considers only the location of your former home. It does not take into account the location of your new home."

Author's note: Don't blame me if this sounds confusing. Blame your members of Congress. It's hard to believe that someone actually thinks of stuff like this.

   In order to help you, I have illustrated this rule in Figure 13-1.

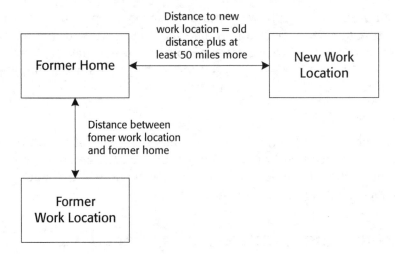

Figure 13-1. Distance test to deduct relocation expenses.

Example: Jan lives 20 miles away from her current office. She's transferred to a job location that's 60 miles away. If she moves, she does not qualify to deduct her relocation expenses because the distance between her old home and her new office isn't at least 50 miles more than her previous commute.

Discrimination Is Okay

As far as I can tell, you can discriminate in determining who gets relocation expenses covered and who doesn't. If your corporation reimburses you and your family for your moving expenses, this would be acceptable. I would, however, establish a class of people who would qualify, such as only officers or only senior officers. This would make it less likely that the IRS would challenge the reimbursement of relocation expenses as being only for the benefit of stockholders.

The Bottom Line

If you're incorporated, have your corporation reimburse you and any employees for qualified moving expenses—people, possessions, and lodging. Self-employed people can deduct qualified moving expenses for themselves and their employees as well.

Company-Provided Transportation, Limos, and Chauffeurs

Generally, if your corporation provides you with free transportation to the job by taxi or limo, it's taxable. However, there's an exception that applies in some rare instances. This transportation can be provided at a phenomenally low cost to the employee of $1.50 each way,[72] regardless of cost, if you meet the following criteria:

- The transportation is provided because of unsafe conditions.
- There's a written policy that transportation is provided only for commuting and not for personal purposes.
- An unrelated third party provides the transportation. (Thus you should use your son or the owner's brother to drive the employees.)
- The person transported must be a qualified employee. (Here's the catch.)

Let's examine what all this means. *Unsafe conditions* means that "under the facts and circumstances, a reasonable person would consider it unsafe for the employee to walk or use public transportation at the time of the day the employee must commute."[73] Thus the employee would ordinarily have to have either walked to work or taken public transportation. If he or she had driven, this exception presumably wouldn't apply unless you could show that there was no safe parking near the job location or that walking to or from the parking lot would have been dangerous.

Author's note: If you're going to use this exception, you want to think like a prosecuting attorney. You want to show the history of crime in the area surrounding the employee's workplace *or* residence at the time of the day of the commute. Perhaps getting a police recommendation to take a cab to and from work because of the unsafe conditions would be very compelling to the IRS. After all, an IRS agent is a sort of police officer, so he or she should respect a police recommendation.

You can provide this benefit only to qualified employees. These are people who are not highly compensated and are not exempt from the Fair Labor Standards Act.[74] This simply means that if they put in overtime, they will be paid at least time-and-a-half.

Example: Perry Mason is a staff lawyer who works long hours for his firm. Even if Perry's commute, which ordinarily would have been by train, could be proven dangerous, he wouldn't normally be a qualified employee because most lawyers are not paid overtime. If he were paid overtime at overtime rates for work beyond the 40 hours, he would qualify.

Finally, self-employed people cannot qualify for this benefit unless they're incorporated. Bah, humbug! They can, however, provide this benefit for their employees.

Author's note: Company-provided taxis and chauffeurs may become fully deductible as a working-condition fringe benefit if these services are provided for deductible stops. For example, if you are meeting various clients, a taxi or chauffeur may be provided to drive you to each business stop.

The Bottom Line

Although this fringe benefit is interesting, it has a very limited use, and corporate owners and officers will not be able to use it unless they're not highly compensated. Moreover, any employee who wants to use this benefit must be subject to the Fair Labor Standards Act and be paid for overtime. Thus it would be available to traditional employees. The next fringe benefit, in Chapter 14, has some similarities but will be more widely useful.

Notes

1. Section 132(d) of the IRC.
2. Letter Ruling 199929043.
3. Section 1.131-5q of the ITR.
4. Letter Ruling 199929043 and Section 1.132-1(b) of the ITR.
5. Letter Ruling 199929043.
6. Section 1.132-5n of the ITR.
7. Ibid.
8. Section 132(d)(1) of the IRC.
9. Section 132(j)(1) of the IRC.
10. Section 129(a)(1) of the IRC.
11. Sections 129(a)(2) and 129(b)(1) of the IRC.
12. Sections 129 (e)(3) and 129(e)(4) of the IRC.
13. Section 129(a)(2) of the IRC.
14. Section 129(c) of the IRC.
15. Section 137(b)(1) of the IRC.
16. Section 137(a) of the IRC.
17. Sections 137(b) and 137(c) of the IRC.
18. Section 212 and 213 of the IRC.
19. Section 106(a) of the IRC. In 2002, the deduction for self-employed businesses and for partnerships was 70 percent of the premium.
20. Section 1.105-5(a) of the ITR.
21. Section 7702B(a)(1) of the IRC.
22. Revenue Ruling 67-360, 1967-2 CB 71.
23. Letter Rulings 9603011 and 9850011.
24. Revenue Ruling 61-146, 1961-2 CB 25.
25. Section 9802 of the IRS.
26. *Seidel v. Commissioner*, T.C. Memo 1971-238.
27. Sections 105(a) and 105(c) of the IRC.
28. Section 105 of the IRC.
29. Sections 105(a) of the IRC and 1.104-1(a) of the ITR.
30. Letter Rulings 8027088 and 9741035.
31. Sections 105(g), 105(b), and 137(a) of the IRC and Letter Ruling 9320004.
32. Section 1.132-6(f) of the ITR.
33. Section 132(e)(1) of the IRC.
34. Section 1.132-6(e) of the ITR.
35. Section 1.132-6(d)(1) of the ITR.

36. Section 1.132-6(d)(2) of the ITR.
37. Section 132(a)(2) of the IRC.
38. Sections 132(K) and 132(c)(1)(B) of the IRC.
39. Section 1.132-3(e) of the ITR.
40. Sections 132(c)(1) and 132(k) of the IRC.
41. Section 1.132-8T(b)(3) of the ITR.
42. Section 132(j)(4)(B) of the IRC.
43. Section 1.132-1(3) of the ITR.
44. Section 1.132-1(e)(4) of the ITR and Letter Ruling 9029026.
45. Section 132(a)(7) of the IRC.
46. Section 132(m)(2) of the IRC.
47. Section 7872(a)(1) of the IRC.
48. Section 7872(c)(3)(A) of the IRC.
49. Section 7872(f)(10) of the IRC.
50. Sections 1.7872-5T(a) and 1.7872-5T(b) of the ITR.
51. Ibid.
52. Section 1.7872-5T(c)(1)(i) of the ITR.
53. Section 1.7872-5T(c)(1) of the ITR.
54. Sections 127(a)(1) and 127(c) of the IRC.
55. Section 1.132-1(f) of the ITR.
56. Section 1.132-5(d)(2) of the ITR.
57. IRS Publication 508 (2000), p. 6.
58. Section 274(a)(3) of the IRC.
59. Section 1.132-5(s)(1) of the ITR.
60. Sections 1.132-5(s)(1) and 1.132-5(s)(3), ex 1 of the ITR.
61. Ibid.
62. Section 1.132-5(s)(3) of the ITR.
63. Revenue Ruling 63-144, Q&A 48, 1963-2 CB 129.
64. Section 1.132-5(t)(1) of the ITR.
65. Section 274(m)(3) of the IRC.
66. Payments for the spouse's expenses would be tax-free as a working-condition fringe benefit. See also Section 1.132-5T(1) of the ITR.
67. *Harris Bradley v. Commissioner*, 324 F. 2d 610 (4th Cir. 1963).
68. Section 1.165-9(a) of the ITR.
69. See footnote 67 and Letter Ruling 9626026.
70. *Thomas L. Karston*, T.C. Memo 1975-2000.
71. Sections 132(a) and 217 of the IRC.
72. Section 1.61-21(k) of the ITR.
73. Section 1.61-21(k)(5) of the ITR.
74. Section 1.61-21(k)(6) of the ITR.

14

Fringe Benefits You Will Love, Part 2

Corporate-Provided Transit Passes, Vanpools, and Parking

This fringe benefit really deals with three related benefits: corporate-provided vanpools, transit passes, and parking. I'll discuss them separately. I should note that there's an overall limit for corporate-provided transit passes and vanpools—a maximum total of $110 of benefits per month.[1] Anything beyond this monthly limit becomes taxable to anyone who receives these benefits.

In addition, all these benefits must be provided to employees, but not self-employed individuals, independent contractors, or stockholders who own more than 2 percent of the stock of S corporations.[2]

Author's note: Darn! However, if you have a regular corporation, you may provide these benefits even if you own more than 2 percent of the stock and may even provide them on a discriminatory basis.

Chapter Overview
- Understand how to get corporate-provided parking, transit passes, and vanpools tax-free.
- Learn how to get company-provided automobiles either tax-free or at a very low cost (such as $1.50 each way).
- Learn why cafeteria plans can result in thousands of dollars of tax-free fringe benefits and give a host of wonderful benefits.
- Learn how to get property such as stock tax-free for services rendered.
- Learn about providing the same top benefit that CEOs of major companies get—incentive stock options.
- Learn how to provide meals and eating facilities tax-free. Yum, yum.
- Learn why every business should set up a qualified profit-sharing plan, a SEP, or a SIMPLE IRA and stash away a ton of money tax-free.

Qualified Vanpools

You can provide qualified vanpools for employees and for yourself (if you are incorporated with a regular corporation) if you meet the following condition[3]:

Chapter Overview (Con't.)
• Find out which fringe benefits can be provided just for the owners and which are nondiscriminatory—and what you have to do to bulletproof these benefits from any IRS attack.

• The van qualifies as a commuter highway vehicle. This means that it has a seating capacity of at least six people, at least 50 percent of the actual seating capacity when used consists of employees, and 80 percent of the mileage is used for transporting employees.[4]

Example: Big Bucks Corporation (BBC) provides a stretch limo for its employees' commute to and from work every day. If the vehicle seats at least six people and uses 80 percent of the mileage for transporting employees to and from work, it would qualify as a commuter highway vehicle.

Author's note: Thus you must keep a log showing that business use for employees is 80 percent or more.

The company can own the van, lease the van for employee use, or hire an independent third party whose business is transporting persons to provide this service in the company-owned or -leased van. However, there's an overall limit of $110 in benefits for both this and for transit passes that a company can provide tax-free to employees. Anything above this limit would be taxable to the employees.

Example: If the monthly cost of the limo service, plus gas and insurance, were $800 to transport five employees, the extra $300 per month spent on the vehicle would be taxable to the five employees pro rata, which means that each employee would pick up taxable income of $60 per month.

Qualified Transit Passes

Congress wanted to encourage workers to use mass transit. Accordingly, companies now can provide transit passes or vouchers for mass transit tax-free to their employees, up to $110 per month for each employee who will use it.[5] Again, this benefit is not available tax-free to self-employed individuals, independent contractors, or 2 percent or more stockholders in an S corporation; however, you can discriminate when providing these benefits. In addition, as with the other benefits noted earlier, self-employed owners and S corporations can provide this benefit to their employees, just not to the owners.

Example: Big Bucks Corporation provides a qualified vanpool only to its officers. This would be allowed.

Sandy's tax tip: Although owners of 2 percent or more of the stock of an S corporation can't receive the full transit pass benefit, they can receive up to $21 of transit pass benefits (by paying the difference, if any) as a de minimis fringe benefit. This may not seem like much, but it's an extra $21 per month that you can get tax-free.

Qualified Parking

In addition to qualified vanpools and transit passes, corporations can provide qualified parking to any employee, as noted earlier. The limit here, however, is different. You can provide qualified parking up to $215 per month in 2007.[6] This amount goes up each year with inflation. Again, this can't be provided to self-employed people, independent contractors, or 2 percent or more stockholders in an S corporation. If, however, you are the sole owner of a regular (C) corporation, you can receive this benefit.

Author's note: As you can see, being a regular corporation gives some better fringe benefits to major stockholders and senior officers. However, this has to be compared with the potential savings in Social Security with an S corporation and the other drawbacks to being an S corporation. (See Chapters 9 and 11.)

The Bottom Line

Vanpools, transit passes, and free parking are great fringe benefits. Vanpools and transit passes have a total limit of $110 that can be given tax-free, and parking can be paid tax-free up to $215 per month. Vanpools have some strict requirements on seating and use by employees.

All benefits noted here, however, don't apply to sole proprietors and 2 percent or more stockholders of S corporations; although the stockholders of an S corporation can have up to $21 of transit passes. C corporations can have these benefits provided to even the owners and senior officers.

Company-Provided Vehicles

There seems to be a great misunderstanding about how company-provided vehicles are taxed. This section will clarify most questions that I have received over the years.

The general rule is that when a corporation provides a company vehicle, the employee is taxable on the personal use of the vehicle.[7]

Example: Financial Destiny is a corporation owned by Art that conducts a multilevel business. The corporation provides Art with a nice Mercedes and pays all the bills. Assuming that Art uses the car 75 percent for business, he would be taxed on his personal use of 25 percent.

Author's note: I've emphasized throughout this book the importance of keeping a good tax diary or tax organizer. When company cars are provided, keeping a good tax organizer becomes twice as important because it will document how much of the car was used for business and how much was used personally, which is the taxable portion. It's critical, then, for every employee who receives a company vehicle to meticulously document business versus personal use.

This is the easy part of the discussion and the part that most people probably know best. But how do you compute what's taxable on personal use?

There are three methods of calculating the taxable portion of a vehicle based on personal use. These approaches provide very different results. Use the approach that provides the least amount of taxable income if—and this is a big *if*—you can use the approach.

Method One: Annual Lease Value Method

This is the general rule that the Internal Revenue Service (IRS) wants most companies and employees to use.[8] Since the IRS likes it, you probably can guess that it's the least beneficial to employees because it maximizes the amount of taxable income.

Author's note: In case I didn't make it clear, if one of the other methods is available to you or your employees, don't use this method! The table used in this method is found in Figure 14-1.

For an automobile with a fair market value greater than $59,999, the annual lease value is (25 percent × fair market value) + $500.

To use this table, find the fair market value of the vehicle provided, and then use the annual lease value that corresponds with the fair market value times the personal use. If the vehicle is owned, that value is normally the cost of the vehicle plus any taxes. If the vehicle is leased, the suggested list price is plus sales tax less 8 percent.[9] The following example will illustrate this.

Example: If Art's corporation purchases a BMW for $38,000 (which includes all applicable taxes), the annual lease value would be $10,250. If his personal use were 25 percent, he would record as additional compensation $2,562.50 (25 percent of $10,250).

The annual lease method includes insurance and repairs and doesn't get reduced if the employee pays any part of the insurance or repairs. Thus, if you're using the annual lease method, *don't* have the employee pay the insurance or repairs. Have the corporation pay these.

Strangely, however, the annual lease approach does not include gas. If the employer provides the gas, the receiving employee is taxed at 5.5 cents per mile,[10] which is a very good deal. However, if the employer reimburses an employee for the gas, then the employee is taxed on the full reimbursement.

Automobile Market Value	Fair Annual Lease Value	Automobile Market Value	Fair Annual Lease Value
$0-$999	$600	22,000-22,999	6,100
1,000-1,999	850	23,000-23,999	6,350
2,000-2,999	1,100	24,000-24,999	6,600
3,000-3,999	1,350	25,000-25,999	6,850
4,000-4,999	1,600	26,000-27,999	7,250
5,000-5,999	1,850	28,000-29,999	7,750
6,000-6,999	2,100	30,000-31,999	8,250
7,000-7,999	2,350	32,000-33,999	8,750
8,000-8,999	2,600	34,000-35,999	9,250
9,000-9,999	2,850	36,000-37,999	9,750
10,000-10,999	3,100	38,000-39,999	10,250
11,000-11,999	3,350	40,000-41,999	10,750
12,000-12,999	3,600	42,000-43,999	11,250
13,000-13,999	3,850	44,000-45,999	11,750
14,000-14,999	4,100	46,000-47,999	12,250
15,000-15,999	4,350	48,000-49,999	12,750
16,000-16,999	4,600	50,000-51,999	13,250
17,000-17,999	4,850	52,000-53,999	13,750
18,000-18,999	5,100	54,000-55,999	14,250
19,000-19,999	5,350	56,000-57,999	14,750
20,000-20,999	5,600	58,000-59,999	15,250
21,000-21,999	5,850		

Figure 14-1 Table for calculating fair annual lease value.

Example: Art's corporation pays for the gas on his BMW. Art normally gets 15 miles to the gallon and pays $2.00 per gallon. If he's taxed using the annual lease method, he would pay tax at only 5.5 cents per mile, or 82.5 cents per gallon. The remaining cost of $1.175 per gallon would not be taxable. Not a bad deal! If, however, Art gets reimbursed for the gasoline, he would pay tax at the full $2.00 per gallon on any personal mileage.

Author's note: If you're subject to the annual lease method, have your corporation provide the gas by obtaining a corporate credit or gas card.

Method Two: The Cents-per-Mile Method

The good news is that this second method results in less tax than the annual lease method. The bad news is that it's limited to inexpensive cars.

To use this method, you must meet the following three criteria[11]:

- The cost of the vehicle must be no more than $15,300.
- The company reasonably expects that the vehicle will be driven regularly for its business by the employee, which means that generally more than 50 percent of the mileage must be for business,[12] or that it will be used as a commuter highway vehicle, or that the employee will put on at least 10,000 miles and use it for commuting.
- If the car is provided for less than a year, then all mileage requirements are prorated.[13]

Example: Lori Ann owns a corporation that she uses for her consulting business. If the corporation provides her with a car for only half the year, all mileage requirements are prorated. Thus, under the usage test, she needs to put on only 5,000 miles.

Example: Lori Ann buys a used car for $12,000. As long as she either uses it more than 50 percent for business or regularly commutes in the car and drives it 10,000 miles per year, she can use the cents-per-mile method.

Author's note: I don't know what the members of Congress were thinking when they placed a $15,300 cost limit on the cents-per-mile method. I guess this method is ideal for cheap cars, such as Daewoo, Kia, or Suzuki, or used cars. In addition, keeping a good tax organizer or diary will establish your 50 percent business usage or that you drove over 10,000 miles.

If this isn't a good enough deal, the cents-per-mile method *includes* insurance plus repairs and company-provided fuel. Thus anyone who uses this method should not be paying for any of this. Let the corporation pay for all these items.

Method Three: The Commuting Value Method

This may be the best and cheapest method to be taxed on a company car; since Congress makes the rules, this method is the most limited for owners and officers. The main benefit is that you're taxed only at a ridiculously cheap flat rate of $1.50 each way for commuting.

To use this method, however, you must meet the following four criteria[14]:

- The company must own the vehicle, not lease it.
- The employee must use the vehicle for commuting to work.
- The company must provide in writing that any employee must use it for business and cannot use the vehicle for personal use. (This part is easy.)
- Except for de minimis use, the employee in fact doesn't use the car for personal purposes.

Here's the catch: The employee cannot be any director, any officer who earns at least $80,000, any employee who earns at least $160,000, or a 1 percent or more stockholder. In addition, this method is available only to company-owned cars. Thus sole proprietorships can't use this method for the owner but can use it for an employee of the proprietorship.

Example: Fred owns a corporation that sells products. If he provides himself with a car, he cannot use the commuting method because he owns more than 1 percent of the stock or more than 1 percent of the ownership of the business.

Author's note: The restriction that's applicable to 1 percent owners applies to any type of entity, even regular corporations, which is very unusual.

The Bottom Line

- If your corporation provides you or an employee with a vehicle, it's vital to maintain a good tax diary showing business usage. This will drastically cut back on what's taxable to you or the employee.
- Anyone who receives a corporate-owned or -leased car is taxed on the fair market value of the personal use. Business usage is not taxable.
- The annual lease method is the general way that you would compute the taxable portion of the personal use—and the most expensive method. If you use it, don't pay for repairs or insurance because they're included in what is being taxed to you.
- The cents-per-mile method is great, but it's available only for cheap cars that cost $15,300 or less. I wonder what most members of Congress are driving these days?
- The $1.50-per-commute approach is fabulous, but it doesn't apply to directors, officers who make at least $80,000, employees who make at least $160,000, or 1 percent or more stockholders. Thus you the owner can't use this method.
- A car can be provided on a discriminatory basis.

A Cafeteria Plan Can Provide Thousands of Dollars of Tax-Free Benefits

How would you like to get a host of fringe benefits for yourself and your employees tax-free by implementing one benefit? You can with what's known as a *cafeteria plan*. A cafeteria plan, as its name suggests, allows employees to pick and choose among benefit options. In fact, there must be at least two options to choose from.[15] Each employee then chooses specific benefits that he or she wishes to have. There are lots of potential choices; in fact, cafeteria plans can provide the following benefits as choices in the plan:

- Medical insurance
- Long-term care insurance
- Disability insurance
- Group term life insurance
- Dependent-care assistance
- Qualified pension or profit-sharing plan
- Adoption assistance[16]
- Qualified group legal services (Although this isn't clear, it seems to be allowed in a cafeteria plan. Outside of one, however, these benefits would not be tax-free.)
- Credits for additional paid vacation weeks

Example: You make $50,000 per year from your corporation and have $2,000 in unused credits. If you wish, you can take $1,000 of the credits in cash and an extra week of vacation in addition to the normal two weeks provided by the company. This would result in taxable income of $51,000 and three weeks' vacation.

Author's note: Cafeteria plans are almost the ideal benefit. By implementing one benefit, you can offer your employees many benefits that I've discussed; thus you will save a lot of time, legal and accounting fees, and money. The only problem, which will be discussed below, is that Congress stupidly limited the cafeteria plan from helping most owners and officers of a business. Because a cafeteria plan generally is available for nonowner employees, many small businesses have not implemented cafeteria plans. I guess the thinking of small-business owners is that "if I can't benefit, I won't use it for my employees either."

Criteria for Bulletproofing This Benefit from the IRS[17]

- It generally must be provided to all employees on a nondiscriminatory basis, although you can have a waiting period for eligibility of up to three years.[18]

Author's note: Actually, there's a limited amount of discrimination allowed. You can worry yourself and your accountant about this to see if you meet the various percentage tests. I suggest, however, that you simply cover everyone equally who has at least three years of service and let your accountant live longer.

- The participants must choose from two or more options.
- The participants must make a specific election of the benefits they're choosing and make this election at the beginning of the year or when they start work, whichever comes first.

- The cafeteria plan must be in writing and contain specific information about the plan. In other words, you have to notify your employees about all the choices and what they have to do in order to elect various options. You just can't keep it quiet and hope that they choose nothing. Sorry, that won't work.
- The plan cannot discriminate in the benefits provided.
- Over 25 percent of the total of the nontaxable benefits cannot go to highly compensated employees, officers who make over $130,000, or 5 percent or more stockholders. In addition, individuals who own over 1 percent of the stock can't obtain more than 25 percent of the benefits if they earn in excess of $150,000.

Author's note: Thus it's difficult but not impossible to benefit the owners of the business with a cafeteria plan, even if it doesn't discriminate, unless you earn less than $150,000 in taxable compensation.

Example: Happysue Corporation, a corporation formed for the practice of law, provides all employees with credits of up to $10,000. They can use these credits as they like to obtain various benefits, such as medical insurance, pensions, and vacations. If Happysue doesn't discriminate on the eligibility for this benefit and the owners/key employees receive less than 25 percent of all the actual benefits used, this plan will meet the IRS requirements.

The Bottom Line

A cafeteria plan is a fabulous plan for rank-and-file employees and even for owners if the corporation doesn't discriminate and doesn't provide more than 25 percent of the benefits to the owners or certain key or highly compensated employees.

Receipt of Restricted Property and Restricted Stock Tax-Free for Services Rendered

Most small businesses are not publicly traded; thus they do not normally provide stock, especially with the securities rules requiring lots of legal work in order to provide stock legally. This would be especially true if one or two people own all the stock because there would be no incentive to giving the owners more stock. However, there are occasions when a company agrees to provide stock or other property to an employee for future services.

Generally, employees are taxed when they receive the stock or other property unless there's a "substantial risk of forfeiture."[19] What this means is that an employee who receives restricted stock is not taxed on it if he or she has to perform future service in order to sell the stock or benefit from it. Taxation ordinarily would occur at the *earlier* of two dates: when the employee sells the stock or when the risk of forfeiture ends. The employee is taxed at ordinary income rates on the fair market value of the stock at this time. Any appreciation thereafter would be a capital gain.

Example: Anita is a staff member of a small advertising consulting corporation, Better Sales or Else, Inc. (otherwise known as BESI). If she receives 100 shares of stock worth $10,000 today but she must work for two years in order to be able to sell it or pledge it for a loan, she's not taxed on the stock because there's a substantial risk of forfeiture. She may not work another two years for BESI. If in two years, when the risk of forfeiture ceases, the stock is now worth double, she would be taxed on the whole $20,000 as ordinary income.

Author's note: When you receive restricted stock with a risk of forfeiture, you have the option of paying tax on the stock now. If you do this, you then would report any appreciation in the future as capital gain and not as ordinary income.[20] This can be a two-edged knife because the stock might depreciate after you paid tax on a higher value. Even worse, you must make this election within 30 days of the date of the transfer of restricted stock. Thus make this election only with a lot of care.

Phantom Stock

Many small businesses want to make employees feel that they own "a piece of the rock." However, if they give the employees stock, there are all sorts of legal security problems that require heavy legal fees in order to comply with. However, some great tax attorney came up with the concept of phantom stock in order to avoid all these security and legal issues.

Phantom stock is simply a promise of a bonus equivalent to either the value of company shares or the increase in that value over a period of time. Phantom stock is treated as if the employees received actual shares in the company. If the stock appreciates in the future, the employees will be paid that appreciation. They might even be eligible to receive dividends. Thus it's like owning the stock without getting any actual shares. Phantom stock allows employees to participate in the appreciation of their employer's stock. Phantom stock is taxed much like any other cash bonus, as ordinary income at the time it's received.

Criteria for Bulletproofing This Benefit from the IRS

The IRS has stated that employees are not taxed on any phantom stock or appreciation until they actually receive payment, under two conditions:

- The employer owns and is the beneficiary of any assets or stock that this benefit is based on.
- The stock or assets are subject to the employer's general creditors.[21]

In other words, the corporation keeps any stock in treasury and doesn't issue it to the employees.

Example: I will use my company as an example. The Tax Reduction Institute (TRI) of Germantown, Maryland, wanted to give our staff the feeling that they participate in the growth and benefits of our company. Thus I provided some employees with phantom stock. If there is any sale of the company, or if we go public, any price received above what it would be worth at the time of the grant would go to them. When they receive this benefit, they will pay tax, and TRI will get the deduction.

Author's note: There are two observations about both phantom and restricted stock. First, the stock can be given to anyone, even if the benefit discriminates in favor of officers and highly compensated employees. Second, no deduction accrues to the employer until payment is made on the phantom stock or until the employee is taxed on the restricted stock.

The Bottom Line

Phantom stock is a greatly underused fringe benefit. It usually makes employees feel as if they are owners (which, in essence, they are) yet doesn't involve any significant legal fees to provide as with regular stock. It also can be combined with a restriction that the employees must work a certain number of years, thus tying the employee to the company and increasing retention.

Qualified Stock Options

How would you like to provide your employees with the same incentives as receiving phantom or restricted stock but with the employees taxed only at capital gains rates? This is the major benefit of providing qualified stock options, the most significant benefit that public companies are using for their top management.

What Are Stock Options (Calls)?

The stock options that we are discussing are not stock. They give the employee the right to purchase the stock at a fixed price over some period of time.

Example: Mary has the right for two years to buy company stock for $100 per share. Assuming that the stock goes to $150 per share, Mary has the right to purchase this stock for only $100 per share. This is called *exercising the option*. The price that she gets to pay ($100) is called the *strike price*. The option will benefit Mary if the stock appreciates in value. If it decreases in value below the strike price, she won't exercise the option. Who would pay more for a stock than it's worth?

Tax Consequences

The employer gets no deduction on the grant or exercise of these options by the employee.[22]

Author's note: Since the corporation gets no deduction on either the grant or the exercise of these options, this is not my favorite benefit for corporations. However, for employees, this is a terrific benefit.

When the employee sells the option, as long as he or she has held it a for certain period, to be discussed below, all gain is long-term capital gain.[23]

You may have read about companies that have overstated their earnings in order to boost their stock values. The use of qualified stock options may have been a major factor in this overstatement of earnings because qualified stock options aren't deductible by the corporation either on grant of the option or on the exercise of the option. Depending on the size of the options, this can cause a substantial overstatement of earnings.

Criteria for Bulletproofing This Benefit from the IRS

Since there are such great benefits to employees, you probably can guess that Congress has lots of requirements in order to obtain these nice benefits. If you thought this, you made a good assumption. If you don't do it right, these benefits will be treated as the receipt of any other stock or option and will be taxable to the employee as ordinary income. Thus you must follow everything said in this book to the letter!

The following requirements are necessary to obtain all the wonderful tax benefits promised above[24]:

- There must be a written plan to offer the option with an option price and a set period of time during which the employee can buy the stock. The plan should show the total number of shares that will be issued and which employees are eligible to receive the options.
- It must be stock of the employer, the employer's parent, or a subsidiary of the employer.
- There must be a formal stockholder approval of the plan, even if all the stock is owned by one person or family within 12 months before or after the plan is adopted.
- The option must be granted within 10 years of the *earlier* of two dates—the date the corporation adopts the incentive stock options plan or the date that the shareholders approve the plan.

Author's note: In order to avoid any potential problem, I usually recommend that the option be granted within nine years of the earlier of the two dates. Thus there should never be a mistake.

- The written plan must provide that the employee must exercise the option within 10 years of the grant of the option.

Example: Amy receives an option in December 31, 2002. She must exercise the option by December 30, 2012.

- The option price must be at the fair market value of the stock at the time of the grant using any reasonable valuation method.[25]

Example: Thus, if the stock in a corporation is worth $100 per share based on an appraisal, the employee must pay the strike price of at least $100 per share in order for the options to be deemed qualified stock options.

- The option can be exercised only by the employee who was given the option. If the recipient dies before exercising the option, his or her estate or the beneficiary named in his or her will can exercise the option.

Author's note: Thus this option cannot be transferred.

- The employee can't have owned 10 percent or more of the voting power of the stock at the time the option was granted.[26] Thus incentive stock options won't benefit many small corporate owners. It's for the employees who either don't already own stock or own less than 10 percent of the stock.

Author's note: Just like most things in life, there are exceptions. A 10 percent or more stockholder can get incentive stock options if the strike price is 110 percent of the fair market value *and* the option can't be exercised more than five years from the date of the grant.[27]

- The total value of optioned stock can't exceed $100,000 per calendar year.

Example: Sonia has the right to exercise 1,000 shares at $100 per share. This would fall within the $100,000 limit. If she had the right to exercise 2,000 shares, only 1,000 shares would qualify as incentive stock options.

In addition, you have two holding periods to worry about.

- You must *not sell* stock for at least two years after the option is granted.
- You must hold the stock for at least one year after you actually receive the stock.

Sandy's warning: If you don't hold the stock long enough, you'll be taxed on the gain as ordinary income when you sell it. Yuck! Take my warning to heart.

Author's note: Whew! I told you that there were all kinds of strict congressional requirements. However, if both the corporation and the employees meet the rules, then the employee really comes out ahead. But if the employee doesn't hold the stock long enough and therefore makes a sale that disqualifies the option, the proceeds from the sale are considered as ordinary income, and the corporation obtains a deduction. I can almost hear most corporate owners wishing for their employees to make a mistake on the holding period when they sell the stock, so the corporation can obtain a deduction.

The Bottom Line

Incentive stock options are fabulous for employees in that income from selling them is taxed at the long-term capital gains rate, which is currently only 20 percent, rather than at regular tax rates, which go up to 37.6 percent plus a Medicare surcharge.

Tax-Free Lodging

Under limited conditions, a company can provide tax-free housing to its employees. This is a great benefit if it's available to your business.

Criteria for Bulletproofing This Benefit from the IRS

You can provide lodging and meals to any employee if you meet the following conditions[28]:

- The lodging is for the convenience of the employer.
- The lodging and/or food is provided on the business premises of the company.
- The lodging must be accepted by the employee as a condition of employment.

One of the big issues is, "What does *convenience of the employer* mean?" This can be proven in a variety of ways. If the employee is on 24-hour call and must be available for duty, this would qualify, or if the employee can't perform the services unless the lodging is furnished, this would qualify.[29]

Example: A prison guard is required to live on the premises in accommodations supplied by the government. The guard must be available if there's a prison riot or break. The lodging can be provided tax-free.

Example: James and Sheila accept a position as managers of a bed and breakfast facility. Their job is to manage the facility, supervise the housekeeping to ensure clean rooms, and provide breakfast for guests. They're required to stay in the facility and handle emergencies. Their lodging and food would be tax-free.

Author's note: In order to have the meals and/or lodging tax-free, the employer must pay for them and provide themt directly.[30] Do not have the company reimburse for any meals or lodging.

Exclusion for Meals

As you might expect, the exclusion for meals alone is a bit easier; meals only have to be provided for the convenience of the employer and furnished for a noncompensatory business reason.[31] There are a number of situations where employers can provide tax-free meals. In fact, most small businesses will be able to use this benefit very much.

The following are some illustrative examples of situations in which your company can provide tax-free meals to employees:

Short business meal during working hours.[32] A corporation can provide meals to employees during working hours if there's a required short lunch period, which is usually less than 45 minutes. However, there's a catch: The employees cannot eat elsewhere in the short time allowed for lunch.

Example: Many times my staff is required to break for lunch no longer than 30 minutes because of the number of customers calling at lunchtime. We normally could furnish meals tax-free to my staff even though there's a Burger King near us. (Who doesn't have a Burger King or McDonald's near them?) The reason is that there's little chance that my staff would be able to stand in line, get their meals, and then eat within the short break. Thus we could furnish employees lunch on these crunch days tax-free.

Example: Alice, John, and Mary work for a Sockittotheirs, Inc. The office is located on the East Coast. During lunch, usually around 12 p.m., many customers from the West Coast call up the company. Because there's a great deal of work during the lunch periods every day, the company can provide free meals.

Meals furnished for employees who are required to live on premises. If an employee can be provided tax-free lodging, as discussed earlier, because he or she is required to live on the company premises as a condition of the job, the company also can provide tax-free meals as part of the deal.[33]

Meals furnished to restaurant employees are almost always tax-free, whether furnished before, during, or after their shift.[34]

Author's note: It amazes me that more restaurants aren't using this benefit more often. It would be a great tax-free fringe benefit and a great way to retain employees.

Meals can be furnished tax-free if the employee is available for emergency calls during his or her lunch period. Thus, if the company provides an employee with meals at his or her desk in order to field calls that come in during lunch, these meals are tax-free.[35] To receive this tax-free benefit, the employee can't perform personal errands during the lunch period.

Example: A medical corporation provides lunch for all staff members and the doctors because emergencies occur during the day, and the corporation wants the staff available for these problems. Lunch can be provided tax-free.

Meals can be furnished if there are insufficient eating facilities near the workplace.[36] If employees have few or no facilities for lunch within a reasonable distance of work, the company can provide meals. It certainly will be important to show that you've checked the Yellow Pages for eating facilities in the area and made estimates on how long it would take to get to and from any facility and to eat lunch there.

Meals furnished to over 50 percent of all employees will be tax-free. This is a great way for any company to provide meals tax-free. As long as the company furnishes the meals on the premises to over 50 percent of all employees, the meals are tax-free.[37]

Example: A hospital provides 210 staff members out of the total 230 staff members and doctors with free meals. Supposedly it's to keep them available for emergencies, but these emergencies rarely occur. However, because the hospital provides free meals to more than half the employees, all meals provided are tax-free to the staff.[38]

Example: We at the Tax Reduction Institute provide a free lunch once a month and discuss business over lunch. Since we provide lunch to more than half the employees, all meals are tax-free, even to me.

Lunch conferences are deductible, even outside the company premises and even if only to senior officers.[39] There is one important case that you'll like. A company provided daily lunches for its officers where attendance was compulsory. The lunches were in a hotel conference room rented by the corporation. The officers discussed daily events and any upcoming activities necessary for the day and shared their experiences. The tax court allowed the corporation to provide tax-free meals even though it was done off the company premises and was done daily.

Author note: You should notice that meals, especially for good business reasons, can be furnished to officers and directors on a discriminatory basis.

Other Interesting Exceptions for Meals

There was an interesting case that may provide a lot of small-business owners with tax-free meals and company provided housing, *F. R. McDowell.*[40] It involved a husband and a wife who were the sole owners of a large farm, which was leased to a corporation owned by McDowell's children. Thus the only business that the McDowells' corporation had was to lease out the land. The tenant, the children's corporation, was engaged in ranching operations and was required to keep the buildings and other improvements in good condition. McDowell retained the right to inspect the property. McDowell actually lived on the land through most of the year and made daily inspections of the leased land. The tax court held that the meals and lodging furnished by the corporation to the McDowells were tax-free.

What does this mean to you? This case has many implications. Here are some examples of how you may use this case to your advantage.

Example: Tiffany is an antique dealer. She runs her business out of her home using a corporation. She's required to work out of her home and to provide security for the antiques. She receives phone calls at home from potential customers and past customers. Tiffany may have her corporation provide housing and meals for her business.

Author's note: Although there is no case on this, I wonder what would happen in this hypothetical situation. A network marketing professional runs her network marketing business out of her home using a corpo- ration. She gets calls daily from distributors and from customers in her home. She meets with her distributors at least weekly and stores inven- tory and marketing materials in her home. Her corporation provides that she must be available to handle all calls on a 24-hour basis. It would appear that, based on the *McDowell* case, she might be able to receive corporate meals and lodging tax-free. Let me warn you, however, that there is no case on this. Thus this benefit may need to be tested in the courts.

Author's note: I also should note that this would work only for network marketers and other home-based business owners who are incorporated. It will not work for the owners of a sole proprietorship.

Qualified Pension and Profit-Sharing Plans

Without question, this may be the most important fringe benefit that you can provide. It not only allows a large deduction but also can provide a great deal of legal protection against lawsuits because some qualified plans are exempt from creditors.

Author's note: Just ask O. J. Simpson.

Everyone should be stashing away at least 10 percent of what they make for retirement. Having a qualified plan is a great way for most peo- ple to achieve their retirement goals. There are wide varieties of plans; in fact, I could also write a book on just this one topic. However, to keep this topic manageable, I want to discuss the most popular and most recom- mended plans among small businesses today.

Profit-Sharing Plan

This plan allows you to put away in any business for any employee up to 25 percent of his or her wages or, if you're self-employed, up to 25 percent of the net income of the company. There's a maximum contribution of $45,000 per year per employee.[41]

What's great about a profit-sharing plan is its flexibility: The amount of an employee's wages that you can contribute can vary from year to year. Thus, if you want to contribute 25 percent of all wages to the plan in one year but only 10 percent in a less profitable year, you can do so. Thus flexibility is the name of the game with profit-sharing plans.

I would unqualifiedly recommend this plan to all business owners. However, there are some drawbacks to this plan. First, it's nondiscriminatory. You generally must cover all full-time employees. You can have a three-year waiting period before coverage, but all employees must be covered under the plan. Second, as with most qualified plans, these are expensive to set up and require filing expensive forms with the IRS, thus enriching your accountant.

Author's note: Despite the disadvantages of a profit-sharing plan, I like them a lot, especially because of their tremendous flexibility. This is one plan that you should consider.

Simplified Employee Pension (SEP) Plan

In many ways, this plan is similar to a profit-sharing plan. It allows you to contribute up to 25 percent of your net income if you're self-employed or 25 percent of an employee's wages. Again, this plan has a maximum contribution limit of $45,000.[42]

As with a profit-sharing plan, a company can vary its contribution from year to year. Thus a company can contribute up to 25 percent of wages this year and much less or even nothing next year. It thus has the same flexibility as profit-sharing plans. However, a SEP has some benefits over a profit-sharing plan. First, SEPs are inexpensive to set up. You simply fill out IRS Form 5305-SEP, but you don't file it with the IRS; you keep the form with the company records. Second, there are no complex annual filings as with other qualified plans, so administrative expenses are very low.

A SEP plan, however, has the same drawbacks as a profit-sharing plan in that it is nondiscriminatory.

Author's note: I love SEPs. If you have few or no employees, a simplified employee pension is the way to go. This also can be used by sole proprietorships.

Defined-Benefit Plan

This is a very different type of qualified plan. Most plans require you to contribute a set percentage of wages. A defined-benefit plan uses an actuary to compute how much you or your employees may contribute in order to get a set retirement income. Thus you figure out how much you need at retirement and, in effect, work backwards. Because of this, a defined-benefit plan normally allows you to contribute much more than other plans, especially if the worker is 50 years of age or older. Since the older the worker, the less time there is available to build up to the desired goal, older workers can contribute much more than younger workers. The maximum yearly contribution to the defined-benefit plan is a whopping $180,000 as of this writing.

With this wonderfully high contribution limit, you would think that I would be wholeheartedly recommending this plan. However, this is not the case because this plan has two major drawbacks. First, a defined-benefit plan is the most administratively expensive plan available. You need not only a good accountant to file some complicated forms but also a yearly actuary to design contributions each year. Second, if this isn't bad enough, there's very little flexibility to this plan. You must contribute a set amount each year, as determined by the actuary, regardless of profitability. Given their lack of flexibility, I normally don't recommend defined-benefit plans.

Author's note: A defined-benefit plan is ideal for older owners who are 50 years of age or older and for firms that have net incomes that don't decrease significantly from year to year.

SIMPLE IRAs

In many ways, this is my favorite plan, especially if you have employees. This also works for all sole proprietorships and even for the owner of the proprietorship. A Savings Incentive Match Plan for Employees (SIMPLE) IRA is like a traditional IRA, except that with an IRA, you can contribute up to 100 percent of your wages, with a maximum contribution of $4,000. What is so different and beneficial about a SIMPLE IRA is that the employee, and not the employer, makes most of the contributions. The employer need only match an employee contribution if the employee makes a contribution for the year.

A SIMPLE IRA allows an employee to contribute up to $10,500 in 2007. In addition, the employer need only match the employee's contribution, if any, up to 3 percent of their wages, up to a maximum of $225,000 in wages for 2007. This means that the maximum employer contribution would be $6,750.

Example: Stitchem, a medical corporation, provides a SIMPLE IRA for all its employees and doctors. If the doctors contribute the maximum amount of $10,500, Stitchem may contribute up to 3 percent of the doctors' wages, up to another $6,750, for a total contribution of $17,250. Not a bad deal! The doctors get $17,250 put away for them because they contribute $10,500, and the corporation contributes $6,750.

Example: Sarah is a receptionist for Stitchem and earns $25,000. If Sarah makes no contributions to the SIMPLE IRA, Stitchem need not make any contributions on behalf of Sarah.

Example: Let's assume that Sarah contributes $2,000 to the SIMPLE IRA. Stitchem would have to match Sarah's contribution, but only up to 3 percent of her wages. Thus, since she earns $25,000, Stitchem would contribute only $750 for Sarah.

Author's note: Many medical and legal firms set up SEPS or profit-sharing plans because they allow a much greater contribution, $44,000. However, if there are other employees, this can be very expensive. If there are several employees, I recommend considering setting up a SIMPLE IRA. The overall contribution by the owner may be less than with a SEP, but the benefit of not contributing as much for employees may greatly offset this. If, however, a company wants to contribute as much as possible on behalf of employees, a SEP may be the better choice.

Notes

1. Section 132(f)(2) of the IRC.
2. Section 132(f)(5) of the IRC, Section 1.132-9(b) of the ITR, and IRS Notice 94-3, Q-5b, 1994-1 CB 327.
3. Section 132(f)(1) of the IRC.
4. Sections 132(f)(5) and (f)(1) of the IRC.
5. Notice 94-3, Q-3a, 1994-1 CB 327; see also Section 132(f)(2) of the IRC.
6. Revenue Procedure 2001-59, 2001-52 IRB 623.
7. Section 1.61-21(a) of the ITR.
8. Section 1.61-21(d)(2)(iii) of the ITR.
9. Section 1.61-2(d)(5) of the ITR.
10. Section 1.61-2(d)(3)(ii)(c) of the ITR.
11. Revenue Procedure 2002-14, 2002-5 IRB 450.
12. Section 1.61-2(e)(1)(4) of the ITR.
13. See note 86.
14. Section 1.61-21(f) of the ITR.
15. Section 125(d)(1) of the IRC and Section 1.125-1 Q&A 8.
16. Notice 97-9, Section II, 1997-1 IRB 365.
17. Section 125(d) of the IRC.
18. Section 125(g)(3) of the IRC.

19. Section 1.83-1(a) of the ITR.
20. Section 83 of the IRC and Section 1.83-2(a) of the ITR.
21. Revenue Ruling 72-25, 1972-1 CB 127.
22. Section 421(a)(2) of the IRC.
23. Section 14a-422(a)(1), Q&A 1 of the ITR.
24. Section 422(b) of the IRC.
25. Section 422(c)(1) of the IRC and Section 1.421-7(e) of the ITR.
26. Section 422(b)(6) of the IRC and Letter Ruling 8238113.
27. Section 422(c)(5) of the IRC.
28. Section 119(a) of the IRC.
29. Letter Ruling 8002003.
30. Section 119(b) of the ITC.
31. Section 1.119-1 of the ITR.
32. Section 1.119-1(a) of the ITR.
33. Section 1.119-1(a)(2) of the ITR.
34. Ibid.
35. Section 1.119-1(a)(2) of the ITR and Revenue Ruling 71-411, 1971-2 CB 103.
36. Section 1.119-1(a)(2)(ii)(C) of the ITR.
37. Section 119(b)(4) of the IRC.
38. Section 1.119-1(f), Example 9 of the ITR.
39. *Mabley v. Commissioner*, T.C. Memo 1965-323.
40. *F. R. McDowell*, T.C. Memo 33 CCH TCM 372 (1974).
41. Sections 404(a)(3)(a), 404(a)(8)(D), and 415(c)(1) of the IRC.
42. Ibid.

Part 4

Miscellaneous Tax Strategies

15

The Four Most Overlooked Real Estate Tax Deductions in America

Unquestionably, there is progress. The average American now pays out almost as much in taxes as he formerly got in wages.

—**H.L. Mencken**

What's the Point of Mortgage Points?

Buying homes in America is as American as apple pie. Everyone seems to be getting into the act. In fact, in June 2002, President Bush even proposed broad incentives that would enable more Americans than ever before to purchase their own home.[1]

Although everyone dreams of owning their own personal "piece of the rock" that they can call home, there are some stiff expenses involved in buying a home. One big, misunderstood, and often overlooked expense deals with points.

Chapter Overview
- Learn about when you should deduct all mortgage points paid to banks.
- Understand a real estate deduction most often overlooked: unamortized points.
- Learn why making repairs in investment property is much better than making improvements.
- Learn why making improvements on a principal residence is much more important than making repairs.
- Learn how to IRS-bulletproof your designation of repairs or improvements.
- Understand the new universal exclusion that allows you to avoid up to $500,000 of gain.
- Learn about new untapped markets where you should be buying because of the universal exclusion. (This is a killer.)

Points, otherwise known as *loan origination fees* or *loan processing fees*, are normally incurred when you obtain a loan at a set interest rate. Many times, paying more in the form of "upfront" points results in a lower interest rate than if no points are paid.

> **Chapter Overview (Cont.)**
> • Learn why it's a tragic tax mistake to purchase the family's home as part of a divorce (which, sadly, is done all the time).

Author's note: You can tell how many points you paid by looking at your settlement statement. It will note exactly how much your points are. In general, points are a percentage of your loan. Thus, if you have a $100,000 loan and pay two points, you would pay 2 percent of the loan in points, which would be $2,000.

Rules for IRS-Bulletproofing Deduction of Your Points

The good news is that you may fully deduct all points paid in the year that you pay them, even if they are paid out of the loan proceeds and even if they are VA or FHA points, provided you meet five conditions:[2]

- You use them to either purchase or improve your principal residence; thus, you can't fully deduct points incurred for a second home, a rental property, or refinancing a home. (We'll discuss this below.)
- Your down payment exceeds the charge for the points.
- Your principal home fully secures your loan. In other words, your home is collateral for the loan.
- Charging points is a normal, established practice in your area.
- The points charged are not excessive. This means that they do not exceed the usual charge for points in your area.

Example: John and Mary purchase their main home for $250,000. They make a down payment of $50,000. In order to get their 6 percent loan, they have to pay two points, $5,000. They may deduct the full $5,000 on their tax return as interest. It would be reported on Schedule A, Itemized Deductions.

Authors' note: Many people overlook this deduction because the bank doesn't send any information form. You just have to recognize it on your settlement statement and know that these points are deductible. If you've purchased a home within the last three years, check out your settlement statement. If you didn't deduct the points, you can file both federal and amended returns for up to three open tax years.

Moreover, the IRS used to require that people pay the points separately, using a separate check, in order to deduct the points. Recently, the IRS yielded on this requirement and now allows you to deduct points even if you did not pay the points in cash or use a separate check. In fact, you can have the points paid from the loan proceeds.[3] However, and this is the catch, you can claim the deduction only if the money that you bring to the settlement (down payment, recording fees, etc.) exceeds the charge for points.

Example: Jack and Jill incur $5,000 in points to purchase their lovely house on the hill. These points are to be paid from the loan. If Jack and Jill want to deduct the $5,000, they must make a down payment of at least $5,000 at the closing. If they pay only $3,000 down, then only $3,000 of the points would be immediately deductible.

Author's note: I wonder if the people at the IRS are actually developing a heart.... Nah!

Points Paid by the Seller

Sometimes a seller agrees to pay points. This often happens when the contract provides that the loan points be split between buyer and seller. The tax consequences are great. The seller treats these payments as selling expenses and you, the buyer, get to deduct the points paid by both you and the seller as interest, as long as you reduce your purchase basis by the seller's payment of the points.[4] Isn't this a great country?

Example: Bob purchases a home with a $100,000 loan. Bob has to pay two points ($2,000) for this loan. The real estate contract provides that Bob and the seller will split the points. Even though Bob pays only $1,000 in points himself, he may deduct the entire $2,000 of points paid. He must, however, reduce his basis in his home by the $1,000 paid by the seller.

Amortize All Other Points Paid

As I noted above, you can deduct the points paid only if you meet certain specific conditions, such as incurring them for the purchase of a principal residence. If you don't meet these specific conditions, you can't immediately deduct all the points. This can occur in many situations. You can incur points to buy investment property or a second home or to refinance a loan rather than using the loan proceeds to purchase or improve the home. In these cases, you cannot deduct the points immediately; you must amortize the points over the life of the loan. This means, in plain English, that you must deduct the points ratably over the number of months of the loan. The following example will explain this.

Example: Howard refinances his home and pays $3,600 for a 15-year loan (180 months). Since this loan is not used to purchase or improve his principal residence, he may not immediately deduct all the points. He must write them off over the life of the loan. Thus, the loan is for 180 months, he would deduct $20 per month or $240 per year.

The main question, which applies to almost everyone, is what happens if you don't hold the house for the full loan term or keep the loan for the full term of the loan? The answer is that you get to deduct all unamortized points in the year that you either sell your home or refinance the loan that you incurred points on.

Example: Let's assume that, in the above example, after you deduct only $240 of the $3,600 of points paid, you refinance your loan. You would deduct the remaining, undeducted portion of the points—$3,360 in unamortized points!

Author's note: From my many years of experience in taxes, I've found that almost everyone fails to notice this major deduction and, of course, to take it on their tax returns. Why? Most people don't know about it and their banks don't send them any notice about this. Also, it requires that you or your accountant check the settlement statement that you received when you purchased the property or incurred the loan to find the amount of the points, which most people forget about because of the time that's passed since the closing. If you've sold your home or refinanced a loan within the last three years, check whether you have any unamortized points. If so, you can file an amended tax return (Form 1040X) for up to the last three years and claim the deduction. Even better, many states allow you to claim this deduction in computing state taxes, too.

Repairs vs. Improvements: Which Is Best?

The second most overlooked real estate deduction deals with the difference between improvements and repairs. When should you try to make an improvement and when should you try to make repairs? At first, they seem similar, but learning to classify and structure them correctly can result in thousands of dollars of extra benefits to you. Much of the answer is a question of facts; however, how you present and structure the facts can result in two entirely separate tax results.

I should note that this issue is even tough for the IRS; the agency's internal manual states that "it is a difficult issue requiring maximum use of judgment."[5]

The key is that, with rental and commercial properties, you always prefer to have fix-ups classified as repairs *and not as* improvements. The reason is that repairs are deductible now, while improvements on rental property are capital items that must be depreciated over a recovery period of 27.5 years for residential rental property and 39 years for commercial property.[6] What would you rather have, a deduction now or over many years?

Example: Dan spends $10,000 fixing up his residential rental property. He can deduct the $10,000 now as a repair or take deductions of $364 per year for 27.5 years if he classifies it as an improvement. But the $364 per year is not really $364 in today's dollars. We must consider the time value of money. If the time value of money is 6 percent, the $364 per year improvement deductions for 27.5 years are worth $4,840 in today's dollars, compared with the $10,000 repair deduction. To put it another way, a repair deduction is twice as valuable as an improvement.

With your residence homes, in contrast with rental or commercial properties, you have a different attitude. Any repair made to a residence is completely non-deductible. You don't get to add it to your basis and you don't get a deduction—nothing, nada, zip! Improvements, on the other hand, get added to the basis of the home and help reduce the gain, if any, when you sell the home. So, with a residence, you want improvements and not repairs.

When is a fix-up a repair and when is it an improvement? That's the big question.

To repair means to restore to a sound state or to mend. You make a repair to keep the property in ordinary, efficient operating condition. It does not add to the value of the property or appreciably prolong its life.[7] Repairs merely keep the property usable and operating over its probable life.[8]

Improvements make the property better in some way. You make improvements when you do one or more of the following:

- You increase the value of the property.[9]
- You make the property last much longer.[10]
- You adapt the property to a new or different use.

Author's note: When does fixing up a roof cease to be a repair and become a partial replacement (improvement)? In situations of this sort, careful tax planning, careful understanding of what's in this book, and complete records can yield big tax savings.

Fortunately, there is a great but little known case that will show you what to do in order to get the right classification for your property.[11]

Roger Jacobson bought a four-unit apartment for $30,000. It had one tenant, but the building was in poor shape. Jacobson spent $6,247 to have a contractor do the following:

- Remove tree limbs that were rubbing on the roof
- Repair water damage
- Clean the carpet, floors, and exterior
- Repair the cracked front porch
- Install new cabinet doors
- Install new counter tops

Although the IRS tried to classify all the work as improvements, the tax court allowed $5,000 as a repair deduction. The only improvements were the new cabinet doors and new counter tops. In siding with Jacobson, the court noted that:

- There was a tenant in residence, whose presence meant that the property was commercially active.
- $6,247 in total and the $5,000 allowed were not material based on the $30,000 building price.
- Most items were fixed using the same or similar materials.

Author's note: The word "new" signals improvements and not replacement or repair.[12]

Eight Great Strategies to Ensure Repairs

Based on the Jacobson case, here are eight great strategies that could ensure that you get the classification that you want.

1. Segregate repairs from improvements. If you're going to renovate the place, but also make certain repairs, you must segregate the repairs from the improvements to deduct the repairs.13 In fact, the IRS says in its audit manual that fix-ups that would be a repair when made separately would be an improvement when made as part of a general overhaul of the building.[14]

Example: Karen wants to fix up her rental property. Unfortunately she both needs a new roof, which would be an improvement, and needs to clean out and fix the clogged gutters, which are repairs. If she does it all in one job and gets one combined bill, the entire project would be considered an improvement that would be depreciable over 27.5 years. She should get an itemized bill for the roof and a separate bill for the gutter work. The gutter work would be deductible as a repair.

Author's note: Make sure repairs are not part of an overall plan and, if possible, have repairs done by a different contractor. Certainly, you should get a separate bill for the repair work.

2. Fix a minor portion only. If you're replacing an entire wall, roof, or floor, you're often making an improvement.[15] If you repair only part of a wall, roof or floor, you're generally making repairs.[16]

3. Use similar, comparable, or less expensive materials. If your purpose is to mend and restore to a sound state, you should use comparable materials[17] If your purpose is to improve, you use better-quality or improved materials.[18]

Example: If, in the above example, Karen fixed her ducts with much better materials, she would have an improvement rather than a repair.

4. Fix damaged areas only. If you repair, you replace or restore worn-out, broken, or deteriorated areas of the property.[19] When you expand your repair to areas of the property that are not worn out, broken, or deteriorated, you make an improvement.

Example: Mark has an air conditioner that suddenly stops working. If he fixes only the compressor, it's a repair. If he puts in a whole new unit, it's an improvement.

Example: Marcia has a leak in her roof. If she needs to replace only half the roof to fix the repair and she uses similar materials, this would be a repair. If she puts on a whole new roof or uses better materials, such as slate instead of shingles, this would be an improvement.

5. Repair after an event. Generally, you think out an improvement in advance.[20] With a repair, something happens that calls your attention to the need for the fix-up.[21] A broken water pipe requires repair. Wear and tear produces a need to repaint. Events made it necessary to repair the pipe and paint the building.

Example: Your floor is damaged. If you resurface it, it would be a repair.

Example: Your building is sinking because of the subsoil. If you shore up the building and replace a good portion of the floor because of this problem, you would probably have a repair. If you put in more than is required, such as a new wood floor to replace linoleum, you would have an improvement.

Author's note: With rental properties, many times repairs occur as a result of calls by tenants. You should document that a tenant called you in order to fix a problem. You can put your tax diary or organizer to good use here.

6. Repair during occupancy or between tenants. The IRS audit manual says that people may buy a property, renovate it, and then try to expense the cost instead of treating these expenses as rightful improvements.[22] The IRS tells its agents to watch for such situations and propose adjustments. You avoid a lot of scrutiny when you own the property for a time before making repairs. Also, you have a much stronger argument for repairs when you have tenants in place when you make the repairs.

7. Classify the fix up as a repair (or improvement) on your books. The bean counters should put the beans in the right spot. If you classify them as improvements on your books, the IRS will use this against you.[23]

8. Try to replace less than half of any wall, ceiling, or floor. If you put in a whole new wall, this would be an improvement; however, if you fix part of the wall, this would probably be deemed a repair.

Author's note: Your best proof may be a photograph. Take pictures before and after. If they look alike, that suggests a repair. Make sure you get the photo processed with a date stamp on the prints. Many digital cameras will date-stamp the photos too.

The bottom line: A combination of good planning and good records of proof—such as tenants calls, photos, separate bills for repairs and improvements—is critical toward getting the repair deductions that you want. If you want your fix-ups to be deemed improvements, as with your residence, you would do the opposite of what's recommended here. Remember: for rental properties, repairs are best, because they give a deduction now. For your home, you want improvements, because they're added to your basis. Repairs give you nothing.

The Universal Appeal of the Universal Exclusion

Prior to 1997, you were able to exclude up to $125,000 of gain on the sale of your principal residence if you were 55 or older. However, this discriminated against most of the population and it involved some complex requirements to obtain this exclusion. Many people felt this was unfair. To simplify the law dealing with residences, Congress passed a terrific law in 1997.[24]

Requirements Needed to Audit-Proof the Universal Exclusion

The general rule is that you may exclude up to $250,000 of gain from the sale of your principal residence ($500,000 if married filing jointly, which will be discussed below) if you meet the following requirements:[25]

- You owned the residence for any two of the last five years.
- You occupied your residence for any two of the last five years.
- You haven't used the exclusion within the last two years.

Author's note: As you can see, you can't have used the exclusion within the last two years. However, this also means that you can use the exclusion every two years!

Example: Tony sells his home for a $200,000 gain and uses the exclusion. He then moves into his summer home in Hyannis and lives there for two years. After the two years, he sells his second home. He may use the exclusion again.

Author's note: You can use the exclusion with every home that you own, by simply moving into it and making the home your new principal residence. You would live in it for two years and then sell the home and take the exclusion. Thus, you can avoid all or most of your gains on every home that you own. Isn't life great?

If you're married and filing a joint return, you may exclude up to $500,000 of gain if you meet these three requirements:[26]

- You *or* your spouse have owned the residence for at least two out of the last five years.
- *Both* you and your spouse have used the house as your principal residence for two out of the last five years.
- Neither spouse is ineligible because of using the exclusion within the last two years.

Ownership vs. Residence Test

The two-years-out-of-five requirement is applied strictly, with some exceptions, to be discussed below. To use the $250,000/$500,000 exclusion, either you or your spouse must have owned the residence and used it as your principal residence for any two out of the last five years.[27] The key, however, is that the ownership period may differ from your use period, as long as you satisfy both tests within the previous five-year window. Like the prior law, the two years need not be consecutive.[28] You can even count short absences for vacations as periods of use even if you rent out the home.[29]

Example: Matt and Lisa rent and live in a home in year 1. In year 2, they purchase the home and live in it until the end of the year. In year 3, they move out and rent the home to Smith until the end of year 5, when they sell the home. They have owned the home for two out of five years (years 2,3, and 4) and used it as their principal residence for two out of the last five years (years 1 and 2), so they qualify for the exclusion.

Even if you are living apart from your spouse and file jointly, each of you can claim the $250,000 exclusion for your individual residences if you meet the ownership and use rules.[30]

Example: Bill and Hillary file jointly, but live in different homes. They have each met the two-year ownership and use requirements for their respective homes. Each may avoid up to $250,000 of gain on the sale of each of their homes.

The general rule is that you can use the exclusion once every two years. Thus, if you use the exclusion less than two years ago, you must wait until the two-year period has passed.[31] However, remember my favorite saying: "Where there's a will, there's a lawyer." There are several exceptions to both the two-year ownership rule and the use rule.

If you or someone in your family becomes physically or mentally incapable of self-care,[32] you are deemed to meet both the ownership and use requirements if you've owned and used the home for only one year out of the last five years.

Example: Myra has been diagnosed with Alzheimer's disease. She lived in her home for one and a half years before she needed to be put into a nursing home for proper care. Despite the fact that she owned and used her residence for less than two years, she will be deemed to meet the ownership and use requirements for the full $250,000 exclusion if her home is sold.

You can even be exempt from all of the two-year rules.[33] Congress specifically allows some leeway to use the exclusion even if you fail the two-year ownership requirement or the two-year use requirement or you've used the exclusion within the last two years.

To avoid all these rules, your sale or exchange must be for one of the following reasons:

- Change in place of employment
- Health
- Other unforeseen circumstances as provided by the IRS.

Example: Warren was told by his doctor to move to a warm climate because of his asthma. If he moves to Arizona after living in his principal residence for only one year, he may still use part of the exclusion. The twoyear ownership and use requirements are waived.

Example: Karen had lived in her home for just one year when her firm transferred her to another city. She moves because of this job change. Despite living in the home for only one year, she may still use part of the exclusion.

As found in much of the recent tax legislation, what Congress giveth, it taketh away. If any of the two-year requirements are waived due to hardship, but you still don't quite meet one or both of the other requirements, the amount of the exclusion is calculated according to percentage of the months out of 24 that you met the rules. Let's take an example to explain this.

Example: Sarah sells her home because she gets a new job in another town. She has not used the exclusion in the last two years and has lived in the home for only six months. If she had both owned and occupied the home for the full two years, she would be able to exclude up to $250,000 of gain. However, since she lived in the house for only six months out of the required 24, by reason of her change in employment, she can exclude only 25 percent of the potential $250,000, so she pays taxes on $187,500 of gain.

Author's note: If she didn't meet the hardship exception, she would have to pay tax on the whole gain. Even though she doesn't get to use the whole $250,000 exclusion, she still avoids taxes on $62,500 of the gain.

IRS "Gotchas" with Prior Depreciation

As I've noted, you can rent out your home or conduct business in part of the home and still qualify for the exclusion. However, there's something that you should know about depreciation taken on your home.

If you've taken any depreciation on your home after May 6, 1997, any gain up to that amount of depreciation will be taxable at your normal rates, up to a maximum of a special long-term capital gain rate of 25 percent, as long as you have owned the property for at least one year.[34]

Example: Samantha sells her home in 2003 for a $200,000 gain. She used her home as a home office and claimed depreciation on part of her home. If the depreciation taken after May 6, 1997 was $5,000, Samantha must pay tax on the $5,000 at the rate of 25 percent. If Samantha had held the property for less than 12 months, the tax rate on this depreciation would be at her ordinary income tax rates.

Author's note: Frankly, I don't consider this payback of the allowable depreciation to be a problem. If you were in the 36 percent tax bracket when you took the depreciation, but you have to pay back the depreciation at only the 25 percent maximum rate, you're still coming out way ahead by taking any allowable depreciation.

Especially Beneficial for the Wealthy

Being able to use the exclusion every two years is very beneficial to the wealthy. Many wealthy people have second homes or vacation homes that have substantially appreciated in value. By being able to use the exclusion every two years, rich people can avoid much of the gain on both their principal residence and the gain on their vacation home by moving into the vacation home for at least two years.

This exclusion can also dramatically benefit people who are very handy with their hands. They can buy a "dog" of a home in a great area, fix it up, live in it for two years, and sell it for little or no taxable gain. If you were to specialize in properties of this type, you would get rich.

This exclusion can be valuable if you own rental property. How would you like to avoid paying tax on the sale of most rental property? Well, you can avoid a lot of tax using the exclusion. If you owned a rental house that had appreciated in value, you would simply move into the house for two years. Upon sale, you would avoid most of the gain, except for any depreciation taken.

Example: Lori owns a house that she rents out and that has appreciated by $200,000. Let's assume that she's taken $16,000 in depreciation. If she sells the house, she would have to pay tax on the entire $200,000 of gain, of which all but $16,000 could be at the 20 percent capital gains rate (25 percent on gain attributable to the depreciation taken). Thus, she may have to pay $40,800 in taxes plus any applicable state income tax. However, if she moves into the house for two years, she only has to pay tax on the depreciation taken. This would result in tax of only $4,000. She would have saved $36,800 in taxes. This surely would more than pay for the move plus the hassle of moving.

Author's note: If spouses who file jointly move into the rental property, they can exclude up to $500,000 of gain.

Transfers of Property as Part of a Divorce

One of the most overlooked real estate tax traps affects millions of Americans yearly as a result of divorces. If you sell your home to your exspouse as part of the divorce, his or her basis in the home is equal to the old joint basis and any gain or loss is measured against this old basis. Any payments your ex-spouse makes do *not* increase that basis.[35] The following example will illustrate this disastrous problem.

Example: Marc sells his share of his home to his ex-wife for $300,000 as part of the divorce. *If* they paid $40,000 for the house 10 years ago, her basis for gain or loss remains at $40,000. She gets no benefit from the $300,000 payment. Thus, if she sells the home for $600,000, she would have to pay tax on the entire $560,000 gain (less the $250,000 universal exclusion). Thus, she gets hit twice: when she pays $300,000 to buy her exhusband's share of the house and the second time when she sells the house and must pay tax on all the gain above the original basis. Yuck!

Author's note: In a divorce situation, neither spouse should purchase the house. Instead, the home should be sold to a third person. Each spouse can then buy a new home with his or her share of the tax-free money!

Summary

- Deduct all points incurred in purchasing and improving your principal residence.
- If you're going to finance the points, make sure that your down payment at least equals the amount of the points.
- If you pay points for any purposes other than to purchase and improve your home (such as to refinance a loan or to purchase a second home), amortize the points over the life of the loan.
- Any points paid by the seller are deductible by the buyer!
- Deduct all unamortized points when the loan is refinanced or when the property is sold.
- Try to structure all fix-up expenses on rental property as repairs rather than improvements.
- Try to structure all fix-up expenses on residences as improvements rather than repairs.
- To qualify for a repair, do the following:
  - Segregate repairs from improvements in the bill.
  - Fix minor areas only. Don't replace a whole wall or roof.

- Use similar, comparable, or less expensive materials.
- Fix damaged areas only.
- Repair after an event or after a tenant complains about a problem.
- Make repairs during occupancy or in between tenants.
- Classify the fix-up as a repair (or improvement) on your books.
- Try to replace less than half of any wall, ceiling or floor.
- Take advantage of the universal exclusion when selling your principal residence. Follow these three rules for the exclusion:
  - Own your residence for any two of the last five years.
  - Use your home as your principal residence for any two of the last five years.
  - Wait at least two years before you use the exclusion again. (Note: if you're married filing jointly, both you and your spouse must use the house as a principal residence for two out of the last five years.)
- The two years of ownership and the two years of usage don't have to be the same two out of five years.
- There's a partial exclusion from the rules if you sell your home as a result of a change in employment, health, or other unforeseen situation.
- Consider buying fixer-uppers and living in them for two years in order to use the exclusion.
- Consider moving into your rental houses for two years before selling them. You would avoid most of the gain.
- If you divorce, don't buy a home from your ex-spouse as part of the divorce. Instead sell the home to a third party and use the tax-free money to purchase a new home. You can even buy the home back as long as it isn't part of a prearranged plan.

Notes

1. Dana Milbank, "Bush Calls for Increasing Minority Home Ownership," *Washington Post,* June 18, 2002, p. A2.
2. Section 461(g)(2) of the IRC; see also Revenue Procedure 92-12A, 1992-1 CB 664.
3. Revenue Procedure 92-12, 1992-1 CB 663.
4. Revenue Procedure 94-27, 1994-1 CB 613.
5. *Internal Revenue Manual,* Section 4843.22.
6. Section 168(c) of the IRC.
7. Section 1.162-4 of the ITR.
8. *Illinois Merchants Trust Company v. Commissioner,* 4 BTA 103 (1926).
9. Section 1.263(a)-1(a)(1) of the ITR.
10. Section 1.263(a)-1(b) of the ITR.
11. *Jacobson v. Commissioner,* 47 TCM 499 (1983).
12. Ibid.
13. *Allen v. Commissioner,* 15 TCM 464 (1956).
14. *Internal Revenue Manual 4232.7, Techniques Handbook for Specialized Industries: Construction,* Subsection 72(18).

15. Section 1.164-4 of the ITR; see also *Ritter v. Commissioner*, 47-2 USTC ¦ 9378 (6th Cir. 1947) (new roof).

16. *Kingsley v. Commissioner*, 11 BTA 296 (1928), *acq.* VII-2 CB 22.

17. *Illinois Merchants Trust Company v. Commissioner*, 4 BTA 103 (1926).

18. *Abbot Worsted Mills, Inc. v. Commissioner*, 42-2 USTC ¦ 9694 (NH Dist. 1942).

19. *Sanford Cotton Mills v. Commissioner*, 14 BTA 1210 (1929).

20. E.g., *Jones v. Commissioner*, 24 TC 563 (1955).

21. *J.F. Wilcox and Sons v. Commissioner*, 28 BTA 878 (1933) (broken glass replaced).

22. *Internal Revenue Manual* 4232.7, *Techniques Handbook for Specialized Industries: Construction*, Subsection 72(18), Expensing of Capital Items.

23. *Farmer's Creamery Company v. Commissioner*, 14 TC 879 (1950).

24. H.R. 2014, Congressional Committee Report Accompanying Taxpayer Relief Act of 1997, Section 312.

25. Section 121(a) of the IRC.

26. Section 121(b)(2) of the IRC.

27. Section 121(b) of the IRC.

28. Section 121(b)(1) of the IRC.

29. Section 121(d)(6) of the IRC. By mandating depreciation recapture, Congress allows the home to be used in part as a business or as a rental.

30. See footnote 24, noted above.

31. Section 121(b)(3) of the IRC.

32. Section 121(d)(7)(A) of the IRC.

33. Section 121(c)(2) of the IRC.

34. Sections 1250 and 1(h)(1)(D) of the IRC.

35. Section 1041 of the IRC.

16

Making Colleges Less Expensive With Tax Planning

*Binghamton University Motto,
"We're only 207 road miles from Yale"*
—Tony Kornheiser, Washington Post

Chapter Overview
- Understand why most people should set up qualified tuition plans for their kids' future education.
- Learn the great benefits of both the Lifetime Learning Credit and the Hope Tax Credit
- Understand the rules of deducting student loan interest.
- Learn how to deduct up to $4,000 of college expenses.

Introduction

Towards the end of 2005, we were investigating colleges for my daughter. When I heard about the current tuition and fee rates, I was having an "out of body experience." Most private schools charged between $24,000 to $38,000 per year for tuition alone! When you filter in the outrageous fees that colleges are now surreptitiously adding plus the high cost of room and board and books, the cost can easily equal or exceed $50,000 per year. Imagine having to buy a BMW every year, which is what paying for college is akin to.

Although the public schools were a lot less expensive, they too have been increasing their tuition rates from 6 percent to 10 percent per year, with many experience double digit increases in tuition.[1]

In fact, over the last 30 years, college tuition costs for both public and private schools have risen far more than our cost of living. College costs today are much less affordable to the average American than they were for our parents.

The good news is that Congress added some great tax benefits to help reduce the sting of high tuition and fees. These benefits provide tax free savings accounts for colleges, otherwise known as Qualified Tuition Plans, and tax credits, which reduce your taxes on a dollar-for-dollar basis. In addition, you may now be able to deduct some student loan interest if you meet the rules and may even deduct some of the college tuition costs. Yes, you read this correctly. Thus, if you have dependents going to college, or are in college now, or even if you are considering attending college; this chapter could be a gold mine for your bank account.

Deductibility of Educational Expenses

I get asked many times if, "I can deduct the cost of college, or the cost of taking a course, or of going for a graduate degree."

General Rule

For courses to be deductible they must either maintain or improve skills required by your present job, trade or business or must meet the express requirements of your employer, or must be required in order to retain your salary, status, or rate of compensation.[2] If you meet these tests, you can deduct your tuition, fees, books, and certain travel and transportation expenses.[3]

Example: Sally takes some courses in order to maintain or improve her job as an accountant. She may not only deduct the tuition and fees, and books but also her round trip transportation to the school.

Example: Gina is a teacher who is taking a college course related to teaching English as required by her school. She may deduct all the costs related to this course.

Exceptions to the general rule

Although the above-noted general rule sounds easy to understand and apply, it is a bit misleading. Congress and the courts have carved out some exceptions to this rule. The main exception is that despite meeting the requirements of the general rule, the education isn't deductible if it either meets the minimum educational requirements for qualification in your current trade or business (or job) or is part of a program of study that would qualify you for a new trade or business.[4] The question thus becomes, "whether the course or program of study qualifies you for a completely different task than you were previously qualified to perform."[5] Let me give you some examples of those courses and programs that would be deductible and also those that wouldn't be deductible. This will give you a feel for what you can and cannot write off.

Courses and programs that were held to be deductible

- A night manager for a store could deduct a food market management program.[6]
- An aeronautical engineer was allowed to deduct the cost of a graduate degree in business management and administration since he also performed some administrative and management duties in his job.[7]
- Even obtaining a Masters in Business Administration (MBA) was held to be deductible if you have a current job that involved skills and tasks related to the MBA such as cost analysis, marketing, advertising, managing etc.

Caution: The costs associated with obtaining an MBA wouldn't seem to be deductible if you didn't have a current job that involved duties and skills related to the MBA.

- Costs involved in becoming a specialist in your profession would also be deductible.[8] Thus, a lawyer who pursues masters of law in tax would be deductible if that lawyer is currently employed as a lawyer or accountant.
- Other examples would be an elementary teacher studying to teach secondary school, a math teacher studying to teach science, or a classroom teachers studying to be a guidance counselor.

Examples of courses that would not be deductible because they qualify for a new trade or business

- Obtaining a law degree or taking a bar review course.[9]
- Taking a CPA review course.[10]
- The costs associated with obtaining an undergraduate degree are not normally deductible because they are deemed to qualify you for a new trade or business.[11]

The Bottom Line

If your program of study simply maintains or improves your current job skills, the program would be deductible *unless* such a program qualifies you for a new trade or business.

Deduct up to $4,000 of college expenses even if they don't improve any job skills

Even if you can't deduct your kids' college education costs because they qualify them for a new trade or business, don't be forlorn. Congress provides a yearly $4,000 expense election (or a tax credit, which will be discussed below) for college tuition costs and related expenses in 2007.

Caution: You cannot take this deduction and take the various college credits noted below. It is one or the other. In addition, what Congress gives, they take away. The deduction phases out for single taxpayers whose modified adjusted gross income is between $65,000 and $80,000. Thus, if you are single and make over $80,000 of modified adjusted gross income, you can not get this deduction. If you make between the numbers noted above, you will get some deduction, and if your modified adjusted gross income is less than $65,000, you can deduct the full $4,000 of college costs. I should note that if you are married filing jointly, the phaseout occurs between $130,000 and $160,000.

Qualified Tuition Programs (QTPs) and Prepaid Tuition

Wouldn't it be great if you could set up a special savings account that would earn tax free interest and tax-free gains and can be used for most college expenses? The answer is that you can with a Qualified Tuition Program (QTP).

There are essentially two types of these programs. The first is a prepaid tuition program that is used mostly for state universities. Here you would prepay a set amount that covers all tuition. The second is a form of investment fund that can be used for all qualified higher education expenses and for any school, whether it is a public supported or privately supported.

Tax consequences of QTPs

QTPs are *not* tax deductible[12]; however, the benefits are tax free to the extent that they are used for qualified higher education expenses.[13]

Example: Juan prepays $25,000 to the University of Maryland. Six years later when this money is used to pay for the tuition of his daughter, the proceeds are all tax free.

Author's elaboration: Prepaid tuition programs, unlike that of other QTPs, are only usable to prepay tuition and not room and board. They usually cover all four years regardless of the cost of living increases. Some of them, such as that of the one set up in Maryland, can even be used for other non Maryland state schools. The state of Maryland will pay what they would have been the highest in-state tuition for a Maryland state university. Thus, if your state has a program akin to that of Maryland, they can use the money for any school. However, you really need to check out what happens if your kids don't attend your state university. Not all states have such as consumer friendly program.

Also, transfers to the QTP qualifies for the annual gift tax exclusion, which is $12,000 per year per beneficiary if you are single and $24,000 per year, per beneficiary if you are married.[14] Thus, there is no gift tax if you limit the per person contribution to less than or equal to these amounts.

What are qualified higher education expenses?

This is the great part that you are going to like. Qualified higher education expenses consist of tuition and required fees, books, required supplies, and required equipment.[15] It also includes room and board for eligible students who attend at least half-time.

Example: Rich has a daughter attending college and covered by a QTP. Her tuition, room, board and books total $32,000. The QTP distribution can cover all of the $32,000 on a tax-free basis

Author's Hot Tip: No income limitations for QTPs: Unlike that of other educational benefits and credits, there are no income initiations for using QTPs. In addition, the Kiddie Tax rules, discussed in chapter 4, don't apply to earnings in QTPs. Thus, you could be making millions of dollars annually and still be eligible to set up and fund a QTP. With the Kiddie Tax age increased to age 18, use of a QTP is even more important now than ever.

QTPs can also be used to pay expenses of special needs beneficiaries for any expenses involved in either enrollment or in attendance at the school.[16]

Author's elaboration: If you have children who are handicapped and need special services such as wheel chairs, readers for exams, etc. QTPs could presumably be used to pay for these services.

Contributions to QTPs

All contributions must be made in cash or by check or by credit card. Thus, you can't contribute your stock portfolio to the QTP.

Caution: In addition, there are few limitations noted on the QTP. IRS, however, is a bit of a kill joy here. They have published some private letter rulings noting that either the QTP has to pay for the anticipated qualified higher education expenses for each dependent, which should presumably include a cost of living increase,[17] or, alternatively, up to five times the cost of tuition at eligible colleges.[18] Thus, this area is in flux, and you need to see a good financial professional in order to determine what maximum amount of contribution you are allowed for each dependent. In fact, you should see a good financial planning professional about setting up a QTP plan, other than that of a prepaid tuition plan, which is usually covered by your state.

Many types of qualified beneficiaries can be covered

What is so great about a QTP is that you can cover just about any person. In fact, if the person covered decides not to use the plan, you can transfer the proceeds, on a tax-free basis to any other qualified beneficiaries. This is a huge list of people:

- Spouse
- Any descendant of your or of your spouse
- Stepson or stepdaughter
- Stepfather or stepmother
- Any in-law such as daughter-in-law or son-in-law. Even a brother-in-law or sister-in-law qualifies
- Spouses of any of the above-named people.

Author's elaboration: As you can see, you have a host of people that you can cover with a QTP. However, you should also take note that your cousin is not a qualified beneficiary.

Author's Hot Tip: *Can Use Hope Tax Credits on QTP expenses:* Later on, you will learn that many middle class taxpayers can claim a Home Tax Credit on the first two years of college tuition expenses.

Series EE and Series I government bonds

This is a great way for lower and middle income parents to save for college costs for their dependents. The interest from these bonds is normally taxable for federal income tax but usually exempt from state income tax. However, if the bonds are used to pay for qualified tuition and fees for higher education for you, your spouse or your dependents, the interest could be tax-free.[19]

Qualification for tax-free status

There are certain qualifications that must be met to make the interest on series EE and series I bonds tax-free:

  a. **It can only be used for higher education expense:** Higher education expenses are tuition and required fees only. The cost of room, board and books don't qualify, unlike that of other tax credits and QTPs. Why Congress didn't allow for room and board here, as it does for other tax provisions, is a mystery. This is just another example of "tax simplification."

  b. **It must be purchased for the education of the taxpayer, their spouse or for their dependent:** If you use the bonds for your education, your spouse or for your dependent children, you would qualify for the tax-exempt status of the interest, assuming that you meet the other tests. However, if the bonds were purchased by a grandfather for his grand kids, the interest would be fully taxable unless the grandkids qualified as his dependents.

  c. **You must be on the cash basis:** With series EE bonds, you have a choice of being taxed each year on the interest, which is known as being on the accrual basis, or you can wait until you cash in the bonds and become taxed on all previous interest at the date that you received the cash for the bonds, which is considered the cash basis. You can't have made an election to be taxed on each year's interest, which is the accrual basis.

d. You must not earn too much money: This is Congress's gotcha! To have all the interest tax free for educational expenses, you can't earn too much money.[20] The benefits of receiving tax free interest from saving bond used for education phaseout as follows for 2007:

For single filers and heads of households: $65,600–$80,600
For married filing jointly: $98,400–$128,400
For married filing separately, there is no exclusion. Yuck!

Author's elaboration: What these phaseouts mean is that if you are a single taxpayer or head of household and earn over $80,600 of modified adjust gross income or if you are a married taxpayer who files a joint return and has a modified adjust gross income of over $128,400, you won't get any tax-free benefit from the savings bonds even if you meet the other qualifications. If you make less than these amounts, you will get a benefit. If you feel that you meet these rules, you should definitely see your accountant in order to see if you qualify. Getting tax free interest from federal savings bonds can be a great way to save for college.

Wonderful tax credits for education

Instead of taking a $4,000 deduction, Congress gives you two terrific tax credits for College tuition. As a reminder, a tax credit is better than a deduction because it results in a dollar-for-dollar reduction in your taxes.

Hope Scholarship Tax Credit[21]

This provides you with a tax credit for the first two years of college. The credit is 100 percent of your college tuition up to $1,100 plus 50 percent of the next $1,100. Thus, the total credit for each of the first two years would be $1,650.

This credit is available for you, your spouse and for each of your dependents. Especially nice is the fact that you can claim this credit for each eligible dependent. Thus, the $1,650 maximum credit is per individual and not per tax return.

Example: John has three kids in college. (I definitely feel sorry for John). He pays tuition of $5,000 for Jeremy, $18,000 for Matthew, and $34,000 for Allison. He may claim the maximum $1,650 credit for each kid, which totals $4,950 for each of the first two years of college.

Caution: *Phaseout of benefits:* Sadly, Congress can't make anything simple. The benefits of this credit start phasing out for married taxpayers filing joint returns if your modified adjusted gross income (MAGI) exceeds $94,000 in 2007. It completely is eliminated if your MAGI equals or exceeds $114,000. For Single taxpayers, the phaseout limits are between $47,000 and $57,000; so much for tax simplification!

Author's hot tip: *Don't claim your kids as dependents and give them the tax credit:* If your income exceeds the phaseout amount so that you can't get the credit, don't be forlorn. Remember, where there is a will … there is a lawyer. If you don't claim them as a dependent, they should be able to get the credit for themselves. This will reduce the taxes that they would pay on earnings from jobs or on investment earnings. I should note that they can't claim this credit if you claim them as a dependent.[22] Thus, you would need to not claim the child or relative who is taking the credit as a dependent on your tax return.[23]

Author's elaboration: Because this provision excludes a student enrolled in a secondary school from the definition of an eligible student, it appears that the credit is not available for the expenses of a high school student taking courses at a college or university.[24]

Caution Convicted drug felons: The Hope credit is not allowed for any student who has been convicted of a federal or state felony drug offense.[25] Presumably, if your kids were convicted of treason, murder, rape or robbery, they would still be eligible for the Hope Tax Credit. How stupid can Congress be?!

The Bottom Line

This is a nice benefit that Congress gave to middle income taxpayers. It's too bad that they didn't give it to everyone.

Lifetime Learning Credit

This is the second tax credit for tuition and related expenses such as tuition, books, supplies and required equipment. The amount of the credit is 20 percent of tuition and related expenses up to $10,000 per year. Thus, the maximum yearly credit is $2,000.[26] This credit is doubled for students in Gulf Opportunity Zone such as New Orleans students.[27]

Difference between Lifetime Learning Credit and Hope Tax Credit

Since you can only use either the Lifetime Learning Credit or the Hope Tax Credit for a specific dependent per year[28], you need to know the differences between the two credits.

   1. **Different Credit amounts:** The Hope Tax credit gives you 100 percent credit for first $1,100 of tuition and 50 percent for next $1,100 for a total credit of $1,650 per student per year. The Lifetime Learning Credit gives you a 20 percent credit for tuition and related expenses, which includes

fees, supplies and required equipment for a total maximum credit of $2,000 per year.

2. **One is per student, and one credit is per year:** You can take a Hope Tax Credit for each student's tuition for post secondary education. Thus, if you have three kids in college during in their first two years of college, you can get three Hope Credits. The Lifetime learning credit is one credit per year per tax return. Thus, your maximum credit is $2,000 regardless of the number of kids in college.

Example: Kevin takes the Hope Tax Credit for the first two years of college for his daughter Karen. For the remaining years of Karen's education, Kevin can claim the Lifetime Learning Credit.

3. **Hope Credits are only for the first two years of college:** The Hope Tax Credits are only for the first two years of post-secondary education. The Lifetime Learning Credit can be used for any year of post-secondary education and even for graduate school.

4. **Unlike that of the Hope Tax Credit, there is no half-time requirement for education:** The Hope Tax Credit requires that a student spend at least half-time pursuing a degree. This means that they must take enough credits to equal one-half of a full time workload for at least one academic period.[29] There is no similar requirement for the Lifetime Learning Credit. The Lifetime Learning Credit can be used for any course or program of study that either leads to a degree by an accredited college or can be used for any course(s) that helps the student acquire or improve job skills.[30] It can actually be used to take as few as one job related course.

Example: Christy, a professional photographer, enrolls in an advanced photography course at a local community college. Although the course is not part of a degree program, Christy enrolls in the course to improve her job skills. The course fee paid by Christy is a qualified tuition and related expense for purposes of the lifetime learning credit.[31]

Author's hot tip: In the same taxable year, a taxpayer may claim a Hope scholarship credit for each eligible student's qualified tuition and related expenses and a lifetime learning credit for one or more other students' qualified tuition and related expenses. However, a taxpayer may not claim both a Hope credit and a lifetime learning credit with respect to the same student in the same taxable year.[32]

Example: In 2007, Dan has two daughters in college. His daughter Allison is a first year, full-time student. His daughter Karen is a college junior. Dan may claim the Hope Credit for Allison and the Lifetime Learning Credit for Karen.

The Bottom Line

Take the credit that gives you the best results.

5. **Deducting Student Loan Interest:** With ever escalating college costs, many kids are saddled with a lot of debt as a result of their educational expenses. Congress came to the rescue in the past few years by allowing up to $2,500 in interest on qualified student loan debt to be deductible per year. Sadly, this deduction starts phasing out for single taxpayers whose modified adjusted gross income exceeds $55,000 and is completely phased out for modified adjusted gross incomes of $70,000. For married taxpayers filing joint returns the phaseout limits are between $110,000 and $140,000.[33]

Author's hot tip: In the event that you can't deduct part or all of your student loan interest for you or your family member, consider taking out a home equity loan to pay off the loan. You may deduct interest on home-equity debt up to $100,000.[34]

Author's hot tip: If your modified adjusted gross income prevents you from claiming the student loan interest as a deduction, consider having your kids pay off the loan. If you don't claim them as dependents, and they are jointly liable on the loan, they should be able to take a deduction for the interest as an adjustment from gross income.

Author's observation: I find it extraordinarily idiotic that Congress has different phaseout amounts in order to determine eligibility for the tax credits, tax-free series EE bond interest, and for deducting student loan interest. In addition, Congress based the eligibility on modified adjusted gross income instead of simply using adjusted gross income, which you can easily determine from your tax return. I truly believe that something negative happens to the common sense of Congressmen and Senators when they are in office too long.

The Bottom Line

There are certainly a number of good tax credits and benefits for middle class taxpayers that help ease the sting of high college costs. In addition, using Series EE bonds and especially Qualified Tuition Programs are a great way to save for your dependents' college expenses. It certainly is better to use a QTP than trying to save up for college paying tax on the earnings.

Summary

- You can deduct all the ordinary and necessary educational expenses that maintain or improve either your trade or business or job performance. They are not deductible, however, if they either meet the minimum educational requirements of your current trade or business or is part of a program of study that qualifies you for a new trade or business.
- Deduct up to $4,000 of college expenses even if those expenses do not improve job skills. However, this deduction starts phasing out as Modified

Adjusted Gross Income (MAGI) for single taxpayers exceeds $65,000 or for married filing jointly of $80,000.

- Qualified Tuition Programs (QTPs) are used to pay for post-secondary educational expenses. They are tax free to the extent used for qualified expenses such as tuition, required fees, supplies, required books and required equipment. There is no income limit for QTPs; thus, they are available to everyone.

- Prepaid Tuition plans are a form of QTP. They are normally used to prepaid state tuition and usually cover four years of tuition.

- QTPs are portable. Their benefits can be transferred to most lineal descendants, ancestor, or spouses of descendants or ancestors.

- Hope Tax Credits can be used on educational expenses paid with QTP funds.

- Series EE and Series I bonds are great ways to save for tuition and required fees for you, your spouse, and your dependents. Be aware, however, of the phaseouts of this benefit if you make too much money.

- Don't forget the Hope Tax Credit, which can save you in taxes $1,650 per student. This applies to you, your spouse and your dependents. However, this is available only for middle-income taxpayers. Thus, you must be aware of the phaseout of these benefits as your modified adjusted gross income increases.

- The Hope Tax Credit is available only for the first two years of post secondary school education and only if the student attends school at least one-half of what a full-time schedule would be. Thus, if a full time schedule would be at least 12 credits, students would have to take at least 6 credits to qualify.

- The Lifetime Learning Credit gives up to $2,000 per tax return and not per student. It is available for students for any courses that improve their job performance or qualify them for a new trade or business. This credit has the same phaseout limit as that of the Hope Tax Credit.

- If you can't qualify for either credit because of the income phaseouts, consider not claiming your kids as dependents and have them get the credit on their tax returns.

- Don't forget to deduct student loan interest of up to $2,500 per year. You can only do this if your modified adjusted gross income does not exceed the phaseout limits. If you can't qualify for the deduction because of your earnings, consider not claiming your kids as dependents and have them pay the loan interest; at least, this would be a deduction for them on their tax return.

Notes

1. *Chronicle of Higher Education.*
2. Section 1.162-5 of the Regulations.
3. Ibid.
4. Section 1.162-5(b)(3) of the Regs.
5. *Diaz v. Commissioner,* 70 T.C. 1067 (1978), Aff'd 607 F. 2d 995 (2nd. Cir. 1979).

6. *Granger v. Commissioner*, T.C. Memo 1980-60.
7. *Beatty v. Commissioner*, T.C. Memo 1980-196.
8. Section 1.162-5(c)(1) of the Regs.
9. Section 1.162-5(b)(3)(ii) of the Regs. See also *Sharon v. Commissioner*, 591 F. 2d 1273 (9th. Cir. 1978).
10. *Cooper v. Commissioner*, T.C. Memo 1979-241.
11. *Garwood v. Commissioner*, 62 T.C. 699 (1974).
12. Section 529(c)(3)(B) of the IRC.
13. Ibid.
14. Section 529(c)(2)(A) of the IRC.
15. Section 529 (e)(5) of the IRC.
16. Section 529 (e)(3)(A) of the IRC.
17. PLR 200030030.
18. PLR 200024055.
19. Section 135(a) and section 135 (c)(2)(A) of the IRC.
20. Section 132(b)(2)(A) of the IRC. See also Rev. Proc. 2005-70, 2005-47 I.R.B. 979.
21. H.R. Report #220, 105th. Congress, 1st. Session (1997). See also Notice 97-60, Section 2, Q&A 6, 1997-46, I.R.B. 8. See also Section 25A(a)(1) of the IRC.
22. Section 25A(g)(3)(A) of the IRC.
23. Section 1.25A-1(f)(1) of the Regs.
24. Kleinrock's Analysis and Explanations, Section 31.2 (2006).
25. Section 25A(b)(2)(D) of the IRC.
26. Section 25A(c)(1) of the IRC.
27. Section 14000 of the IRC.
28. Section 25A(c)(2)(A) of the IRC.
29. Section 25A(b)(2)(B) of the IRC.
30. Section 25A(c)(2)(B) of the IRC.
31. Kleinrock's Analysis and Explanation, Section 31.2 (b) (Hope Scholarship and Lifetime Learning Credits, Example 1.
32. Section 1.25A-1(b)(1) of the Regs. See also footnote 31, noted above.
33. Section 221(b)(2) of the IRC and Rev. Proc. 2005-70, 2005-47 I.R.B. 979 (2006).
34. Section 163(h)(3)(A) and section 163 (h)(3)(C) of the IRC.

17

The Top 10 Tax Questions

The questions answered in this chapter have universal appeal, have been asked numerous times at my seminars, or are very interesting. I hope you enjoy reading them as much as I've enjoyed answering them.

Question Number 10

"As a part owner of my corporation, I am paid a salary as an employee and receive bonuses as part of my salary. If I were to travel on business and incur some expenses that aren't reimbursed, can I deduct the excess unreimbursed expenses on my tax return as an itemized deduction? For example, I may stay at a nicer hotel, but my company may reimburse me for a lower amount."

Sandy's Answer
You can deduct any excess travel expenses incurred by you as employee business expenses, a miscellaneous itemized deduction on Schedule A of your tax return. However, I would not do this. Have your corporation reimburse you for all your travel expenses. The reimbursement would not be taxable to you, and the corporation would get a deduction (although it would deduct only one-half of the meal costs). The reason is that miscellaneous itemized deductions are deductible only to the extent that they exceed 2 percent of your adjusted gross

income (gross income from wages, dividends, and pensions less certain deductions, such as moving and IRA contributions, etc.). Thus you would lose some or all the deductions as a result of this threshold. However, you will not have this problem if your company reimburses you for all your reasonable travel expenses. Thus here's the bottom line: If you're operating as a corporation or partnership, get your business to pay for all business expenses. This is much better than taking any unreimbursed employee business expenses as an itemized deduction and losing some of the deduction.

Question Number 9

"I have been told that I can deduct up to $25,000 of rental property losses that might exceed rental property income and use those losses against any other form of income, such as my wages. Is this true? Also, I am a part-time property manager (working about 300 hours per year). I heard that being in real estate or property management can allow me to take all the rental loss deductions without limit and regardless of income. Is this true?"

Sandy's Answer

You're asking a very good question that affects a lot of people. For many years, real estate investors were allowed to deduct all rental property losses against any form of income. Real estate was the best legal tax shelter available. Starting in 1987, Congress limited rental property losses to rental property income and other passive income. However, there are two little known exceptions.

The first exception, which you noted in your question, applies to real estate professionals. If you're in the business of real property development, construction, acquisition (such as Donald Trump), management, leasing, or sales and you meet two tests, there are no limits to being able to use rental property losses. In fact, if you're in any of the occupations listed, your real estate losses are deductible against any other form of income, with no limitation. However, to meet this exception, your real estate business must meet either of the following two tests:

- You perform more than half your business working hours in the real estate business.
- You perform more than 750 hours of this type of work during the year.

Since it seems that you do not meet either of these tests, you do not qualify for the real estate professional exception.

However, you may qualify for the second exception. If you actively manage your real estate investments—such as making the management decisions of approving tenants, deciding on rental terms, and approving repairs and improvement expenditures—and your income is under a certain ceiling (this is the congressional "gotcha"), you can deduct up to $25,000 of rental property losses against any other form of income.

The ceiling for that maximum loss allowance is an adjusted gross income (AGI) of $100,000 for either single or joint filers or $50,000 for married filing separately. If your AGI is over $100,000, the maximum gets phased out by $1 for every $2 that you earn over $100,000. But you can carry over to future years any remaining unused losses; the same limits apply. You also can use the losses against any gains from the sale of rental property.

Let's take some examples.

Example: David and Kari earn $120,000 AGI together. They have substantial rental losses that exceed their rental income. Since they earn over $120,000 AGI, they may only use $15,000 of the losses against their wages (the $25,000 maximum less 50 percent of the $20,000 excess AGI over $100,000). They can carry over the remaining unused losses, subject to the same limits.

Example: Deb and Donald earn $180,000 AGI and also have the same amount of rental property losses. They may not use any of the rental losses above their rental income because their AGI exceeds $150,000, which is the top for the phaseout ($25,000 less 50 percent of the $80,000 excess AGI over $100,000).

Question Number 8

Here is a vital question dealing with pension distributions. If you terminate your relationship with your company and you get your vested pension in cash, this question and answer will save you a bundle!

"I got a pension distribution made to me when my job got terminated. If I want to avoid any gains, I was told that I would have to roll over the contribution to my IRA within 60 days of receipt of the distribution to avoid all gains. The problem is that my company took out 20 percent of the distribution as a withholding for the IRS pursuant to IRS requirements. What do I do now? I can't rollover the withheld amount."

Sandy's Answer

You're right in noting that you have to pay tax on all pension, 401k, and IRA distributions (other than the new Roth IRA) if you don't roll over the distribution within 60 days to another qualified plan or IRA. If this isn't painful enough, you also could be hit with a 10 percent penalty if you're younger than 59½.

Because the distribution was sent to you, the prior plan trustee *must* withhold 20 percent of the distribution. Your only choice is to contribute other money to the IRA to make up for the withholding. You would therefore not be taxed on any of the distribution and will get a refund of all withholding.

The better solution, which is too late for you, would have been to require the plan trustee to directly roll over the funds to your IRA and not to distribute the money to you. In this way, you would have avoided withholding.

Question Number 7

This question does not have universal appeal. However, as you'll see, I had fun with the answer.

"I have begun a photo enhancement/alteration service in which I can turn any 'would have been a good shot if only…' photo into something worth displaying. My biggest target markets are the consumers and business providers of the equestrian (horse) industry. Currently, I have a display at the public stable where my horse resides. If I display it on my horse's stall door, can I deduct my monthly board that I pay to keep the horse there? I view this as being similar to taking a home office deduction for displaying products and services in a home office."

Sandy's Answer

This is a great question. I met a couple on my travels who were "equine expression specialists." I wonder if that was you and your wife.

As for your question, the home office rules are very specific. They apply only to a residence that you live in. Thus, unless you live with your horse—and I doubt that your horse is cute enough to warrant this—the home office rules are not applicable.

Having a display at a public stable probably wouldn't alone allow for a deduction of the boarding fee of the horse; you probably could get a display posted even if your horse weren't there. You may, however, be able to deduct the stable fee if you run your horse business like a business and not just "horsing around" like a hobby.

The following are some factors that the IRS would look for:

- Do you race or breed your horse?
- Are you making money?
- If you're not making money, what steps are you taking to make money?
- What consultants or specialists have you used?
- What training have you attended?

If you're considered to be running your horse business as a business, this could be a " horse of a different color" as far as the IRS is concerned. See pages 145 to 149 of the workbook in my *Tax Strategies for Business Professionals* series.

Question Number 6

If you own some investment property, such as rental property, you'll find this question and answer very useful.

"I currently own some houses that I rent out. I want to sell the houses but don't want pay tax on the sale. I guess I want to have my cake and eat it too. Any suggestions, Sandy?"

Sandy's Answer

You can indeed avoid all capital gains on your real estate by structuring a *like-kind exchange*. This is where you trade one investment property for another. You may trade an apartment building for land or a commercial building for residential rentals, etc. The exchange must, however, be investment property for investment or commercial property. You can't have a like-kind exchange for your residence. Moreover, you cannot receive anything in exchange, such as cash or other property, or you may have to recognize gain to the extent of the other property received.

In addition, you don't even have to know which property you want to receive in the exchange. You can have a deferred exchange, where you would identify the property that you want within 45 days of the contract and then acquire the replacement property within 180 days of the contract. Check with your accountant and a good realtor who specializes in this type of transaction.

Question Number 5

This question is for you "party animals." It involves entertainment and alcohol.

"I am having a business party in my home. I will be following your advice about sending out an announcement that I am celebrating 10 years in business and will have displays of what I do. I intend to serve alcohol, and in my state, there is a special alcohol tax like a sales tax. Can I deduct the cost of the alcohol just like deducting food, and can I deduct the tax?"

Sandy's Answer

Alcohol is treated like any other beverage. It would be as deductible as food. The tax on the alcohol also would be deductible, as would any tax on food. I should note that generally entertainment is 50 percent deductible, unless you're having a sales presentation in your home. Also, there's no limit to how much you can spend on the party. So have a good time—and let the government pay part of the bill. Cha, cha, cha!

Question Number 4

This question will have universal appeal. It deals with the issue of when you can start taking business deductions. This is a vital issue for all new business people.

"I just bought some investment real estate. It's in bad shape and needs some work. When can I start deducting the depreciation and maintenance on the property? Also, my wife is opening up a restaurant. When can she start deducting expenses related to the restaurant?"

Sandy's Answer

These are good questions that apply to many small businesses. You're deemed to be in business and therefore able to deduct business expenses when you're open for business. Thus you must be able to sell services or products or take customers. It's at this point that any reasonable business expenses that you incur become deductible.

In your real estate investment business, you would reach this point when your property becomes habitable, and you start advertising for a tenant. In your wife's restaurant, she would reach this point when she is able to accept customers.

Some businesses, however, incur some expenses before they open the business, such as investigation expenses, legal and accounting fees incurred for the startup, copyrights, etc. These would be nondeductible.

However, where there's a will, there's a lawyer. The IRS gives you an out. You may elect to amortize your preopening expenses over a period of at least 60 months. You must, however, elect to do so on your tax return. See your accountant about making a protective election for your startup expenses.

Question Number 3

I get this question a lot. Network marketers in particular frequently ask it. It applies, however, to any business. It entails one of the biggest myths that surround the tax law.

"I am in the network marketing business. I have some losses in my business during my first two years of operation. My accountant told me that I have to have a profit for three of the last five years in order to take the losses, so he won't allow me to deduct these losses against my salary. Is this true?"

Sandy's Answer

You need to get a new accountant immediately. As for needing a profit in three of the last five years, this is probably the biggest myth in tax law. Rightfully, you want to be construed as a business and not as a hobby. The implications are enormous.

If you're in business, you get to deduct all ordinary and necessary business expenses on a dollar-for-dollar basis. In addition, if your expenses exceed your income, you will have a tax loss that you can use against any form of income, such as wages, dividends, and pensions. You can even use it against your spouse's earnings.

Example: Scott earns $40,000 in salary from his job. If his side business generates a $10,000 loss, he may offset the salary with the loss and pay tax on only $30,000.

If the loss from your business exceeds your yearly income, you may either carry back the loss two years (for 2002, it's five years owing to a special rule) or carry forward the loss 20 years and offset up to the next 20 years of income.

If you're a hobby, however, all expenses related to the hobby constitute miscellaneous itemized deductions, which must exceed 2 percent of your adjusted gross income to be deductible. Even worse, all net losses from hobbies are limited to the income from hobbies: You cannot carry over or carry back any of the losses. Thus you rarely, if ever, want to be classified as a hobby.

The Internal Revenue Code notes that if you have a profit for three of five consecutive years (two of seven for horses), you're presumed to be a business. However, even if you don't have the necessary profit in the three years, you can still have many years of losses *if you run your endeavor with a reasonable expectation of profit.*

There are a number of factors that the courts use in making this determination. One of the biggest and most important factors is whether you have a business plan. This is a five-year projection of income and expenses. The projection should at some year show a profit. I cannot overstate the importance of this. You also should have a marketing plan built into your business plan to show your projected marketing activities.

Another factor is documentation. Businesses have correct detailed records. Businesses keep tax diaries. Hobbies do not.

You also should work your business regularly. This means at least 45 minutes per day, four or five days a week. It's much more beneficial in establishing a business motive to work a business four hours a week than to put in eight hours in one week and none in the second week.

Business owners go to training that should be documented. In addition, if business owners don't have a profit in one year, they don't repeat the same mistakes. Insanity is expecting different results from doing the same thing from year to year. Business owners change marketing strategies if they don't work and they consult with experts.

There's much more that I can add to this answer, but it should give you a good review of what's necessary. See also the in-depth discussion of this subject in Chapter 8.

Question Number 2

This question deals with a major issue that is misunderstood nationwide. There are millions of people who take out home-equity loans unnecessarily because they don't understand this issue.

"I am self-employed and use the IRS mileage deduction for my vehicle. Therefore, I do not deduct gas, insurance, repairs, etc. However, my question is whether I can take the interest deduction incurred on my car loan and deduct a percentage for business."

Sandy's Answer

This is a great question and an example of one of the biggest misunderstandings in the tax law. You're allowed to deduct your car interest and/or sales tax to the extent that you use your car for business. Thus, if you use your car 80 percent for business, you can deduct 80 percent of the year's interest and 80 percent of any taxes incurred on the car for that year. This point is also true *regardless* of the method that you use to deduct your car, whether it's the IRS mileage approach or the actual expenses (such as deducting gas, repairs, insurance, etc.).

Sadly, many people don't understand that you can deduct interest on car loans to the extent that the vehicle is used for business. Thus they take out home-equity loans to accomplish this. This could be a bad mistake. If they fail to pay off the loan, they could lose their home. Moreover, home-equity loans have limits of up to $100,000 of credit. If you use a loan to purchase a car, this would reduce the available amount of the loan that you could use for other purposes.

I should note that employees who don't have a side business cannot deduct the interest and taxes incurred on their vehicles. You must use a car in business to get this benefit.

Question Number 1

This is the question I get most frequently. Someone asks this question on my Web site, www.taxreductioninstitute.com, almost every week. If you have a network marketing business, you probably have wondered about this yourself. However, this question also would apply to other businesses, such as franchises, where there may be a minimum purchase requirement.

"I have a multilevel marketing business. I am required to purchase $100 a month of product in order to receive any check. May I deduct the cost of this required monthly purchase?"

Sandy's Answer

In my opinion, and that of IRS personnel with whom I spoke, you cannot deduct your monthly purchases. The reason is that these items usually can be resold, so they would be nondeductible inventory, or you probably consume the products monthly, which would make these purchases personal and nondeductible.

However, as I'm fond of saying, "Where there's a will, there's a lawyer." There are a couple of ways that would entitle you to get a deduction for these purchases.

One way is to give them away to prospects as samples. You would have to note in your diary answers to the following questions:

- Who did you give the product to?
- What did you give?
- When (the date) did you give it?
- How much did it cost?
- Why did you give it (such as for samples or demonstration)?

If you write down the answers to these questions, you may deduct your monthly purchases to the extent that you gave the products away as samples.

A second method is to sell the products. As I mentioned, they're considered inventory, so they're not deductible until they're sold.

The third method is to donate them to charity, such as to your local college or religious organization. You then would take a charitable deduction for the donation as a nonbusiness deduction. Don't forget to get a receipt from the charity!

Author's note: There are tax professionals who disagree with my opinion on this issue. Their reason is that there is no case or IRS ruling on this issue. In addition, requiring product purchases in order to receive a check seems like it is ordinary and necessary to the network marketing business. I should note that this answer to question 1 is my opinion; however, it is also the opinion of IRS personnel whom I have questioned. If you try to take this deduction, be prepared to have to fight with the IRS about this issue. Who knows? You may win the case, and I can cite you in forthcoming books!

Appendix A

2007 Tax Rates

Single Individuals
  Standard Deduction = $5,350

Taxable Income Over	But Not Over	Pay	+	% of Excess	Of the Amount Over
0	$7,825	0		10%	0
$7,825	$31,850	$782.50		15%	$7,825
$31,850	$77,100	$4,386.25		25%	$31,850
$77,100	$160,850	$15,698.75		28%	$77,100
$160,850	$349,700	$39,148.75		33%	$160,850
$349,700	-	$101,469.25		35%	$349,700

Married Individuals Filing Joint Returns and Surviving Spouses
  Standard Deduction = $10,700

Taxable Income Over	But Not Over	Pay	+	% of Excess	Of the Amount Over
0	$15,650	0		10%	0
$15,650	$63,700	$1,565.00		15%	$15,650
$63,700	$128,500	$8,772.50		25%	$63,700
$128,500	$195,850	$24,972.50		28%	$128,500
$195,850	$349,700	$43,830.50		33%	$195,850
$349,700	-	$94,601.00		35%	$349,700

Heads of Household
  Standard Deduction = $7,850

Taxable Income Over	But Not Over	Pay	+	% of Excess	Of the Amount Over
0	$11,200	0		10%	0
$11,200	$42,650	$1,120.00		15%	$11,200
$42,650	$110,100	$5,837.00		25%	$42,650
$110,100	$178,350	$22,700.00		28%	$110,100
$178,350	$349,700	$41,810.00		33%	$178,350
$349,700	-	$98,355.50		35%	$349,700

Married Individuals Filing Separate
  Standard Deduction = $5,350

Taxable Income Over	But Not Over	Pay	+	% of Excess	Of the Amount Over
0	$7,825	0		10%	0
$7,825	$31,850	$782.50		15%	$7,825
$31,850	$64,250	$4,386.25		25%	$31,850
$64,250	$97,925	$12,486.25		28%	$64,250
$97,925	$174,850	$21,915.25		33%	$97,925
$174,850	-	$47,300.50		35%	$174,850

1. The Personal Exemption for 2007 is $3,400; Personal Exemptions are phased out by 2 percent for every $2,500 over:
   a) $156,400 for singles
   b) $195,500 for head of household
   c) $234,600 for married filing jointly or surviving spouse
   d) $117,300 for married filing separately

2. For 2007, itemized deductions are reduced by 2 percent for adjusted gross income over $156,400 ($78,200 for married filing separately). It *cannot* be reduced by more than 80 percent of allowable itemized deductions.

3. $1,000 tax credit in 2007 for each dependent child under age 17. The credit phases out for adjusted gross income that exceeds:
   a) $75,000 for single taxpayers
   b) $110,000 for married filing jointly

4. Dividends are taxed at the maximum rate of 15 percent in 2007.

5. Capital Gains are taxed at a rate of 15 percent; however, for taxpayers in the 10 to 15 percent tax bracket, capital gains are taxed at a rate of 5 percent in 2007.

Appendix B

How to Find a Good Accountant

The question that I get asked most frequently at seminars is, "How do I find a good accountant?" Sadly, it is very tough finding the right, knowledgeable accountant.

First, not all accountants specialize in taxes. Many accountants perform audits, computer studies, and the like. Second, many accountants are timid! They would love for you to send in 100 percent of your income (less their accounting fee).

Accordingly, there are some questions that you can ask in order to see an accountant is right for you. Here are some suggestions:

1. What designations or credentials do you have?

Look for enrolled agents (people who pass a special IRS examination), certified public accountants, ex-IRS agents, attorneys, etc. I like preparers with legal backgrounds, because they tend to be more aggressive.

2. Are you in practice full time?

Hopefully, the answer will be yes.

3. How many years' experience do you have in tax practice?

You don't want a rookie experimenting on you!

4. Do you prepare all returns by computer?

Handwritten returns ended with the '80s.

5. What are your fees and do you have a written fee schedule?

Cheaper is not necessarily better. You may get what you pay for!

6. Can you provide references from other businesses similar to my own?

Many accountants, rightly, don't give out names of clients. However, all firms should have some happy clients who will be willing to speak to you. When you call them, ask them, "What do you like about the accountant?" and "What would you improve about his/her services?"

7. Do you use any checklists to maximize my deductions?

8. Test your accountant.

Tell him/her that in a tax reduction book and seminar it was suggested "to hire your spouse and make that person the primary insured so you can deduct medical insurance premiums and set up a self-insured medical plan." Ask what the accountant thinks of this strategy.

9. Do you teach any tax courses or have you written any tax publications?

The more, the better.

10. Are you conservative, aggressive, or somewhere in the middle?

11. What review process do you use in order to ensure a quality product?

12. May I look at your tax library?

Accountants need to look things up. The more sources, the better. They should have at least two separate tax research sources.

13. Do you specialize in taxes?

They should say yes!

14. What percentage of your practice relates to taxes? What other accounting services do you personally perform?

15. What is your attitude toward tax audits?

Unfortunately, many tax preparers recommend not taking legitimate tax breaks at all if it could possibly trigger an audit. These accountants are a "hazard to your wealth."

16. How do you treat gray areas?

The best advisors will tell you that the area is gray and give you your options. Stay away from advisors who say, "The area is not clear, so don't take the deduction."

17. What do you do after tax season?

You want to hear that he/she does other accounting work and also does marketing for new clients.

18. How often do you take tax courses?

19. Have you ever been disciplined by the IRS or any accounting society?

If an accountant refuses to answer this question or acts insulted, forget it!

20. How many other clients like me do you have?
You don't need hundreds, but more than 10 would be helpful.

21. Do you offer pre-year-end tax planning as part of your tax service? If so, is there an extra fee for this?

22. Do you offer any tax planning during the year?

23. How soon do you return calls from clients?

24. Give me a tax-planning tip based on a recent tax change that may benefit me.

Conclusion

These questions may not be all-inclusive. However, they will certainly "separate the wheat from the chaff" and enable you to make much better decisions as to whether an accountant is right for you!

Appendix C

Overview of HSA's: An HSA requires a trust to be set up for paying qualified medical expenses. The contributions are deductible, and the payments for these qualified medical expenses are tax-free.

Qualifying: You must use the HSA proceeds for qualified medical expenses. In addition, you must have a high deductible medical policy.[1] For both 2007 and 2008, a high deductible plan, for single taxpayers, is one whose annual deductible is at least $1,100. In addition, the amount of the deductible and out of pocket expenses for single taxpayers can not exceed $5,500 for 2007 and $5,600 for 2008.[2]

---

[1] Section 223©(1)(A) of the IRC
[2] Section 223©(1)(A) of the IRC and Rev. Proc. 2007-36 I.R.B. 1335

Contribution Limits[3]:

Tax Year	Self Only coverage Dollar limits	Family Coverage Dollar Limits
2007	$2,850	$5,650
2008	$2,900	$5,800

There are catch up contributions allowed for those who are age 55 or older of $800 per person for 2007 and $900 per person for 2008.

Observation: In my opinion, the self insured medical plan is still the better option since you don't need a high deductible policy, don't need to set up a trust with yearly fees paid to financial institutions and don't have any dollar limitations on contributions other than the fact that the payments must be reasonable for the hours and work performed. An HSA, however, might be advisable if you are single and don't have a C corporation or you don't want to hire your spouse in your business in order to utilize the benefits of the self-insured medical plan for yourself.

---

[3] Section 223(g) of the IRC and Rev. Proc. 2007-36 I.R.B. 1335

Index

About the Author

Sandy Botkin, CPA, Esquire, is the CEO of the Tax Reduction Institute of Germantown, Maryland. Sandy was one of the first lecturers nationwide to teach tax planning and audit-proofing techniques to small and home-based business.

Prior to joining the Tax Reduction Institute, Sandy spent three years in the tax department of the international accounting firm Deloitte & Touche. He then became a tax attorney for the Internal Revenue Service and was one of eight attorneys who taught other attorneys at the IRS. He was one of the founding members of the IRS' elite Tax Shelter Group.

Sandy has authored numerous publications, including a real estate tax planning program, *The Tax Reduction Organizer, Real Estate Tax Strategies of the Rich*. He also provides tax audit insurance and many other tax-related products.

You can get more information on Sandy, his published articles, and his products and seminars by accessing his Web site at **www.taxreductioninstitute.com**.